A HISTORY OF
GOLF

A HISTORY OF GOLF

ALAN ELLIOTT & JOHN ALLAN MAY

CHANCELLOR
PRESS

CONTENTS

The Publishers are grateful to the General Committee of the Royal and Ancient Golf Club of St Andrews for permission to photograph and publish in this book paintings and other archive material at the R & A.

The Publishers also thank the Editor and Staff of *Golf Monthly* (Glasgow) for their assistance in the preparation of photographic material from the magazine's archive.

Endpapers *Golf Beneath Edinburgh Castle*, an 18th-century painting by Paul Sandby.
This spread Royal County Down, Newcastle, Northern Ireland: 1st fairway.

First Published in 1990 by
The Hamlyn Publishing Group Limited

This edition published in 1994 by
Chancellor Press
a division of Reed Consumer Books Ltd
Michelin House
81 Fulham Road
London SW3 6RB

© The Hamlyn Publishing Group Limited

ISBN 1 85152 635 8

Produced by Mandarin Offset
Printed and bound in China

PICTURE ACKNOWLEDGEMENTS

Photographs are reproduced from *Golf Monthly*, whose photographers include Peter Dazeley, Keith Hailey and Phil Sheldon.

The Publishers would also like to thank the following organisations and individuals for their kind permission to reproduce the photographs in this book:

Allsport 150, 156, 157, 196, 204tr, 243t, 244 inset, 245t, 250b, Bruty 139, 143b, 148t, 198, 229b, 245b/Dave Cannon 21, 95, 113, 116, 140, 141t, 144t, 148b, 155, 1621, 166, 169, 184b, 185, 197b, 203r&b, 204t, 210b, 212, 213, 225b, 226t, 228t&bl, 235b, 242b, 243b, 251; The Trustees of The British Museum endpapers; Fujioka CC, Japan 101; Hulton-Deutsch Picture Company 61r, 63b , 79r, 80, 119, 200, 231, 240t; Ladies Golf Union 236; Mansell Collection 17b; Don Morley 147bl, 202b; Bert Neale 19b, 98, 125, 134, 179,-180, 194t, 220c; Popperfoto 40t, 164, 195, 219t, 221t; St Andrews University Photographic Collection 28t&c, 29, 30–1, 36, 44–5, 46b, 48b, 58; Phil Sheldon 91b, 94, 95, 111t, 112t, 114, 115b, 145, 149, 189, 193, 207t, 211, 226t, 238b; Fitz Symms 2091; Bob Thomas 184.

Special Photography at St Andrews
Michael Joy

Publisher's Note
Although every effort has been made to trace the copyright holders, we apologise in advance for any unintentional ommissions and would be pleased to insert the appropriate acknowledgements in any subsequent edition of this publication.

ROYAL AND ANCIENT

Where did it all start?

No one knows where or when golf began, or even if it evolved independently at different times and places. But it seems likely that it borrowed from many stick-and-ball games that had become popular in Europe by early medieval times....

From time immemorial man has been attracted by pastimes which have involved throwing, kicking or striking ball-like objects of various sizes. It seems to be a natural instinct, and although legend tells us that the ball originated in a game associated with Anagella, a native of Corfu, it seems more likely that the habit goes back to the earliest men. The ultimate origins of most ball games are lost in the obscurity of antiquity. Golf is no exception; and although there is no shortage of accounts purporting to explain the evolution of the game, the best that can be said of these is that some are less fanciful

Below *A form of* palle-maille *played at an elevated target. The modern professional teacher might well commend the loose but controlled swing.*

than others. Nevertheless, we know something of quite a number of early stick-and-ball games.

In medieval times there were already in Europe several different types of game, any of which could have had an influence on what eventually developed into golf as we know it. One of the best known of these games was *palle-maille* (which means ball and mallet); it originated probably in France, but was popular in Italy too. It was played with a boxwood ball and a stick which was rather like a small-headed croquet mallet and the object was to drive the ball to a marked point, or through a suspended hoop. It was played in city streets, but by the early 17th century a large purpose-made *palle-maille* court had been built near St James's Palace in central London. (The street later built on this site was given an anglicised version of the name of the game: Pall Mall.) Charles I is known to have played on the St James's court in 1629, and Pepys makes several references to the game in his diary. England probably had the game rather later than Scotland, where the royal ties with France were particularly close.

Another version of the same game was *jeu-de-mail*, but that was played across country rather than in a confined area. It was similarly played to a mark, which might be up to about half a mile away from the start. Mail courses were to be found in many towns in France and the Low Countries, and the game was still played in the city of Montpellier in the 1930s. Phenomenal distances were claimed for strikes of the wooden mail balls: were there, asked Horace Hutchinson (the late-19th-century golf writer), gigantic drivers even in those days, or only gigantic liars?

Chole, played predominantly in Belgium, was a game for the open fields, where elliptical balls made of beechwood were struck with an iron spoon-shaped club, to reach a distant target in as few strokes as possible. The interesting part of this game was that it involved two or more sides, each playing at the same ball. The distant target having been selected, the side which offered to get there in the fewest strokes had first go; three players from this team each then played one stroke at the ball; after this, an opposition player was allowed one stroke, his task,

Above Jeu-de-mail *was played across country. Local inhabitants must have feared wayward shots.*

Pages 6-7 *Golf has been played for centuries on this stretch of land between St Andrews and the Eden estuary. The picture shows part of four courses, including the Old.*

9

obviously, being to play the ball into as awkward a situation as possible. The sequence of play now continued, with three more strokes from the *choleurs* and then another stroke from the next *décholeur*. And so on, until the target was reached. You would think it would have led to a good deal of ill-feeling if a comparison with 'coarse croquet' is anything to go by. The earliest rules of golf made it clear that you might not interfere with your opponent's ball: *chole* was a long way from golf, but it could well have exercised a negative influence on the eventual rules.

Paganica, a Roman word meaning a leather ball stuffed with feathers, was the name of a game in which the ball was struck with a curved stick. It is not known how this game was played, but it may well have been the same as *cambuca* (or 'bandy ball') which was played in England in the 14th century, and which had the

feature of these other games in that it was played to a mark. In a stained glass window in Gloucester cathedral there is a 14th-century pane depicting a figure swinging a club resembling a hockey-stick at a ball; it is likely that this represented a *cambuca* player.

The Teutonic *kolben* (club) was the origin of the Dutch *colf*, the name for a game played largely in built-up areas, and only occasionally relegated to the areas outwith the towns; again, the object seems to have been the striking of a fixed object in the fewest strokes. The wooden balls (usually of elm or beech) showed an alarming tendency to veer off line, and thus were something of a hazard to persons and property in the neighbourhood. *Colf* was soon played with a ball made by stuffing feathers or cow's hair into a leather jacket (a ball-maker is recorded at Bergen-op-Zoom in 1428). In winter the game was sometimes played

Colf in Holland was enjoyed by many – often on the the ice in winter.

Old Time Dutch Kolf.

The Dutch game of kolf was played in an enclosed area with a much larger ball.

on the ice, and many Dutch artists have captured the scenes. *Colf* died out in the later 17th century: apparently it caused too much nuisance to the citizens, and it was superseded by *kolf*, a similar type of game, but played in an enclosed area, often covered.

Golf evolves

It is safe to assume that golf was not 'invented' but evolved over a considerable period of time. It may well have taken ideas and little bits and pieces from the other games, and may well have contributed to these games, too. The old Scots word 'to gowff' means 'to strike', and it is of ancient origin. There are good reasons to suppose that golf was played on the links at St Andrews before the founding of the University in 1411, but there are no written records; this is not altogether surprising if it was an activity largely of the common people, for the historian was interested not in what they were about, but in high affairs of state.

The first written reference comes from a Statute of Parliament in 1457, prohibiting golf as it was interfering with the practice of archery – the equivalent of the modern infantry man's training on the rifle range. Parliament found it repeatedly necessary to inveigh against unmartial exercise: in 1491 (the year before Col-umbus discovered America) we find that 'in na place of the realme there be usit Fute-ball, Golfe or uther sik unprofitabill sportis'. The fine for avoiding archery practice was 'fourtie shillings', a dire penalty in those days and indicating the seriousness of the offence. By the early 16th century, however, the King himself was spending money on golf, as is shown in the accounts of the Lord High Treasurers. Throughout the century there are records of punishments meted out to those who dared to play golf on the Sabbath at 'the time of the sermonnes'. It is clear that the game was popular along the east side of Scotland. By the end of the 16th century, golf has evolved into something akin to the present-day game: the ball is played into several consecutive holes, and the courses (greens – the term in its original sense includes every playable part of a golf course) cover a considerable area of ground.

Robert Clark in *Golf: A Royal and Ancient Game* (1875) begins his introduction thus: 'Golf is a game peculiar to the Scots, and may indeed be called par excellence the National Game of Scotland.'

From whatever sources it came, the game of golf as we know it is of Scots origin, and its development through the centuries, and to all parts of the globe, owes much to the Scots.

The links game

The modern game of golf developed as a national pastime on commonland known as links – those extensive strips of close-cropped turf and rough-grassed dunes that lie behind the foreshore on the east and south-west coasts of Scotland....

By the 15th century golf was flourishing on the Scottish links. It was played by all sorts of people; it helped that these included the aristocracy and the gentry. Numerous town games were still being played, some resembling *colf* or *chole*, some more akin to hockey and shinty. These games lost their popularity as town councils provided more in the way of law and order; and with the increase in trade, merchants were more concerned for their property. Much less damage and nuisance were caused outwith the town walls, and it was then that this priceless asset, the links came into its own.

The word 'links' is sometimes used to refer to any bit of rough ground, but the true links lie by the sea. It is where the coastal sand has, over the years, been blown into dunes and become grass-covered; but the cover is not proof against the penetrating winds: sand hollows form, and dunes move, so the area becomes undulating. Links grasses tend to be short, but the activities of grazing animals and rabbits help to keep them shorter; and scrapes in the grass may gradually erode into natural bunkers. Because of the sandy texture of the ground, drainage is excellent and it is not often that play is suspended even during the heaviest downpours today; it is noticeable that, when play does have to be suspended, the unplayable area is usually that which has been carefully worked upon by man: the putting greens.

'Links' is a word of Scottish derivation, and a case where the plural may be used as the singular. Many, but by no means all, the links on the east coast of Scotland have been taken for golf, from the Dornoch Firth to south of Dunbar; they are less common along the fjord-like west

Right *On the the island of South Uist, in the Outer Hebrides, the course at Askernish resembles closely the links on which earlier golfers played.*

coast of Scotland, but there are large areas to the south of the Clyde which now hold many courses. In north-west Scotland the links area by the sea is called the 'machair': golf has never been a popular sport in these northern areas, but there is an interesting course at Askernish on the Atlantic coast of South Uist in the Outer Hebrides. It is now about 100 years old, and was laid out by Old Tom Morris. Here we find a course which perhaps more closely resembles some of the early links courses, where there were few artificial features. Our ancestors played on the land as they found it, and simply took the most convenient features for their game; each hole would be at a reasonable length from the previous one, and scooped out in a more or less flat piece of ground. The whole playing area was called 'the green' – retained nowadays in the expression 'through the green' and in the 'green-keeper'.

It is only with the advent of inland courses in comparatively recent times that man has started to make his own features. The bulldozer has enabled him

to construct much more easily the bank, the hollow, the cutting – and that inevitable feature of many new courses, the artificial lake. Before the time of the vast earth-moving machines, the work was done by large gangs of labourers; before that, the golfer got on happily with what was provided by nature. It is interesting to note the comment of Curtis Strange – until recently a rare visitor to Britain – after he had played on the Old Course at St Andrews in the 1987 Dunhill Cup:

Above *Dornoch – an ancient links. The naturally springy turf was kept short by the sheep.*

'Many of our course designers would learn a great deal by coming and playing on this course'.

Royal patronage

There are records of gentlemen golfers playing on the Leith links from at least the 15th century. Balls were expensive, and *colf* balls were frequently imported from Holland. James VI, after he had moved his court to London in 1603, appointed his own club-maker and sold the monopoly for ball-making.

The links were common ground, and available for grazing as well as for pastimes other than golf. When gentlemen played golf, they would often employ a caddie ('cadet') to carry their clubs; also necessary on crowded links was a 'fore-caddie' to see that the way was cleared ahead. And the links *were* often crowded: 'Lords of Session and cobblers, knights, baronets, and tailors might be seen earnestly contesting for the palms of superior dexterity'.

Golfing references can be found throughout the 17th century. The first Marquess of Montrose, a famous general in the 1640s, was a keen player, and frequented St Andrews links from the time when he was a student at the university there; he played at Leith, too, where two golf balls cost him 10 shillings, and at Montrose, where he again expended sums for balls, and also for clubs. He was a dashing and successful player, though he obviously found trouble from time to time, for he needed regular repairs to his 'bonker clubbis'.

The Stuart kings were for the most part keen on their golf. Charles I, a pious man, commanded that his subjects should not be molested in or for their lawful recreations on the Sabbath, having first done their 'duetie' to God. Charles himself received news of the Irish rebellion in 1642 while in the middle of a match on the links of Leith; he was so upset by the news that he abandoned his match at once and returned to his palace at Holyrood. (Horace Hutchinson wondered, with deplorable cynicism, whether the king was 'down' in his match at the time of receiving the news; but the score was not recorded for posterity.) James VII and II, when Duke of York, was a player of note. When in 1681 he was based in Edinburgh, he was challenged by two English noblemen attending the Scottish Court to find a partner and to play against them for a large stake to prove which country had the better golfers: this was the first international match of significance. The Duke chose for his partner one John Paterson, a shoemaker, who was amongst the best players of the day, coming from a family of well-known golfers. The Duke and his partner won, and Mr Paterson was rewarded with a half share of the winnings: with this he was able to buy himself a house in the Canongate. The Duke was accustomed to use a forecaddie called Dickson – the first recorded named forecaddie; this Dickson became a noted clubmaker, and founded a firm which flourished for many years.

In 1724 another match attracted noble followers as well as a substantial crowd. This match, for a wager of 20 guineas, was between Alexander Elphinstone (who won) and Captain Porteous, the ill-fated central figure of the Porteous Riots, when the reading of the Riot Act took place for

This picture was presented to the Royal & Ancient Club in 1847. It shows a match in progress on the links, the dress of the players suggesting a date around 1700. The view of St Andrews shows features on the skyline which are still there today. The building on the right is an old windmill without its sails; its site is remembered by the present-day Windmill Road nearby.

the first and only time in Scotland. Historical figures, too, had their relaxations, and golf was one of them.

The first golf societies

It was not until the 18th century that golf clubs and associations began to appear. The earliest records show that golf was not always the main reason for the groups of players to form an association: some of these groups, for instance, consisted of freemasons, who thought it beneficial to play golf as healthy exercise before proceeding to their dinner meetings. In 1744 the Gentlemen Golfers of Edinburgh (later to become the Honourable Company of Edinburgh Golfers) persuaded the Edinburgh City Council to present them with a silver club, to be competed for on the Leith links. The winner of the trophy became 'Captain of the Golf' for the year, and all disputes about golf were to be settled by him.

As there was a prize at stake, the Gentlemen Golfers were requested to frame a set of rules to cover the competition: thus came about the first set of rules for the game, the Thirteen Articles. It is worth a look at a resumé of these, to see how they correspond to today's rules.

1 You must tee your ball within one club's length of the [previous] hole.
2 Your tee must be upon the ground.
3 You are not to change the ball you strike off the tee.
4 You may not remove stones, etc. for the sake of playing your ball 'except on the Fair Green, and that only within a Club's length of your Ball'.

5 If your ball is in water you may lift it out and tee it behind the hazard, but 'must allow your Adversary one stroke'.
6 If the balls touch each other, you lift the first till you play the last.
7 'At Holing you are to play honestly for the Hole and not upon your Adversary's ball'.
8 If you lose your ball, you go back to where you struck it and drop another ball 'and allow your Adversary a stroke for the misfortune'.
9 When Holing you may not mark your way to the hole with a Club or anything else.
10 If a ball is stopped by an outside agency it must be played where it lies.
11 If you have started on the down swing, your stroke counts.
12 'He whose Ball lyes farthest from the Hole is obliged to play first'.
13 A local rule, to cover conditions peculiar to the Leith Links.

It is on these that all subsequent sets of rules have been based, though with frequent variations. There was always the insistence that you must not interfere with your opponent's ball, though for a

Top *From early times the common ground was used for many purposes, including golf. This view of Leith links was drawn by John Smart in 1893.*

Above *Leith links as it is today, an open green area within the town. The stone mound and plaque commemorate one of the earliest courses in Scotland.*

short while there was a code which permitted it: if you thought your ball was unplayable, your opponent was permitted, if he wished, to play two strokes at it; if he managed to shift it, then the two strokes counted; otherwise you were allowed to drop it in a playable position for a penalty of one stroke. It conjures up some interesting pictures. It was not until 1897 that the Royal & Ancient Club of St Andrews, by then pre-eminent, by popular demand appointed a Rules of Golf Committee, which frames standard rules.

In 1754 the Society of St Andrews Golfers was formed. They, too, played for a silver club and the connection with the competition at Leith is clear. But it is also of note that the University of St Andrews had a Silver Arrow trophy for archery in a tournament of earlier origin; each winner attached a medal to the arrow (a winner's medal dated 1618 is in existence); and several of the founders of the St Andrews Society of Golfers were past winners of the arrow.

The winner of the silver club at St Andrews became the captain, (as with the Company of Edinburgh Golfers). After a time, it became the custom to decide who should be captain, and the scores in the competition were then suitably 'arranged' so that the chosen captain turned out to have the lowest score. Now each new captain still plays for the silver club, and he plays just one shot to win. The winning is surrounded by much ceremony. At 8am on a morning of the Autumn meeting, the captain-elect drives from the first tee on the Old Course; his ball is teed up by the honorary professional to the club. As the captain drives off, a small cannon is fired; all the local caddies stand on the fairway, and the one who retrieves the ball returns it to the new captain, and is rewarded with a gold sovereign. There have been occasions in the past when some of the more knowledgeable caddies stood rather closer to the tee than was consistent with tact. The playing of the one shot ensures that the captain wins, as there are no other competitors. He is then entitled to attach his silver ball to the club; on occasions when a member of the Royal Family has been captain, he has attached a gold ball.

During the reign of King William IV, the club was authorised to use the title 'Royal' and became 'The Royal & Ancient Golf Club of St Andrews'. The King became patron of the club, and presented a gold

Right *Extract from the minute book showing the early rules of the St Andrews Club. These rules follow closely those of the Gentlemen Golfers of Edinburgh, formulated in 1744.*

Opposite, upper left *A picture taken early this century of the caddies scrambling for the ball as the new captain of the Royal & Ancient drives himself into office.*

Opposite, upper right *Francis Ouimet was the first American to captain the Royal & Ancient. He is seen here at his driving-in ceremony in 1951.*

Opposite, below *A founder member of Royal Blackheath. Gentlemen golfers were colourful figures in their uniforms. The caddies carried the clubs; there were no golf bags till the later part of the 19th century.*

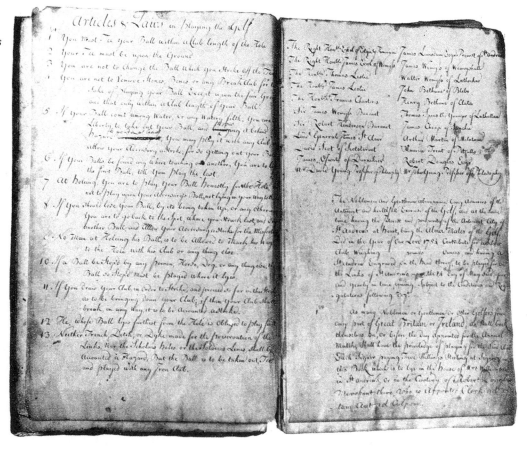

medal in 1834, which is competed for annually. In 1838, the King having died, Queen Adelaide became patroness, and she too presented a medal to the club. It is said that she found difficulty in distinguishing the captain of the club amongst all those wearing their red jackets, and she asked that the captain should wear her medal to help visitors to know which he was. This is done to this day.

The membership of Blackheath was predominantly Scottish, and could trace its ancestry almost to James VI's arrival from Scotland. The club was founded in 1766; its ties with the Company of Edinburgh Golfers and with the Society of St Andrews are clear, and many of the customs of the clubs are similar. When in 1768 a new Golfing House was prepared for the Company of Gentlemen Golfers at Leith, Blackheath and St Andrews were represented at the laying of the foundation stone by William St Clair of Roslin, at that time the Grand Master Mason of Scotland and a keen and proficient golfer. The Edinburgh Burgess Golfing Society (1735) used the Bruntsfield links in Edinburgh, as did also the Bruntsfield Links Golf Club (1761). The Musselburgh Golf Club, a few miles east of the capital, was founded in 1774.

Although in the early 19th century some of the societies and clubs had financial troubles, yet golf remained a popular game for all, and the links were well used. Golf had come a long way in 400 years; but it was still played only in a limited area till the later 19th century.

TODAY'S CLASSIC LINKS

The springy turf, formidable bunkers, subtle greens and testing, ever-changing winds of the great links courses offer a unique examination of a player's skill and cunning.

All the courses used for the Open Championship are, and always have been, links courses. Although early records tend to be accidental (royal or parliamentary edicts) or minutes of societies, the links have always been used extensively by the ordinary people for ordinary activities. This is not the stuff of which history is made, so little or nothing has been written of early times. Links such as those at Musselburgh, Leith and St Andrews were common ground, and golf took place amidst many other activities; golfers made use of the ground as it was. The number of holes varied from place to place, and often depended on the extent of the ground available. At St Andrews, play was to a number of holes leading north-westward from the town; then they played homeward to the same holes; at one time it was the custom to play 22 holes, but it eventually settled at 18 and, given the pre-eminence of St Andrews, this became the number of holes for the normal full course everywhere. For convenience of play, there came a time at St Andrews when two different holes in the ground were used at each hole, one for the outward half, one for the inward; and thus evolved the famous (and now unique) double greens on the Old Course; today there are seven of these, some immense.

These old links courses were little changed from their natural form. Today, of course, the putting greens are given much attention, but the basic shape of the holes remains. Prestwick, home of the first 12 Opens from 1860, also uses the natural features to advantage; it originally had 12 holes, and seven of the original greens remain. The last four holes ('the loop') at Prestwick are not long but they are supremely tricky and call for accurate and thoughtful play if they are to be conquered. Musselburgh at first had seven holes; this was increased first to eight and later to nine. Not enough

Left *The Open at St Andrews in 1939, with Henry Cotton putting at the 16th. A feature of the Old Course is the large double greens, this one being shared with the 2nd. The train has stopped at the signal. The railway has been an important out-of-bounds feature of this and many other courses.*

ground was available for expansion, though, and when in 1892 an 18-hole course was needed with the Open to be held, for the first time, over 72 holes, it was switched from Musselburgh to Muirfield, the new home of the Honourable Company of Edinburgh Golfers, at Gullane on the southern shore of the Firth of Forth. Sandwich, on the coast of Kent, was opened as a result of the need for links not too far from London, where the available courses were heavily oversubscribed. It was the case at Sandwich of links purchased for the express purpose of playing golf, and specially laid out for it. The Open was played there for the first time in 1894.

Above *Westward Ho!, the earliest links course in England.*

Below *The 13th at Birkdale: tiger country! Typically of the finest links courses, the subtly contoured fairways tempt the shotmaker, but a slice or hook into the gorse spells disaster.*

Westward Ho! – the first links course of all in England – 'is a course of supreme naturalness', said Bernard Darwin. 'It looks for all the world as if some golfing adventurer had merely to stroll out with a hole-cutter, a bundle of flags, and perhaps a light roller, and had made the course in less than no time.' Hoylake, a difficult course, now the home of Royal Liverpool Club, has suffered from a lack of space about it and has not hosted the Open since 1967; it is a pity that this fine and testing course is no longer on the circuit.

At Lytham & St Anne's there are some artificially constructed hillocks, and part of the course is set within a leafy suburbia beyond sight of the sea; but it is another difficult test which usually finds the right winner.

The nature of links golf

What are the differences between the links and the inland courses? Winds are often stronger by the coast, and moreover may change from offshore to onshore during the playing of a round. On links courses, vegetation tends to be low and trees, when they are there at all, stunted; so the wind blows almost unimpeded; on inland courses, often with many trees, and sometimes with tree-lined fairways, and with lush vegetation as well as shelter provided by undulating ground, the force of the wind is broken and its overall effect less. Links courses often

Royal Troon: the short 8th from the tee to the elevated 'Postage Stamp' green, amply guarded by ferocious bunkers. At the 1973 Open the 71-year-old Gene Sarazen scored an ace here.

look wide and inviting, but with subtle changes in the wind causing infinite problems, drives need to be hit to pinpoint accuracy if the player is to have a reasonable chance of being near the hole after his second stroke. Links courses usually drain better and their greens become hard and fast very quickly. The modern tendency to water (indeed, over-water) greens has taken away some of the difficulty, but there are occasions still when fiery fairways and glassy greens ensure that only the most skilful golfer can cope. Bunkers are a natural feature on the sand; on links courses these can be ferocious hazards: often small in surface area but pitilessly deep and steep-sided.

On true links the rough really is rough because only the toughest, most wiry grass, not to mention whin (gorse), can prosper in face of the wind. Somewhere about 1847, the short 11th hole (the High) on the Old Course at St Andrews suffered from erosion and often the green was unplayable because of blown sand. A local nurseryman planted sea-lyme grass behind the green to keep the sand steady, and it succeeded. Incidentally, this 11th hole was the first to have the hole protected with a cast iron rim so that it might keep its shape. The designers of inland courses often make sure that they are well-

manicured and straightforward; rough does not often provide a hazard if a player is reasonably straight. On the links, the 'tiger country' is often uncomfortably near the fairway and, when the almost inevitable cross-wind is blowing, a small lapse in compass-direction can invite major trouble – as in the Opens at Sandwich in 1985 and Turnberry in 1986.

Above *The shape of some large bunkers is often maintained by massive timberwork. Here Ben Sayers views the result after playing from the redoubtable 'Redan' on the 15th at North Berwick.*

Below *In England courses were often laid out on previously little-used links. Sandwich was such a course, and full use is made of the natural dunes.*

The rise of competition

Golf matches, often involving side bets and wagers, are as old as the Scottish game itself. The earliest recorded matches were between golf societies and links clubs. By the mid-19th century, the first great professional champions had emerged. . . .

All games are a form of contest, a chance to show that you are better than your adversary, or that your team is better than his team. Golf is no exception. However, it was not until societies started to keep records that we can see something of what was going on.

Golf in those days was all about matchplay; the idea of counting strokes for the complete round was quite incidental, for matches were decided by holes up, or, when several rounds were played, by rounds up. The foursome – where two partners play alternate shots at one ball against another pair – was a very popular game, and it is still common in the older clubs.

At first, matches often involved wagers. Sir John Foulis of Ravelston showed in his note-books of 1672 his losses incurred while playing at Leith and Musselburgh; the sums lost, even in Scots money, were by no means small. Sir John seems to have been a regular, indeed almost invariable, loser – unless his winnings were recorded in another book. The Honourable Company had their own Recorder, who at first was Clerk to the Betts. All wagers had to be approved by the Captain, and then recorded. A golfer who reneged on a wager was heavily fined – as was a golfer who played in incorrect dress.

Many bizarre wagers were laid. In 1798 a bet was taken that there were not two members of the Edinburgh Burgess Golfing Society capable of driving a ball

over the spire of St Giles' church. Each player was allowed six balls, and the judges were placed (rather insecurely) near the weathercock. The feat was easily accomplished. Some years after this, a similar wager was made concerning the Melville Monument: this was easier to achieve, and one of the parties at least cannot have had knowledge of the earlier event. Then there was a Mr Scott who bet one guinea with a Mr McDowall that he would drive a ball from the Golf House at Bruntsfield links over Arthur's Seat in 45 strokes. Arthur's Seat rises to a height of 823 feet, the distance to be covered was about a mile and a half, and the rise some 600 feet; the first part of the route must have been through several streets, and the last part of the hill would have been very

Above *A mid-19th century photograph of Musselburgh links, which has been used for golf since earliest days. The holes now lie within the racecourse.*

Left *From Bruntsfield links in the north-west suburbs of Edinburgh, the summit of Arthur's Seat looks a long way away. It was a remarkable feat to reach the summit in less than 45 strokes, which was accomplished for a wager at the start of the 19th century.*

Carnoustie has testing courses, where some of the earliest inter-club matches were played. This view of the first hole dates from the 1890s.

rough going. Anyway, Mr Scott lost. A similar contest not long after resulted in a Mr Brown defeating a Mr Spalding by completing the task in 44 strokes.

Cross-country events were not uncommon, but competitions on the links were more important. Meanwhile, normal club activities continued as usual. There is this timeless report from the Bruntsfield Links Club in 1845:

The object of the Meeting being to compete for the Cairns Medal, the Members proceeded to the Green (Musselburgh) and, though the wind blew a perfect hurricane, accompanied by showers, the competition was animated. It terminated in the success of the Secretary, Mr Cameron. The Club dined in the Musselburgh Arms Inn, and spent a very happy evening; but the meeting having been prolonged beyond the period at which the omnibus (in which seats had been taken) started, the Members found it necessary to walk the greater part of the way to town.

A curious bet was made in 1820 between two members of the St Andrews Society: Sir David Moncrieffe, Bart and Captain Whyte Melville had undertaken that whoever lived the longer should present a Silver Putter to the Club with the arms of the two engraved on it. Sir David died in 1833, and the bet was duly honoured. Captain Whyte Melville was elected captain of the Royal & Ancient for a second time in 1883, but he died, at the age of 86,

just before taking office; the captaincy was left vacant for that year.

The links clubs

By the early 19th century new clubs were starting at many places where the links had been used for golf for hundreds of years. The society of golfers at Aberdeen founded their club in 1780, but golf had been played there since at least the 16th century, and as far back as 1642 a town council licence had been granted to John Dickson to make golf balls. The club at first had problems on the links with damage to the course from carts and from football; in the middle of the century they had trouble with fisherman who spread their nets all over the course to dry, making golf impossible; then there was a move to remove some holes to make way for a cricket field; and there was also talk of putting a railway through the links. The club continued despite the difficulties, and late in the century moved to a new course of its own a little farther north.

Perth was another place where golf had been played for a very long time on the Inches. James VI is said to have played on the North Inch before going south to London in 1603. Golf, as on other common land, had to take its chance with every other activity. The Golfing Society was first minuted in 1824, and William IV became patron of the club in 1833, granting it the title of The Royal Perth Golfing Society. It was the first of the 'Royal' clubs. The King James VI Club was founded in 1858, and both clubs played on the North Inch. In the 1890s the course was moved northwards to include Muirton Field, and left ground free at the town end for cricket and football. In 1896 the King James VI Club moved to its present course on Moncrieffe Island.

There were also many clubs and societies not attached to a particular course. One such was the Six-Feet Club, instituted in Edinburgh in 1826. Members had to be at least six feet tall, and the club's officials included two Measurers. The club was founded to promote the National Games of Scotland, and held a Golf Medal in July every year 'over the Links of Edinburgh, Leith or Musselburgh'. It was found necessary to state in their rules for the Golf: 'A stroke is counted if the Golfer, in the act of playing, either strike the ground, or pass the ball with his Club'. Lawyers might well have been needed to interpret that one, though its intent is clear enough. In addition to members of clubs, there were plenty of other golfers who simply wanted to play. The links were open to all, and, for instance, 'many who go to Bruntsfield Links are accommodated with the loan of clubs by the maker for a trifling remuneration'.

There is a record in 1818 of a match over the Bruntsfield links between the Edinburgh Burgess Society and the Brunts-field Links Golf Club. This was the first of many such encounters; then came a match between Bruntsfield Links Club and Musselburgh Golf Club, at Musselburgh; and this too was repeated. Hitherto, clubs had not ventured far from home; but within a few years clubs in all the golf-playing areas of Scotland were beginning to communicate with each other and

EARLY CLUBS AND SOCIETIES

Edinburgh Burgess GS	1735
Honourable Company of Edinburgh Golfers	1744
Society of St Andrews Golfers	1754
Bruntsfield Links GC	1761
Blackheath GC	1766
Musselburgh GC	1774
Crail GC	1786
Glasgow Gailes GC	1787
Cruden Bay GC	1791
Dunbar GC	1794
Burntisland GC	1797
Glasgow GC	1797
Montrose GC	1810
Scotscraig GC	1817
Old Manchester GC	1819
Leven GC	1820
Perth GS	1824
North Berwick GC	1832

Below *Royal Dornoch is the most northerly of the world's great courses. Laid out originally by old Tom Morris, its plateau greens influenced the work of many golf architects, most notably the great Donald Ross.*

Above *The racecourse stand at Musselburgh was once the home of the Honourable Company of Edinburgh Golfers. The ladies seen on the first tee in this late-19th-century photograph must have had restricted swings in such clothing.*

Below *Golf at Wimbledon Park in the early 1900s. Golf was played on the common from the 1860s.*

before long regular fixtures were arranged.

In 1857 a tournament was proposed to the Royal & Ancient by Prestwick; it was to be an amateur club tournament, and it is interesting to see the list of competing clubs. These are the first-round results:

- Royal Blackheath *beat* Royal Perth Golfing Society
- Edinburgh Burgess Golf Club *beat* Montrose Royal Albert
- Edinburgh Bruntsfield *beat* Prestwick Golf Club
- Royal & Ancient *beat* Dirleton Castle Golf Club
- Leven *beat* Musselburgh
- North Berwick: bye

In the final Royal Blackheath defeated the team from the Royal & Ancient.

With the railway network reaching into the most distant corners of the kingdom, club matches began to be a regular feature on the calendar. Elie & Earlsferry entertained the King James VI club in 1860; Royal Perth had matches with Carnoustie Dalhousie and Aberdeen, who also played against each other. In the far north one of the greatest, if least accessible, links in the world is at Dornoch, where golf has been played certainly for 300 years. Originally of nine holes, it had another nine laid out by Old Tom Morris some ten years after the club was founded in 1877. Of the great links on the Ayrshire coast, the club at Prestwick was founded in the 1850s and that at Troon, half a dozen miles to the north, in 1878.

By this time, things were stirring in England, too. The Old Manchester Club dates from 1819, and Scots in the Liverpool area eventually found the coastal links: Hoylake, started in 1869, soon became a famous golfing links; whilst Westward Ho! in Devon had been the first links course in England five years earlier; Wimbledon Common had seen the start of golf there in 1865.

So far little has been heard of the ladies Queen Mary of Scotland had indeed played with her friends in the 16th century; and was also heavily criticised for playing soon after her husband's death. She is known to have played on the Leven links, too. There were girls and their mothers out playing with the men on the links, and there is a minute of the Musselburgh Club in 1810 which allows for prizes to be awarded: 'The Club resolve to

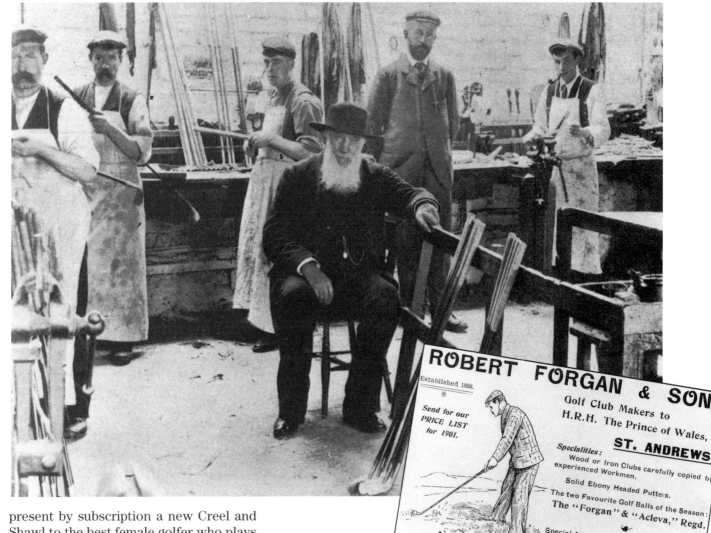

present by subscription a new Creel and Shawl to the best female golfer who plays on the annual occasion on 1st January next, old style (12th January new), to be intimated to the Fish Ladies by the Officer of the Club. Two of the best Barcelona silk hand kerchiefs to be added to the above premium of the creel.' The clubs which were formed in the 18th century were, however, for men.

Until Douglas Gourlay started making balls at Bruntsfield in 1780, they were brought from St Andrews and retailed by tavern keepers. Gourlay worked in the same building as James McEwan, who was a clubmaker. The families were joined by marriage, and their descendants maintained the skills in ballmaking and clubmaking. Gourlay feathery balls were highly prized as amongst the best, but the gutty, when it came, was rapidly incorporated into the business. James McEwan died in 1800, but his son Peter, though only 19, continued the business. By this time McEwan's clubs were being sent all over Scotland, and his agent in St

Andrews was ballmaker David Robertson. In 1819 Hugh Philp was appointed clubmaker to the St Andrews Golfers. Philp was born near St Andrews in 1782, and for many years he dominated the clubmaking scene in Fife. In due course he was joined by his nephew, Robert Forgan; and after Philp's death Forgan took over the business. Under him it expanded, and was a reputable clubmaking firm till the modern era. Old Tom Morris became a well-known clubmaker, and in Musselburgh four other distinguished players, the Parks and the Dunns, were clubmakers of note. Outwith these areas, there were the Patricks of Leven.

The early champions

Many of the caddies who were attached to the clubs at the links were also good players; most of them had played from an

Top *Robert Forgan in the finishing shop with his clubmakers in typical working aprons.*

Above *Although special types of clubs were obtainable on request, most clubmakers were selling individually made clubs at the turn of the century. Mass production was still to come.*

early age and, as they grew older, they became professional players as well as caddies. In these early days the only way to make a living from golf was by playing money matches, and these became common from the middle of the 19th century; many players were also ballmakers or clubmakers.

Allan Robertson came from a ball-making family which had been in the trade at St Andrews for many generations (Allan's father, David, was the agent for Peter McEwan's clubs). Allan was himself a ballmaker. Born in 1815, he became without any doubt the best player of his time: he never lost a match played on level terms. A kind-hearted and gentle-manly person, always fair and honourable in a game, he nonetheless was always determined to prevail. He did much for golf in his time.

One of the first of the great matches was between Allan Robertson and Willie Dunn, of Musselburgh. It was a match of 20 rounds, and they played two a day. Allan won this two rounds up with one to play. In 1849 there was perhaps the most famous foursome match of the time: Allan Robertson and Tom Morris played the Dunn twins over three greens: the Dunns won (by a huge margin) at Musselburgh; Allan and Tom won at St Andrews. The final game was at North Berwick, and with eight holes to go, the Dunns were four up; odds of 20 to 1 were now offered against their losing, but the St Andrews pair made a magnificent recovery, and in the end won at the final hole. There was great excitement among the enormous crowd which had turned up to watch. Allan Robertson was described as the most beautiful swinger of a club. He died in 1858 when he was only forty-three and was mourned by golfers everywhere. He was the superstar of his day; but he never had the opportunity to win the title of Open Champion.

Tom Morris played many matches against Willie Park, Sr, and on the whole results were even. On one occasion, however, at Musselburgh the referee stopped the match because of bad crowd behaviour and interference with Tom Morris's play; Old Tom refused to continue, and finally Willie Park played the remaining holes himself, and claimed the stake. This is not the only time that we come across partisan feelings getting the better of crowds desperate to see their own hero winning.

Often the professionals would be backed by their local club members, and a lot of money changed hands at the big matches. For the players, however, there was nothing for the loser – so it was important to win.

With the coming of the first of the English clubs, the matches took on an international flavour. For a long while the Scottish professionals were supreme: the great players were Willie Park and Mungo Park, Bob Ferguson and Willie Park, Jr from Musselburgh; and from St Andrews Old Tom, Jamie Anderson, the Straths, and the next superstar, young Tom Morris, who in his short life was head and shoulders above the rest.

In 1883 there was an important amateur match with John Ball, Jr from Hoylake against long-hitting Douglas Rolland from Earlsferry. Rolland was nine up after the first 36 holes at Elie. John Ball recovered one hole on the first 18 holes at Hoylake, but eventually went down 11 and 10. Already Ball was an outstanding player, and his local members had not expected him to lose. Another two-round match was hastily arrange for the next day; but Rolland won that one, too.

This chapter should end with two famous challenge matches at the end of the century. In 1896 Willie Park, Jr played a 72-hole match against J.H. Taylor: at Musselburgh, Park was four up. In the second-leg at Sudbrook Park, Richmond, Park was often in trouble amongst the trees, but his marvellous putting kept him in the game. In the end he was left with a fiery four-yard downhill putt for the match. He holed it, and took the £50 stake.

Three years later, Willie Park, Jr and Harry Vardon played. Vardon declined to play at Musselburgh because of partisan barracking which Taylor had suffered there; so the first 36 holes were played at North Berwick. Special trains were run from Edinburgh, and a crowd of 10,000 turned up to watch an exciting game which Vardon won two up. At Ganton in the second game, Vardon won the match 11 and 10.

During the course of the century, then, local contests had grown into national affairs. Golf had started its process of rapid expansion.

A famous group by the Swilcan Bridge at St Andrews. Major Boothby is playing a shot; Jamie Anderson (Open Champion in 1877-78-79) is to his right; behind is Old Da'; Old Tom Morris is on the left; Allan Robertson is to the right on the bridge. Note that they are playing the holes in reverse order, Boothby hitting his approach to the 17th green from the 18th fairway.

Golf spreads its wings

The global spread of golf in the 19th century followed on the heels of British imperial, commercial and social expansion. And wherever the game spread, the teaching and course-design skills of the great Scottish professionals were in demand....

What caused the sudden explosion of the game?

There were many reasons; and they all worked together to produce a growth of staggering magnitude. Without delving into the social history of Victorian times, is is fair to state that a prolonged period of peace coupled with enormous colonial development had meant much increased prosperity and the growth of the middle classes. Many Englishmen followed the monarch northwards to take holidays in Scotland and fell under the spell of golf. Meanwhile, the Scots themselves emigrated to all parts of the Empire as well as to North America – and they took their own game to their new places of residence.

The middle classes all over the white, English-speaking world swiftly took to a game offering many advantages and benefits: it could be readily played by anyone at any standard and of any age; it was a social game and gave ample opportunity for making friends or having conversation – usually between shots; it

Right *The course at Hunstanton in Norfolk. Dating from the 1890s, it is one of the best of the links courses which mushroomed on the east and south coasts of England at that time. It has been used on several occasions for men's and ladies' amateur championships.*

Far right *The famous Putting Course (The Himalayas) at St Andrews. This is the oldest ladies' golf club in the world.*

encouraged healthy if not too strenuous exercise – and the fresh air alone was worth a lot to a man who had spent the week sitting in an office; and it could include wives, too. (Gentlemen in late-Victorian times, however, were not too happy about that and the ladies were often put firmly on their own short courses. But they were not to be denied, and they had organised their own competitions and championships long before the suffragette movement got under way.)

Westward Ho!, as we have seen, was the first links-course club in England, founded in 1864. Hoylake and the Liverpool Club (1869) was followed up the west coast by the scarcely less splendid West Lancashire (1873) and Formby, Lytham & St Anne's, and Birkdale in the 1880s; also at that time came the first Yorkshire courses, while in the far northeast Alnmouth had started in 1869. Courses appeared all along the east and south coasts of England, and from Norfolk (most notably at Hunstanton and Brancaster) round to Hampshire every possible piece of the coast was investigated. The number of players increased

Above *Royal St David's, a picturesque course lying between the sea and the grim walls of Harlech Castle in North Wales. Although short it is a fine test of golf.*

dramatically, and Scottish professionals were in demand to go to clubs, and also to give advice on the laying out of courses. Wales had its first course in 1875, and Tipperary was the first in Ireland in 1879, with other courses following quickly after that. At this time, too, many more courses and clubs appeared in Scotland

With the increase of interest in the game, there followed a rapidly increasing literature, and periodicals started: *The Golfing Annual* was first issued in 1888; and first *Golfer's Handbook* came in 1903;

The course at Mussoori lies at 7,000 feet in the foothills of the Indian Himalayas; the picture, was taken in 1923 soon after it was completed.

the weekly *Golf* started in 1890; *Golf Illustrated* in 1899.

Imperial connections

As early as 1829 golf had started in India, when the Calcutta Club was formed to play on a small course at Dum Dum. It comes as no surprise to find that the first list of members contains a large majority of Scots names. The club prospered, and was soon followed by the Bombay Club (1842); both clubs had close connections with the Royal & Ancient and Blackheath. The Calcutta Club eventually moved to a new course which, after protracted negotiations for buying the land, was opened in 1910, by which time there was a membership of some 700. The Indian Amateur championship was first played in 1892; it is the oldest national championship outwith the British Isles.

The first club on the continent of Europe was in the south-west corner of France, at Pau. There is a story of Scots officers, pursuing their campaign against Napoleon in the Peninsular War (1808-14), carrying their golf clubs amongst their impedimenta and using them when the chance arose. They found an attractive area in the foothills of the Pyrenees, and amazed the local inhabitants with their extraordinary dress and sporting activities. In 1856 the British holiday colony from nearby Biarritz formed the Pau Club.

Suddenly in the 1890s we find that, in addition to the Scots, the Grand Duke Michael of Russia was involved in forming a club at Cannes. He had married the Countess Sophie against the wishes of his brother, the Tsar, and had been banished from his homeland. During his travels, he had come to Scotland, and on going to St Andrews had played golf and had become an enthusiast. In Cannes he set up a course and club, and there was no shortage of applicants to join. Local officials and merchants rubbed their hands at the promise of outstanding chances to expand a lucrative trade. In 1899 there are records of the Prince of Wales (later King Edward VII) playing, and of being judged by the local professional to have a 'promising' swing. The Grand Duke ruled the roast in the golf circle, and the club flourished. Pau may have been the first club in France; in the 1890s Cannes was the first socially.

The first course in the southern hemisphere was in New Zealand: the Dunedin Golf Club was formed at Otago in 1871, thanks particularly to Charles Howden, who had come from Edinburgh 10 years before. A group largely of Scots made up the first members, and shortly after another club was formed at Christchurch. Difficulties arose, and for some years the game was dormant in New Zealand, but

new interest came in the late 1880s and the game, as elsewhere, started to spread all over the country. In Australia, the first club was formed in Melbourne in 1891, though there had been spasmodic attempts to play there from the 1850s; in South Africa, the Cape Club dates from 1885; planters had a course in Malaysia in 1888; and the Hong Kong courses started in 1889.

The first written record of golf in North America was in 1779, when an advertisement in the *Rivington Gazette* was directed towards golf players: 'The season for this pleasant and healthy exercise now advancing, gentlemen may be furnished with excellent clubs and Caledonian balls by inquiring at the Printers.' Was this just a speculative advertisement? It does suggest that the game was played somewhere there by someone, but there is no record of it. A South Carolina Golf Club was formed at Charleston in 1786, and one at Savannah, Georgia at about the same time – but these clubs seem to have been just social, and there is no record of any play nor of any course. *Kolf* had reached Albany, New York in earlier times, but this was clearly the town game. The first golf club in North America was founded in 1873 in Montreal, Canada, and it was not long before the Queen had graciously assented to the 'Royal' prefix. Instrumental in starting the club was Alex-ander Dennistoun, born in Edinburgh in 1821, and two other Scots, the Sidey brothers. There are references to the game in Canada as far back as 1824; even earlier, there may have been play amongst the fur traders in the north. The first club in the United States was the St Andrews Club of Yonkers, New York in 1888. John Reid, a native of Dunfermline, started with some friends a three-hole course in his cow pasture. It was a modest start, but destined, as we shall see, to have repercussions the world over.

EARLY GOLFING EQUIPMENT

The evolution of equipment during the 19th century was made possible by radical developments in the technology and design of golf balls and later by improvements in techniques and in the quality of courses.

The feathery-ball era lasted for about 400 years. The ball had a sewn leather cover with a slit for stuffing: into the wetted cover a top-hatful of wet, boiled goose-feathers was packed, and the slit sewn up; as it dried, the leather shrank and the feathers expanded, producing a hard ball. Unfortunately when used in wet weather it became soggy and disintegrated rapidly. A skilled ballmaker could make only four balls a day, so they were expensive.

The gutty arrived in the 1840s. It did not take on immediately, but was much cheaper, so featheries were soon superseded. Gutties were made of solid gutta-percha, a tropical rubber-like but non-elastic material. Smooth, hand-made gutties ducked in flight, but used and hacked balls flew better, so the surface of new gutties was hand-hammered to improve their trajectory; also, if given time to mature, they performed better. Smooth, then patterned, moulds and even do-it-yourself kits were introduced; so were paints to make the

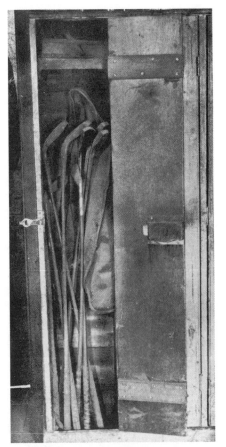

dark-brown balls easier to find in the rough.

From the 1870s onwards, though often still called the gutty, the composite ball became common: there were many experiments with other materials either to mix with the gutta-percha or to use as a core enclosed by gutta-percha. Eventually the wound rubber-thread centre, and later the rubber-thread wound around a core led to the forerunners of the modern golf ball. The feathery, gutty and composite balls were all made in the same series of sizes: as yet there was no standardisation for playing in competitions. The standard diameter for the modern British ball was 1.62in and for the American 1.68in; today, use of the American-sized ball is mandatory for golf events throughout the world.

The changes in golf balls promoted changes in clubs. Featheries were struck with wooden clubs, which were graceful with long thin heads, usually of thorn, and long tapering shafts of ash; but with fairly thick grips, often a wool padding under the leather, as players used a two-handed grip. Long heads made it difficult to play a ball in a tight lie, so the first iron clubs were introduced. The track-iron was designed to hit balls out

Left *Young Tom Morris's locker at St Andrews. His clubs are typical of his day; his clubmaking tools are on the shelf.*

Left *Different types of golf balls including the feathery (front), the gutty (centre right), the composite, the rubber-core.*

Right *This advertisement tempts the modern golfer to speculate how he might play if he could use one of these.*

Below *At Auchterlonie's famous shop in St Andrews, clubmakers still produce handmade clubs.*

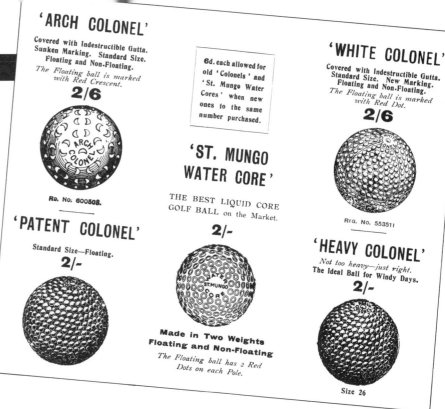

of small holes and the ruts made by cart wheels in the links common-land. Its head was only slightly larger than the ball, its shaft shortish; and it proved useful, too, for getting out of bunkers.

The gutty was very hard compared with the feathery, and to make a successful stroke with a wooden club, the head had to give more. Clubmakers first turned to beech, and then to persimmon; and to make the shaft less whippy they changed to hickory. The gutty was well suited to iron clubs, which in consequence grew in popularity and numbers. The early iron heads were hand-forged by blacksmiths and then given to clubmakers to shaft; later, cleekmakers performed both tasks.

There was a very large range of clubs: drivers or play clubs; spoons, including the baffy, then the brassie with its brass sole; niblicks; lofting irons, leading to mashies (and the socket or shank!); cleeks, as well as being long-hitting irons, were developed for approach shots and for putting; and putters, which have always been singular clubs, exhibiting infinite variety in both style and the manner in which they are used: the wooden putter, the iron, aluminium, brass, wry-necked and centre-shafted – they are legion.

With the change to composite balls, which were much easier to play, there were fewer wooden clubs and more irons; and whereas wooden club heads were still hand-made, the new drop-forged iron heads became more uniform and could be graded. When the overlapping grip became popular, the woollen layer on the grip was omitted to make it less clumsy.

EARLY CHAMPIONS

The professional game was dominated in the mid-19th century by two generations of Scottish champions. By the 1890s, however, the centre of power had shifted south of the border, where The Great Triumvirate held sway.

Tom Morris

(1821–1908)

Tom Morris was born in St Andrews and lived there nearly all his life. He was apprenticed to Allan Robertson as a ballmaker, and spent some years working for him; finally there was a disagreement about the gutty ball, and he set up on his own as clubmaker and ballmaker. In 1851 he was taken as greenkeeper to Prestwick. It was there that his two sons were born. At Prestwick he assisted in the setting up of the Open Championship, which he was to win four times out of the first eight, though he was over 40 when he won for the first time in 1861. He returned to St Andrews at the start of 1865, when he was appointed by the Royal & Ancient Club to be their

Left *Old Tom Morris, one of the great golfing personalities, and four times winner of the Open Championship.*

Right *A well-known portrait of Young Tom, the outstanding golfer of his time, wearing his Open Championship belt – his to keep after winning it for the third year running in 1870. He was also the first winner of the present trophy, the silver goblet, in 1872.*

professional and to have full charge of the greens; he was given a barrow, a spade and a shovel, and was allowed the help of a man on two days a week. He continued to play in competitions and matches, and played every year in the Open until 1896, when he was 75. He was also much in demand as a course designer and adviser, and was closely involved in the original laying out of such superlative courses as Royal Dornoch, Carnoustie, Royal County Down, Nairn, Westward Ho!, and Lahinch (County Clare). He became an institution at St Andrews, and was visited and consulted by golfers old and young, famous and lowly. To all he was the same: a kindly, genuine, knowledgeable person, totally involved in every way with golf, and always ready to give anyone a game if there was time; and he could hold his own with most even in his eighties. He was a good swinger of a club, and master of all strokes – except the short putt; though even that deficiency had not stopped him being a most formidable player. Old Tom died, a greatly respected man, after a fall in the New Club, St Andrews.

Tom Morris, Jr

(1851–75)

Young Tom was playing from his earliest years, and soon showed himself to be very special indeed. As early as 13 he was in a match on the North Inch at Perth against a local youth, much fancied for his skill, and trounced him – to the disgust of his opponent's backers. By the age of 16, he was playing in the Open, coming fourth. He won in 1868, again in 1869, and in 1870 finished 12 strokes ahead of the next player – having played the 578-yard first hole in a staggering three shots. His three consecutive titles won him the Championship Belt outright. When the competition resumed, for the new trophy, in 1872 he won again, completing a sequence of four wins, which has not been repeated.

He played many matches, and would back himself against enormous odds; but he always managed to win. He would take on a group of the best amateurs of the time, allow them strokes, and still win. He took on the best professional players of the time, and won most of those matches, too. All the time he was returning scores well below those of any other player.

It was a tragedy when his wife died. He had been playing with his father against the Parks at North Berwick; when the match was over (and won), he received news of his wife's illness. He hurried home with his father by boat, but he was too late to see his wife alive. He never recovered his spirits, and died soon after.

Left Willie Park, from Musselburgh, was winner of the first Open Championship, held at Prestwick in 1860.

Below His son, Willie Park, Jr, was also Open Champion and famous as a golf-course designer.

Below left An advertisement for Willie Park, Jr golf products in a 1911 issue of Golf Monthly.

time Old Tom won. The series of matches was to continue for many years. Willie played many other matches, and won most of them. He was an exceptional putter, deadly, it was said, from three or four yards; this indeed was remarkable with greens as they then were. When the Open Championship started in 1860, Willie Park was the first winner, and in all he won four times. He was also a skilful and well-known ball and club maker, whose name was carried further afield by his son, Willie Park, Jr, also an Open winner and later famous as a golf-course architect (his masterpiece was Sunningdale).

Willie Park, Sr

(1833–1903)

He was born near Musselburgh and, like so many other top golfers, started as a caddy. A dashing player, he had soon disposed of all local opposition, so he issued a challenge in *The Sporting Life* to play a match for £100 stake; it was addressed to Allan Robertson, Tom Morris, Sr and Willie Dunn, the other three top players of the time. For some time there was no response, but eventually Tom Morris took him on, and lost. At once a return was demanded, and this

Right *This cartoon captures vividly the character of J. H. Taylor, the first of the Great Triumvirate to win the Open.*

THE TRIUMVIRATE

J. H. Taylor

(1871–1963)

He was the youngest of the three, but the first on the championship scene.

Born of a humble family at Northam, North Devon, he left school at age 11 and began his interest in golf as a caddy. At 15 he had a job as a gardener's boy, then as a labourer, and after that, to his joy, was taken onto the greenkeeping staff at nearby Westward Ho! With plenty of opportunity to play, he soon showed excellent form. In 1891 he was appointed professional-greenkeeper at Burnham, and the next year he became professional at Winchester; then he moved to Wimbledon in 1896, and in 1899 to Mid Surrey.

J. H. Taylor – he was always known by his initials, not his first names (John Henry) – first entered for the Open in 1893 and finished tenth, though his 75 in the first round led the field and served notice of what was to come. He won his first Open title convincingly at Sandwich in 1894: it was the first time that the championship had been held in England, and the first time that it had been won by an English professional. Taylor was one of the best players ever seen with a mashie (equivalent to today's 5- or 6-iron); some doubted if he would be able to control it on the hard, fast greens at St Andrews where the Open of 1895 was to be held. He soon silenced his critics with another convincing win there. He was runner-up to Vardon in 1896, second in four consecutive years from 1904; had three more wins in 1900, 1909 and 1913, and was second in 1914. He won the match-play title in 1904 and 1908. He played in his last Open in 1926.

By nature aggressive, he took a great deal out of himself emotionally in every match he played, for he was always striving for perfection. He was sound in all aspects of play, and a very good putter; his early training on links courses meant that he could master the worst conditions and he was superb in windy weather.

Although largely self-educated, he was lucid and clear-thinking as both a writer and a speaker. Instrumental in forming the Professional Golfers Association, he took a full part in their counsels and was largely responsible for lifting the status of the golf professional in the early years of the century. He died in North Devon at the age of 92 in 1963.

Harry Vardon

(1870–1937)

Harry Vardon was born at Grouville, Jersey. Had it not been for his younger brother Tom's success as a golf professional, Harry might well have stayed in his job as a gardener. He was good at all games, but he was persuaded when he was 20 to take a job as professional at Ripon in Yorkshire. His duties there were not arduous, and he found time still to play a good deal of cricket. He moved to Bury, and then, in 1895, to Ganton.

He had entered for the Open in 1894, when he came fifth; but he was not well placed the following year. In 1896 he tied with J.H. Taylor, and won the play-off. Taylor often reckoned that Vardon's win had been influenced in no small measure by the contest the two had had at Ganton a few weeks earlier, in which Taylor had been trounced; certainly Vardon in his early days of competitive play never suffered at all from nerves or the tenseness which has affected so many great players.

Vardon's great year was 1898: he won the Open at Prestwick, but also won matches all round the country; it seemed that he was invincible. He won again in the 1899 Open, and came second in the next three years. In 1900 he undertook a strenuous tour of the United States, playing matches all over the country, and winning the U.S. Open. His name became a byword not only in Britain but also in the United States, and crowds flocked to see him play. He took too much out of himself in this tour, and his health was never the same again. The Open was won in 1902 by Sandy Herd, the only one of the top players using the rubber-cored ball, but in 1903 Vardon won back the title although he was suffering from tuberculosis and almost unable to keep playing. He always thought himself that this was his most remarkable performance of all. After this, he had to pay frequent visits to the sanitorium, and he won nothing for eight years.

Vardon won two more Opens, in 1911 and 1914; the match-play title in 1912; and he was runner-up in the U.S. Open in 1913 and 1920.

A kindly and considerate man of great courage, Harry Vardon's name is one that will live in golf annals. Not only was he the supreme player of his time, but his lovely swing, his rhythm, and his development of the overlapping grip named after him were the link between the style of the early players and the modern approach.

James Braid

(1870–1950)

Born at Earlsferry in Fife, James Braid was a joiner by trade. His parents did not want him to take up golf as a career, but he had cousins who played in the top class, and in 1893 he was persuaded to go to London to work in the Army & Navy Stores as a clubmaker. Here he found more time for playing at the week-ends, and was soon in demand at exhibition matches. Standing over six feet tall, he hit the ball enormous distances, but was an indifferent putter. At this stage, he soon reached the top class, though without achieving major success.

It was after he changed his cleek for a putter that he began to win the titles: his first Open came at Muirfield in 1901. In the next 10 years he added another four Opens and four match-play wins; and he was never far from the top of the field in any tournament. During this time he was almost unbeatable, and he gave a great many exhibition matches with J. H. Taylor and Harry Vardon, sometimes being joined by his fellow Scot, Sandy Herd.

Braid had been professional at Romford, Essex; but in 1904 he moved to the newly opened Walton Heath (one of Herbert Fowler's masterpieces), where he remained for the rest of his life. In 1902 he was one of the founder members of the Professional Golfers' Association, and was elected captain. He remained involved in their

affairs throughout his long career in the game.

As a result of an accident when he was a joiner, he got lime in his eyes, and this eventually caused him so much trouble that he was advised not to play. However, he persisted, though the trouble remained with him. A shy and reserved man, he showed little emotion when he played, whether he was winning or losing. His com-

ments were short and to the point, and he was rarely given to raising his voice in public. In later years Braid was much in demand as a golf-course architect. His best known design is the King's course at Gleneagles; he was also responsible for two first-rate championship links courses – at Southport & Ainsdale in Lancashire and at Hunstanton in Norfolk. Braid died in London in 1950.

AN INTERNATIONAL SPORT

Amateurs and professionals

The last years of the 19th century and first two decades of the 20th saw the emergence of great amateur players – women as well as men – and the spread of professional and amateur national championships all over the golfing world. . . .

Above *Harold Hilton, twice winner of the Open and only British winner of the U.S. Amateur.*

Right *Four Great amateurs of the 1890s: from left, Johnny Laidlay, John Ball, Horace Hutchinson, Peter Anderson.*

Preceding two pages *The vast complex of courses at Pinehurst resort in North Carolina typifies the prodigious expansion of golf in America this century.*

Golf in Scotland and golf in England have always been very different. Although, as we have seen, it was the gentry who started many of the early Scottish clubs, yet all classes of people played from the earliest days, and the game was engrained in the popular culture in a way in which, even now, it is not in England. With the links common ground long ago, the stage was set for the expanding of the Scottish game by the introduction of many public courses, and at the same time there were plenty of private clubs being formed as well; but the accent was on a widespread availability. In England, on the other hand, there was a much more narrow approach, and this narrowness was also to be seen abroad, where golf tended often to be only for the rich. This is why, at first, most of the professionals were Scots.

At the end of the 19th century there were many good amateur players, and some at least could hold their own against most of the professionals. There were John Ball, both Open and Amateur Champion in 1890, and eight times winner of the Amateur before the first war; Harold Hilton, twice Open Champion, and four times Amateur Champion; Horace Hutchinson, finalist in the first three Amateurs, and winner twice, who was also a noted golf writer; Freddie Tait, twice Amateur Champion and twice third in the Open; John Laidlay, second to Willie Auchterlonie in the 1893 Open, reaching five Amateur finals in six years, and twice the

Champion. If these were the top amateur players of the time, there were also many others not far behind.

The list of amateur events grew steadily, and clubs began to run open amateur

tournaments; among the earliest open amateur stroke-play tournaments were the Tennant Cup in Glasgow and the Leven Gold Medal, both of which are still going strong. In 1888 the St George's Challenge Cup was introduced at Sandwich (home of Royal St George's Club), and it is still a major event in amateur golf. The names of the winners through the years indicates the strength of the fields and the status of this tournament; the winners from abroad include Francis Ouimet (winner of the U.S. Open in 1913) and Jack Nicklaus. Another prestigious trophy was the *Golf Illustrated* Gold Vase, instituted in 1909: Abe Mitchell won it twice before he turned professional, and Bobby Jones won it in 1930 – in addition to four other trophies of somewhat greater moment.

Amateur international matches were played between Scotland and England from 1902, and Ireland and Wales played their own first fixture in 1913. The standard in these matches was high, and there

was great competition among golfers to gain international status. In the 1920s there was a number of matches amongst the home countries, but it was not until 1932 that the Home International tourna-

Above *John Ball driving at Portmarnock in the Irish Open Amateur of 1899, when he won for the third time.*

who 'had partnered Harry Vardon in last year's Open'. The country-house round often meant country-house golf on days unsuitable for shooting or fishing; often the golf club, too, became, like the town club, a place where men could meet and relax or talk business. Club golf was played by more and more, and if the aspiring young tiger in the club disappeared into the upper echelons of county and national competitions, the vast and growing majority enjoyed their mediocrity – or worse – and played their regular matches with enthusiasm.

The ladies' game

Ladies' golf had been keeping pace with the men's, and the Ladies Golf Union was founded in 1893 by some ladies from Wimbledon; the moving spirit was Miss Issette Pearson, who became the first secretary. She also lost in the final of the first British Ladies Championship in 1893, and did the same in 1894. The winner for the first three years was Lady Margaret Scott. In the first 22 years of this championship, up to the First World War, it was played only four times in Scotland, showing the dominant English influence on the LGU over the period.

It has been said that at this time ladies' golf was played only by the upper classes; that was no doubt true in England, but

Above left *John Ball and Abe Mitchell.*

Above right *The Prince of Wales (later Edward VIII) at Oxford in 1912.*

Below *The final of the Ladies' Championship at St Andrews in 1908. Maud Titterton, the winner, is driving.*

ment was put on a regular basis, and organised in turn by the four home unions.

There were plenty of well-off young men in England in the Edwardian period who had leisure time. Bertie Wooster (of immortal memory) had friends in the Drones Club who played golf, though there is no evidence of any of them having reached the standard of Cuthbert Banks,

certainly not in Scotland, where everyone played. Ladies' clubs started, frequently connected with, or as sections of, men's clubs. In some cases, ladies had their own courses which were completely independent: examples of such self-governing course-owning clubs are still to be found to-day at Lundin Ladies (1891), Wirral Ladies (1894), Formby Ladies (1896) and Sunningdale Ladies (1902).

The LGU secretary, Miss Pearson, later became Mrs T.H. Miller, and her husband presented a trophy for the winners of the Ladies' Home International tournament. This was first contested in 1905 – a considerable time before the equivalent men's tournament. There were other important ladies' trophies of an early date: the Midland Ladies' Championship began in 1897, while the first of the county championships (Cornwall's) dates from 1896.

Overseas, too, the ladies' game had been expanding, and enough women were playing golf to encourage the institution of national ladies championships in New Zealand (1893), Australia (1894) and the United States (1895).

As with the men, there were many good women players in Britain before the First World War. Apart from Lady Margaret Scott, who had retired after her three consecutive British Ladies' wins, but returned to take the first three Swiss Ladies' championships (1907–9), there were the Misses Hezlet from Ireland; Miss Maud Titterton (Mrs Gibb); Miss Gladys Ravens-croft (Mrs Temple Dobell), who won the British Ladies in 1911 and the U.S. Ladies in 1912; and that most prolific winner Miss Dorothy Campbell (Mrs Hurd) who won two British, three Scottish, three Canadian and two U.S. Ladies' titles before the First World War, and then added a third U.S. title in 1924. Three of the Leitch sisters from Silloth (near Carlisle) played for England, but it was Cecil Leitch who was outstanding: she won the British, the

Above *Gladys Ravenscroft won the Ladies' Championship at Turnberry in 1912. Here she plays from a bunker by the 10th green.*

Below *Cecil Leitch playing against Harold Hilton in 1910. Note the 'Miss Higgins', a belt worn at knee-level to control her long skirt.*

English and the French titles in 1914; won each of them again on their resumption after the war, and altogether won the British title four times, the English twice, the French five times, and the Canadian once. Sadly, she was at her peak during the war years: how many more titles might she have added then?

Professionals' progress

At first the worlds of the amateur and the professional golfers were far apart; professionals were attached to clubs, and were club servants; they were usually responsible, in addition to playing, for a shop concerned with club making, repairing and selling, and also keeping a supply of balls; they were engaged in instruction: many were involved in course maintenance, or planning extensions or alterations to their home courses; and some were concerned with advising about new courses elsewhere. Essentially, though, the professional was a tradesman, and he

Right *The Great Triumvirate: J. H. Taylor seated; James Braid behind him; and Harry Vardon on the right. On the left is Jack White, Open Champion of 1904.*

Below *Commemorating the Golden Jubilee of the Open in 1910, a historic picture to show all the previous winners.*

'used the tradesman's entrance'. He was not a member of the club, and would not be allowed into the club socially except on odd occasions. There was a similar outlook in the other games: in cricket, for example, where the amateurs and professionals used different dressing rooms, and came onto the field by different gates. There was not a great deal of change before World War II. For although in the 1920s and 1930s there was a slow movement amongst the golf professionals towards improving their status, they did not achieve anything approaching social equality at the clubs until after the Second World War.

At the turn of the century, the Triumvirate of J. H. Taylor, Harry Vardon and James Braid ruled supreme: from 1894 to 1914 one of them was usually the Open Champion, they won many of the other tournaments (though there were few of these), and they won most of the challenge matches they played against others, though Sandy Herd, Ted Ray and one or two others proved redoubtable opponents. They went all round the country playing exhibition matches, and were an immense influence on the younger generation of golfers, both amateur and professional. Often they made up their four with the local professional, but their most frequent partner was Herd, who had been Open Champion in 1902, when he had been one of the few to use the new rubber-core Haskell ball. Another way they often arranged to play was with two of the three each taking a local top amateur partner; this was a particularly popular arrangement when they were inaugurating a new course or club.

With the great increase in the number of clubs, both at home and overseas, there was a need for a great many professionals. In the 1890s and early 1900s the opportunities were there, and the Scots came south and went overseas in large numbers; there were many competent players, and also many who had been apprenticed to a trade, and were therefore able to cope with the demands on the club professional. Sometimes whole families would move; sometimes there was opposition from parents: James Braid, for example, did not please his parents when he went south to a job in London; they thought he was throwing up the safe trade as a joiner for a very chancy future.

However, with a growing market, the way was clear for a young man to make what he could of it; and there were many who were outstandingly successful.

In 1901 an association of professional golfers in the London region was founded to look after their interests, and by 1902 this had become the Professional Golfers Association. Its first chairman was J.H. Taylor, and the first captain James Braid; both maintained a life-long connection with the PGA. The first trophy was the Tooting Bec Cup, and although this course in south London has now disappeared, the trophy remains, now awarded to the resident British player who has the lowest round in the Open. There is also the Harry Vardon Trophy, inaugurated after his death in 1937, and awarded to the player who comes top of the annual Order of Merit.

If many of the first professional golfers were Scots, there were soon many good English players who, usually coming from the ranks of the caddies, took up appointments as club professionals. Such a one

Scotland v. England professionals' match, 1912. **Top** *Scotland: standing, Allan Gow, R. Thomson, George Duncan, James Braid, Tom Fernie; sitting, W. Watt, Jack White, Alec Herd, J. Hepburn (capt.), Ben Sayers, L. B. Ayton, J. Kinnell.* **Above** *England: standing, J. B. Batley, Rowland Jones, Tom Williamson, Harry Vardon, T. G. Renout; sitting, P. J. Gaudin, W. E. Reid, G. H. Mayo, Ted Ray (capt.), J. H. Taylor, Tom Ball, J. Sherlock.*

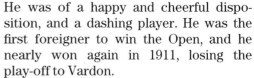

Above *International quartet at the Open in 1913 at Hoylake: (from left) Arnaud Massy (France – first foreign winner of the Open, in 1907), M. J. Brady (United States), Andrew Kirkaldy (professional to the Royal & Ancient); and Johnny McDermott (U.S. Open Champion in 1911 and 1912).*

Below *The Schenectady putter: competitors at the U.S. Amateur of 1912. W. J. Travis is at second right. By this time the row over the centre-shafted putter had erupted.*

was J. H. Taylor, and so too was Harry Vardon's brother, Tom, who persuaded Harry to give up his job as a gardener to be a professional golfer. There were many others, though not as famous. There were enough, however, to ensure that the Professional International match between Scotland and England, which ran from 1903 to 1938, was won by the English every year after the first three.

Up to 1914, then, British golfers held the top place in the world. There had been only two hiccups.

The Open Championship at Hoylake in 1907 was won by Arnaud Massy. He came from the south of France, had been 'discovered' at Biarritz, and sent for instruction to Ben Sayers at North Berwick.

He was of a happy and cheerful disposition, and a dashing player. He was the first foreigner to win the Open, and he nearly won again in 1911, losing the play-off to Vardon.

The Amateur Championship of 1904 was won by Walter J. Travis, Australian-born, who had lived in the United States since he was four years old. He had a remarkable run of success after taking the game up at the age of 34. Already a three-times U.S. Amateur champion, he came to the championship at Sandwich thoroughly dissatisfied with his performance in practice at St Andrews; the night before the opening round he borrowed a putter. It was a centre-shafted 'Schenectady' putter, and with it he recovered his usual immaculate putting. The amateurs of the day had not expected to be troubled by the invader; but he went through round after round, leaving amongst others Harold Hilton and Horace Hutchinson by the wayside. In the final he defeated the long-hitting Edward Blackwell. It was unfortunate that misunderstandings arose between the winner and the local golfers: they had found him stand-offish, and he thought he had been badly treated, and said so for some years. Nevertheless, the golf correspondents gave him full credit for his win, and crowd support for him seems to have been generous.

No one bothered at the time about his putter, but some years later the Royal & Ancient Rules of Golf Committee was asked if a putter with a centre-shaft like a croquet mallet was legal. The Rules of Golf Committee decided that it was illegal. The USGA did not agree, and there were the makings of a first-class row. Common sense prevailed, but the two bodies agreed to differ: and it would be many years before such a putter was allowed by the Royal & Ancient. Nowadays their Rules of Golf Committee holds regular meetings with the corresponding USGA committee to see that the rules and their interpretations are in harmony.

Golf between the wars

The First World War affected golf as it affected everything else. Most of a generation of Britons were killed or wounded, and after four years of conflict the country was tired and resources scarce.

In the years immediately following the war, people tried to pick up the pieces and to carry on as before. In 1920 George Duncan won the Open and Cyril Tolley the Amateur. Then, in 1921, Jock Hutchinson defeated Roger Wethered in a play-off for the Open at St Andrews. Also in the field were Walter Hagen, U.S. Open winner in 1914 and 1919, who had barely forgiven himself for finishing well down the field in the previous Open, and who this time finished in a respectable fifth position; and Robert Tyre Jones, who after a poor first nine holes, blew up at the short 11th, and slipped away, little noticed except by himself: and he did not easily forgive himself. Of the next nine Opens, Hagen was to win four and Jones three.

There was another contest in 1921, when a team of amateurs from the United States played a British team at Hoylake, and won easily. This developed into the Walker Cup, played for in each of the next three years, and thereafter every second year. The Americans were soon to show that they had developed into the best golfing nation in the world, their many great professionals and amateurs dominating the game at every level.

The Oxford & Cambridge Golfing Society had been formed in 1898 and had played a number of matches in each season before the war. In 1920 the society inaugurated the President's Putter tournament, and it has continued annually ever since. This informal but keenly contested event is, somewhat eccentrically, played at Rye in the dead of winter, and the field generally contains many of the top amateur golfers. In the first four years Ernest Holderness was the winner, and he won again in 1929. Roger Wethered also won five times (including a shared win, when the light gave out before a result in the final could be achieved). Cyril Tolley contested three finals before his first win, in the fourth, in 1938. The Society has made a notable contribution to golf, particularly in the south of England.

In 1924 the Halford-Hewitt Cup was presented for competition amongst a number of independent schools. The competition grew to include a total of 64 schools and, with teams of 10, has one of the largest competitive entries. It is play-

Above A distinguished post-war golfer, Sir Ernest Holderness, twice Amateur Champion, playing in the President's Putter at Rye in 1925. The green is white with frost.

Below The Varsity Match of 1920: the Oxford team included Roger Wethered (centre) and Cyril Tolley (right). On the left is R. R. Burton.

ed at Deal and also (after the expansion) at Sandwich, and is another event supported loyally over the years.

Open amateur tournaments continued to flourish: the Prince of Wales Challenge Cup, started in 1927, is played at Deal; the St David's Gold Cross (1930) at Harlech; the Worplesdon Mixed Foursomes (1921); and in Scotland the Glasgow Amateur (1925), the Eden Tournament at St Andrews (1919); the Craw's Nest Tassie at Carnoustie (1927), and the Gleneagles Silver Tassie (1925) are all examples of the appetite for more and more competitive golf. Counties which had not had their own champions before fitted the tournaments into their programme; district championships multiplied; there were county matches, district matches, international matches. And a golfer who had played at all these levels could now hope to reach the ultimate goal – the Walker Cup team.

Golf in Britain had always been a social game; it was played to be enjoyed in itself, and the handicapping system meant that players of widely different ability could have an even game. Of course you tried to win, but it was not a disaster if the result went against you. This is a wide generalisation, but it does show the British approach in most games and sports. The whole world was changing in its outlook, and although the attitude was to look down on those who 'practised beforehand

Above *Bernard Darwin: a top class golfer and an eminent golf-writer. He played in the first Walker Cup team in 1922: he was there to report the matches but joined the team when a substitute was needed.*

Above, right *George Duncan studies Bobby Jones's putting style before the 1921 Open.*

Below *Ted Ray, recently returned from America where he had won the U.S. Open, drives off in a challenge match at Oxhey in 1920.*

and ruined the fun', yet it began to be realised that the British, who had been pre-eminent in most games, were now no longer at the top. It was a hard lesson to learn, but the days of what were called 'the true amateur' were numbered as far as golf's major prizes were concerned.

Transatlantic domination

The lesson was first brought home in the professional field. Throughout the 1920s there was a steady invasion by United States players in the Open. Arthur Havers won in 1923 at Troon, by a single stroke from Walter Hagen: it was to be 11 years before there was another British winner. Meantime the club professionals

flourished, and there were a number of tournaments during the summer season. The Whitcombe brothers, Abe Mitchell (three times match-play champion), Percy Alliss (who won the German Open five times, the Italian twice), Archie Compston (who in a £500 challenge match defeated Walter Hagen comprehensively in 1928 – just before Hagen went on to win the Open), Alf Padgham: these were all players successful through the 1920s and early 1930s, but they never seemed quite good enough to take the major prize. It was left to the young Henry Cotton to see what was wanted, and to spend time playing in tournaments in the United States to try to find the secret of their success. In simple terms it boiled down to practice – and more practice. Henry Cotton was a dedicated person, determined to succeed. He did well enough in the United States, and returned with the will to achieve his object: a win in the Open. This came at Sandwich in 1934, and it was clear that a new star was on the scene. It was the start of a string of English winners up to 1939. Cotton's second win was at Carnoustie in 1937, against a very strong field including the United States Ryder Cup team, which had been the first team to win away from home.

Highlights of the amateur scene were the Hon. Michael Scott's win in the Amateur Championship of 1933 at the age of 54, and the lone Walker Cup victory at St Andrews in 1938.

Although the ladies in the United States did not start a professional tour until after World War II, they too were brought up in a hard school, and proved a handful in encounters with British players. However, they were not able to storm the citadel of the British Ladies', and in the battle for the great prizes, Britain, represented by Joyce Wethered, was supreme. There was a number of excellent British lady golfers during the 1930s after Joyce Wethered had retired from major competition: Enid Wilson won three consecutive British Ladies' titles; Helen Holm won three of her five Scottish championships and two British Ladies' before the war; Diana Fishwick (Critchley) had held off the American challenge in the British Ladies' of 1930; Pam Barton, twice winner of the British Ladies' and twice runner-up, carried the flag overseas and won the U.S. Ladies' in 1936; and Jessie Anderson (Valentine) won her first British Ladies' in 1937, the Scottish Ladies' in 1938 and 1939, and had nervelessly holed a stupendous putt in the 1936 Curtis Cup at Gleneagles to square the whole match.

When the war came in 1939 the game of golf all over the British Isles was flourishing, and players in their thousands filled the private and public courses from Shetland to Scilly.

Left *Diana Fishwick successfully repulsed the challenge of Glenna Collett to win the 1930 Ladies' Championship.*

Below *Lawson Little, a mighty hitter from America, twice won the Amateur Championship in the 1930s.*

FASHION ON THE FAIRWAYS

Styles in golf wear were for long determined less by practicality than by social convention and the stern dictates of modesty. Today more or less anything goes — and the men are often as gaudy as the women.

Originally golfers wore their everyday clothes, but with the forming of societies it became the custom for members to play in club uniform, and there were penalties for those who did not conform. In the mid-19th century the two St Andrews clubs could be distinguished, the Royal & Ancient wearing a red coat and the St Andrews Club a green one. The Aberdeen Club uniform included a lum (stove-pipe) hat, but this proved impractical and was superseded by a velvet cap.

Towards the end of the 19th century, gentlemen wore a jacket (often a belted Norfolk jacket) and tie, and some preferred knee breeches to ordinary trousers, for they are more comfortable and effective wear in wet weather — particularly if one is given to visit-ing the rough. Tight jackets may have been fashionable, but they were restricting.

Largely as a result of golf in other climates, especially in Amer-ica, a revolution occurred, and by the 1920s clothing became not only more comfortable but also more colourful. Top players appeared in striking garments; in this, as in so many other ways, Walter Hagen was prominent, whilst Tommy Armour was another natty dresser. Plus-fours (knickers) appeared, an extension of knee breeches, but with very baggy legs; plus-twos, now so popular, were also worn in the 1930s. In hot climates golfers frequently played in shorts; while in the wetter ones, the all-weather gear consisted of a jerkin and waterproof trousers for men, or waterproof skirt for ladies: by modern standards, they were not

Golf fashions in the ads: top right from 1912; top left from 1920. The Kilton of 1913, above, was presumably for use north of the Tweed.

Below *A 1926 version of the mini-skirt. Some women favoured 'bloomers', too; and the belted jacket had given way to the straight cut with loose belt.*

Right *By 1952 comfort and elegance went together. The Vicomtesse de Saint Sauveur (winner of the British Ladies' in 1950) was considered amongst the best dressed.*

Below *There are some very colourful dressers nowadays: men, especially the professionals, indulge in outfits of matching coordinates. Perhaps the prize is divided between Payne Stewart (seen here) and Rodger Davis.*

the last moment for her match, Miss Gloria Minoprio appeared in a striking pair of black slacks: there was consternation; the accepted dress for championships was a blouse and skirt. Today many women golfers resort to the briefest of shorts and sleeveless shirts for summer; and, for men and women alike, the cool practicality of summer-weight materials is matched by the loudness of their colours and patterns. And even on the gloomiest English day, the more slavish followers of fashion dare not tee off without a sun visor.

very effective. The cloth cap, or bonnet, has remained in vogue throughout.

The ladies, bound by the tyrannical requirements of modesty, were even more restricted by their clothing, and it should have been almost impossible for them to take more than a half-swing; but pictures of Lady Margaret Scott (the first champion) in the 1890s show that she was capable of a full back swing and complete follow through. There was little change before the First World War, though Miss Cecil Leitch favoured a sensibly loose blouse and skirt, and was one of the first to belt the ball a good distance. Skirts were long, but they shortened with the passing years: the flapping skirt, much later on, gave way to trousers.

A startling effect was produced in the 1933 English Ladies Championship at Westward Ho! when, at

TEN GREAT AMATEURS

Ball, Hilton, and above all the immortal Bobby Jones were amateurs capable of beating the finest professionals of their day. Among the women the greatness of Wethered and Collett matched that of today's finest lady pro stars.

John Ball

(1861–1940)

John Ball's father owned the Royal Hotel, Hoylake, built alongside the ground on which was built Hoylake golf course, later to become home of the Royal Liverpool Club. John Ball learnt his golf here and spent much of his youth on the links, developing quickly into an accomplished player. At the age of 16 he first competed in the Open, and finished fourth, ahead of many famous professionals. In 1890 he won the Open: he was the first amateur to do so, and it was the first time that the title had not been won by a Scottish professional. In this year he also won the Amateur (for the second time), and thus was the holder of both championships at the same time: he is the only British player ever to have done this; Bobby Jones was to achieve the same feat in 1930; but it is most unlikely that it will ever be done again. In all, John Ball won the Amateur eight times between 1888 and 1912, as well as three Irish Amateur titles; and he won the St George's Challenge Cup for four years from its inception in 1888. He played for England in all international matches from their start in 1902 till 1912.

An essentially modest person, not given much to talking about himself or his golf, he was described as 'wiry and active, and immensely strong'. Some of his contemporaries were of the opinion that, although he was almost invincible at Hoylake, he did not do well elsewhere. It seems very strange that this should have been said, for it fails to account for the championship titles he won at such diverse and widely scattered venues as St Andrews, Prestwick, Sandwich, and Westward Ho! There seems little room to doubt that he was the greatest-ever amateur produced in Britain.

Left *First amateur to be Open Champion, John Ball won both the Open and the Amateur in 1890. Here he plays a full shot with a straight-faced iron from the Cop Bunker at Hoylake. Only a player of his calibre could contemplate such a shot.*

Harold Hilton

(1869–1942)

Harold Hilton was born at West Kirby on 12 January 1869. It was not far from Hoylake which was opened that same year; and it was there that he played his early golf. Some seven years younger than John Ball, he had that player before him as an example, and to spur him on.

In 1892, at the age of 23, Hilton won the Open; it was the first time it had been played over 72 holes, and it was also the first time it had been played at Muirfield. It is interesting to note that Hilton and Ball were two English amateurs who won the Open before any English professional (the first was

J.H. Taylor in 1894). Hilton won the Open again in 1897, on his home course; but so far the Amateur had eluded him. Finally he achieved it in 1900, and he went on to win four times in all, the last in 1913. One of these victories was in 1911 and in that year he also won the American Amateur at Apawamis. He is the only British player to have won the two titles in the same year. His other wins included four Irish Amateur Championships (including three in a row from 1900), the St George's Challenge Cup in 1893 and 1894, and the *Golf Illustrated* Gold Vase in 1914. He was the first Editor of *Golf Monthly* (launched in 1911) and held the post till the outbreak of war in 1914. He was below middle height, but very powerful and a most determined competitor.

Harold Hilton was twice Open Champion; in 1911 he won both the Amateur and the U.S. Amateur. Like his great rival John Ball, Hilton was a member of Royal Liverpool club at Hoylake.

Freddie Tait

(1870–1900)

Frederick Guthrie Tait was the third son of Professor Tait of Edinburgh University. The family went often to St Andrews, and Freddie had a club in his hands from the age of five on the sands; by seven he was playing on the courses, often all day long; and by the time he was 12 he had been round the Old Course in under 100. From 1884 on he kept a note of all his games, with remarks: his notebooks have been preserved, and make interesting reading. In a match at St Andrews with A.F. Macfie, the first winner of the Amateur Championship (1885), he went round in 77, then a course record; later he lowered it to 72.

Tait first played in the Open in 1891, and in the course of eight entries was first amateur three times, coming third in 1896 and 1897. He won the Amateur in 1896, beating Laidlay, Ball, Hutchinson and Hilton on the way; he won again in 1898; and in 1899 in the final he lost at the 37th to John Ball. He also won the St George's Challenge Cup in 1896-98-99.

He had become a professional soldier, in 1894 being gazetted to the Black Watch. In 1899 he went with his regiment to the war in South Africa, and he was killed leading his men into battle on 7 February 1900. He was a person of great cheerfulness and adventurous spirit, always with a smile on his face. Loved and admired, he was an inspiration to all who knew him.

Below *Twice winner of the Amateur Championship, Freddie Tait was one of the great gentleman golfers of the 1890s. Here he is putting at the 18th in a match at St Andrews; attending the pin is Old Tom Morris.*

Francis Ouimet

(1893–1967)

He was born at Brookline, Mass. and, when he was a youngster, his family moved to a house near the Country Club. Ouimet was bitten by the golf bug, and used to play as often as he could; he took up caddying when he was 11. His family were not well off, and he found himself a job when he was 16 – he could no longer caddy without losing his amateur status. His golf continued to improve, and he had early success in some important local tournaments, taking the Massachusetts Amateur championship in 1913.

It was in the U.S. Open of 1913 that he came to national prominence. He almost did not play in it as he had used up his available holiday time playing in the U.S. Amateur. However, he was persuaded to enter by the president of the U.S. Golfing Association, and his boss agreed to his playing. Harry Vardon and Ted Ray, on tour in the United States and expected to provide the winner, tied, and Ouimet was able to equal their score for a three-way play-off: it

was a situation which captured the imagination of the American people: here was the home-bred youngster pitted against the seasoned British invaders. Ouimet won – and with it kindled the immense popularity of golf in the States, for it showed that an ordinary American from an ordinary home could take on the best.

Ouimet won the U.S. Amateur in 1914 and again in 1931, as well as being runner-up in 1920. He played in the first-ever Walker Cup match, and was included in every team up to 1949 – in the last four as non-playing captain. In 1951 came the final honour from across the Atlantic when he became captain of the Royal & Ancient. A modest and genuine person, he never let success go to his head. He continued to be involved in the administration and running of the game until his death in 1967.

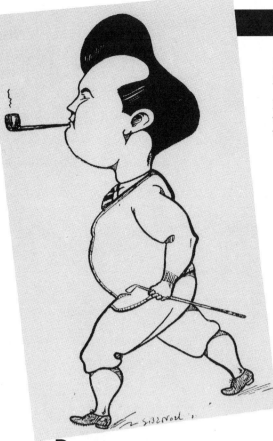

Roger Wethered

(1899–1983)

Cyril Tolley

(1896–1978)

These two players were the dominant British amateurs between the wars. Both started to play golf at an early age, Tolley at Eastbourne and Wethered much of the time at Dornoch. They met at Oxford after the First World War, and went on to many successes.

Wethered was tall and given to hard concentration and not much talk. A great match-player, he was superb with his irons, and had the ability to play recovery shots from almost anywhere. He tied for the Open 1920 after penalising himself for standing on his ball while looking at a line; he lost the play-off. He won the Amateur in 1923, and was runner-up in 1928 and 1930. He appeared in five Walker Cup matches, and won a host of tournaments, including the Royal St George's Cup, the *Golf Illustrated* Gold Vase and the President's Putter (five times). He was captain of the R & A in 1946.

Tolley had a magnificent swing, almost machine-like in quality and rhythm. He always had a confident and majestic air, hit the ball prodigious distances, but was inclined to be careless. He won the Amateur in 1920 and 1929, the French Open twice (1924, 1928), on the second occasion against a very

Right *Bobby Jones in 1929 at Winged Foot, where he won the U.S. Open for the third time.*

Below *1930, the year of the 'Impregnable Quadrilateral': Jones with the British and U.S. Open and Amateur trophies.*

strong field that included Walter Hagen (who took the Open at Sandwich that year). Six times he played in the Walker Cup matches, and he too won many of the main amateur tournaments, including the *Golf Illustrated* Gold Vase on three occasions. He was captain of the Royal & Ancient in 1948.

Bobby Jones

(1902–1971)

Robert Tyre Jones – 'Bob' to his friends, 'Bobby' to the media and his host of admirers around the world – was born in Atlanta, Georgia into a well-to-do family. He started playing golf at the age of five; and he used to say later that he had had the benefit of starting early in life, which gave him an advantage over those who had begun the game only when they had reached maturity. As a teenager in 1916 he won the Georgia State Open, and he played in the U.S. Amateur for the first time in that year. In 1919 he lost in the final. He came to Britain in 1921 and played in the Amateur at Hoylake, losing in the fourth round. It was also in this year that, in the Open at St Andrews, he picked up his ball half-way through the third round as his score was so bad; his re-

marks concerning the course were not complimentary. For ever after he regarded this day as the most shameful of his life and he apologised for his 'demeanour'. He came to love the Old Course as he grew to know it: he is not the only great golfer to have 'discovered' this course through hard experience. Also in 1921 he played in a Great Britain v United States match at Hoylake; this led the following year to the inauguration of the Walker Cup. Jones played in five of the first six matches, losing only once – in a foursome – in his 10 games.

It was in 1923 that he won his first major tournament, the U.S. Open at Inwood, Long Island; he tied with Bobby Cruickshank, but won the play-off. From 1923 till

Joyce Wethered

(Lady Heathcoat-Amory) (1901-

Joyce Wethered was in her time the supreme lady golfer. It was Bobby Jones who said, after playing with her: 'I have never played golf with anyone, man or woman, amateur or professional, who made me feel so utterly outclassed'. There cannot be a better testimonial.

She was noted for a magnificent swing and for phenomenal accuracy; she hit the ball as straight as anyone ever has, and her short pitch shots were played with extreme delicacy. It all came from great application and practice.

She was born in 1901, and learnt to play on the links at Dornoch, where her family went frequently on holiday. She played with her brother, Roger; when he was in the Oxford University team, she played often with him and his friends, all top amateur players, and absorbed much from these games. It was to be a great help to her when she started to play in competitions against ladies; whereas she had been striving to keep up with the men, now she was leaving her opponents yards behind.

Her record in the short time she played championship golf was extraordinary: in 1920 she entered for the English Ladies' Championship, persuaded by a friend to come along with her and play; Miss Wethered reached the final, and there played against the reigning

1930 his success was phenomenal: during this period he won three Open Championships (1926, 1927, 1930); four U.S. Opens (1923, 1926, 1929, 1930) – he was also in a tie in 1928, but lost; five U.S. Amateurs (1924, 1925, 1927, 1928, 1930), and was runner-up in 1926. In 1930 he won the Amateur Championship at St Andrews, and by the end of that summer, he had won the British and United States Opens and Amateurs, a unique quartet of wins which is now beyond even any possibility of emulation.

Bobby Jones' complete domination of the golfing scene in the 1920s won him an immense following both in the United States and in Great Britain. Vast crowds came to see him wherever he played; he seemed almost invincible. He found playing in championships a great strain, however, and, as he was taking so much out of himself, he decided to quit at the end of 1930. He was then 28 years old – an age when he could reasonably have expected to go on improving for at least another five years.

He was in no way finished with golf; but he set himself up in a law practice and golf became a spare-time activity. Amongst other facets of the game, he worked on the setting up of his course at Augusta,

and in 1934 the Masters tournament was launched, in which he enjoyed taking part quietly, without thought of being a serious contender. He served in the U.S. Air Force during the Second World War, and returned to playing in the Masters when it resumed; but he was struck by a debilitating illness in 1947, and after some years he was confined to a wheelchair and often in great pain. Bravely he continued with all the activities he could, and as always his many friends among the golfing great world would gather at Augusta for the Masters. He became an honorary member of the Royal & Ancient Golf Club in 1956 and – at an intensely emotional ceremony two years later – a Freeman of St Andrews after he had come over as non-playing captain of the United States team in the Eisenhower Trophy. The 10th hole on the Old Course, which had no name, is now named after him.

Bobby Jones was a great man: a man of culture and learning, he was blessed also with a huge generosity of spirit and the social grace of the well-bred Southern gentleman. He was also beyond question one of the three or four greatest golfers – amateur or professional – who ever lived.

Below *Joyce Wethered: a study in balance and control at the 1923 Ladies' Championship at Burnham and Berrow.*

Right *Wethered's great rival Cecil Leitch had a most distinguished career. Between 1912 and 1926 she won the Ladies' Championship four times; the English Ladies' twice; the French Ladies' five times; and the Canadian Ladies'. She would undoubtedly have added to these had it not been for the First World War.*

champion, Cecil Leitch, who had already won the English Ladies' twice (1914, 1919) and was holder of the British Ladies' too; almost a cult figure, Miss Leitch had an enormous accompanying support. Miss Wethered won, and she also won the next four English Ladies' titles on the trot. She entered the competition only five times, and won on each occasion. Runner-up to Miss Leitch in the British Ladies' and the French Ladies' in 1921, Miss Wethered defeated her in the 1922 final of the British Ladies', and also won in 1924 and 1925. She then decided she had had enough; but she could not resist returning to play in the British Ladies' at St Andrews in 1929. In the final she played Glenna Collett, the finest woman golfer in the United States.

In a magnificent, fluctuating final Miss Wethered won. This time she really was finished with championship golf.

After playing in the home internationals six times (1921 to 1925, and 1929) she played in the inaugural Curtis Cup match in 1932, lost in the foursomes, but again defeated Glenna Collett (Mrs Vare) in the singles. Thereafter she played competitively only rarely, but she continued to enter the Worplesdon Mixed Foursomes, and, with various partners, won it eight times between 1921 and 1936; and she won the Sunningdale Open Foursomes twice, in 1935 and 1936.

When she took a job in the golf department of Fortnum & Mason's in London her amateur status was taken away; and in 1935 she made a successful exhibition tour in the United States.

Her amateur status was restored after the Second World War. She now lives, a widow, in Devon.

Enid Wilson

(1910-

Enid Wilson was a well-known figure, dressed in her tweed skirt and (when necessary) her long macintosh. A much respected reporter and writer, she was for many years with the *Daily Telegraph* until her retirement in the early 1970s. (She would, indeed, have enjoyed a wider reputation as a superb player if she could have been persuaded occasionally to mention her own play in her match reports.) Her articles and books were always full of knowledgeable comment; play at the highest level and a lifetime's attachment to golf gave her a sound base, and she was not afraid of expressing her opinions. She had, in particular, an expert and wide grasp of every facet of women's golf.

She was born in Derbyshire and first came to prominence at golf as a schoolgirl of 15, when she won the British Girls' at Stoke Poges. County and district titles followed, and in 1927 she was runner-up in the English Ladies'; she won the title in 1928, and again in 1930. In that year, too, she won the Roehampton Gold Cup. Then came a hat-trick of wins in the British Ladies', 1931-3; and this established her firmly amongst the greatest women golfers of her time. Twice (1931, 1933) she reached the semi-final of the American Ladies', on the second occasion winning the medal for the best qualifying round; and she played in the inaugural Curtis Cup match in 1932. It was a most distinguished record, but it came to an end suddenly with the withdrawal of her amateur status, although she had been writing some years.

She worked in a London store selling and designing golf equipment until the war, during which she served as an officer in the WAAF. After the war she took up writing full time.

Left *Glenna Collett shows perfect balance. She had a wonderful competition record and was known as the 'female Bobby Jones.'*

Below *Although Glenna Collett played par golf, she found Joyce Wethered in unbeatable mood at the British Ladies' at Troon, 1925.*

Glenna Collett

(Mrs Vare)
(1903-88)

Glenna Collett dominated American ladies golf for many years during the 1920s and 1930s, and was referred to as 'the female Bobby Jones'.

Born in 1903, she came from a well-to-do family, and was keen on all sports and a naturally gifted player. It was not until she was 14 that she started to play golf – her mother had tried to steer her away from baseball, at which she excelled, and into tennis; golf came more or less accidentally. She was one of the first women to hit the ball with real freedom, and drove great distances from the start; her whole approach to the game was full of bubbling enthusiasm, and she attacked every hole. That was the sort of person she was.

By the age of 18 she had defeated Cecil Leitch, already winner of three British Ladies' titles, in a competition. She first won the American Ladies' in 1922; then again in 1925; and then three in a row, 1928-30; and for the last time in 1935: six times the winner, a feat which has not been equalled. She also won the Canadian Open twice, and many other tournaments.

It was her keen desire to try her hand in Great Britain, and she played in the British Ladies' at Troon in 1925; she lost to Joyce Wethered in the 3rd round, but was only one over par when she lost 4 and 3. In 1929 at St Andrews she again met Joyce Wethered, this time in the final; after a magnificent match of fluctuating fortunes, she again lost. She was runner-up once more the next year. She played in four Curtis Cup matches, and was non-playing captain on a fifth occasion.

She lifted American ladies' golf to new heights; but it was said of her that her charm lay in a freedom of spirit which did not make her feel that success was everything in the world. She was that very rare person, a good winner. She was still playing golf to a respectable standard when well into her 80s.

The transatlantic wave

In the United States the design and construction of courses, the founding of clubs, and the spread of the game itself owed much to immigrant Scots – both businessmen and journeyman professionals – during the three decades from 1890....

The famous tree which gave its name to the Apple Tree Gang, who started golf in the United States at the St Andrews Club, New York. The original course is now built over, but the tree is preserved.

When John Reid, originally from Dunfermline, received from his friend Robert Lockhart, a New York merchant who had also emigrated from Dunfermline, some clubs and balls, he set up (as we have seen) a three-hole course in his cow pasture. This was in November 1888, and the St Andrews Club of Yonkers, New York, was formed. They soon moved to a bigger area, and then to an apple orchard, where they became known as 'The Apple Tree Gang'; there was some opposition to a further move, but it became necessary, and they made a nine-hole course at Grey Oaks. The final move was to their present home at Mount Hope, Westchester County, in 1897; here they had 18 holes and a good clubhouse. The Shinnecock Hills Golf Club, at the eastern end of Long Island, was the first incorporated club, and dates from 1891. Willie Dunn, Jr laid out the first 12 holes, and soon there were courses for gentlemen and ladies there.

The most notable golfer in the United States at this time was Charles Blair Macdonald, whose family came from Scotland. He was sent to the University of St Andrews, and lodged with his grandfather, who initiated him into the mysteries of golf. He was immediately hooked. He quickly became a good golfer, and played with most of the local professionals and top-class amateurs of the time. He used his university years to full advantage. At home he played at the Chicago Golf Club, where he laid out the course. A tournament in 1894 at Newport Club was sponsored by Theodore Havemeyer, a rich business man, and 20 golfers were invited from various clubs. Macdonald came second, but he objected to the tournament being considered as the Amateur Championship as it was a stroke-play event.

In October of the same year, the St Andrews Club ran a tournament, and

Macdonald lost in the final at the 19th. He objected to this tournament, too, on the grounds that it was not open, but by invitation. The result of all this was a get-together of representatives of the five main clubs – Shinnecock Hills, the Country Club at Brookline (Boston), the Chicago Golf Club, St Andrews Golf Club, and Newport Golf Club. From this meeting in December 1894, the Amateur Golf Association of the United States was born; later it became the American Golf Association, and in due course the United States Golf Association (USGA). Its first president was Theo Havemeyer, and each of the five clubs was represented on the first committee. The secretary was Henry O. Tallmadge, from the St Andrews Club; he seems to have been one of the few able to keep in check the tempestuous Charles Macdonald, who was one of the first vice-presidents, and who won the first official U.S. Amateur in 1895. The trophy was provided by the president, Theo Havemeyer. The committee had arranged to have in addition an Open Championship, which was played on the following day, and a Ladies' Championship a month later.

The Scottish legacy

By 1900 there were over 1,000 golf courses in the United States, and each state had at least one. The first public course outside Britain had opened five years before at Van Courtland Park, New York City. To meet the needs of what now amounted to about a quarter of a million American golfers, there was a steady stream of professionals across the Atlantic from Britain, and most of them came from Scotland. There were some who made a quick impact on the tournaments:

An early American course, at Shinnecock Hills, venue of the U.S. Open of 1896 and home of the first incorporated club in the United States.

Pinehurst No 2, the masterpiece of master course designer Donald Ross, once the professional and greenkeeper at Royal Dornoch.

United States in 1899 at the promptings of Professor Wilson of Harvard, a visitor to Dornoch. He worked first at Oakley, but was then also appointed to Pinehurst, a links area in North Carolina, and for some years he spent the summer at Oakley and the winter at Pinehurst. He was a top-class player, finishing fifth in the U.S. Open of 1903 at Baltusrol (NY) and eighth in the Open at St Andrews in 1910; but he was much better known as a golf-course architect, and became the most famous in the country. Responsible for several hundred courses, his greatest masterpiece is Pinehurst No.2, completed in 1907. Remembering his early training under Old Tom, he took immense trouble to make his courses as natural as possible; but his particular trademark was the raised greens that are a feature of the great links course at Dornoch. He supervised personally the construction of as many of his courses as possible. He set his sights and standards high, and a Donald Ross course is always the guarantee that it is in the top class.

In 1900 Harry Vardon came on a tour of the United States; in the course of some months he covered over 20,000 miles, and played exhibition matches wherever he went. At the time he was the leading golfer in the world: he had won the Open Championships of 1898 and 1899, and had also won nearly every tournament and match he had played during those two years, usually with great ease. His modest and friendly manner made a great impression during his tour, and he did much to promote golf. Indeed, the four rounds he played at Pinehurst's crude No.1 course inspired the course's owner to commission Ross's No.2 and the construction of two further courses later on. During his tour Vardon won the U.S. Open at the Chicago Club (J. H. Taylor coming second).

Home-grown talent

The winner of the U.S. Amateur in 1900, 1901 and 1903 was Walter J. Travis, who as we have seen won the British Amateur in 1904. 'The Old Man', as he was known, had started to play golf only in 1896, when he was 34. He was an influential figure in American golf during the first part of the 20th century, and winner of many tournaments. He was not a long hitter but very

Horace Rawlins, who won the first U.S. Open, was only 19, and had only recently come from England when he defeated Willie Dunn, Jr by two strokes. Willie Smith won in 1899, and his brother Alex in 1906 and 1910; the whole family, from Carnoustie (a great source of emigrant golfing talent), was to come to the United States, the parents bringing the youngest brother, Macdonald Smith, the most famous of them all, and one of those with a strong claim to be known as 'the best player never to win an Open'. Then there was Willie Anderson, who won the U.S. Open in 1901, and again in three consecutive years, 1903, 1904 and 1905; and Alex Ross, from Dornoch, who won in 1907. His brother Donald never won that prize but was to achieve even more lasting fame.

Donald J. Ross was born in Dornoch in 1873. Apprenticed as a joiner, when he was 20 he went as apprentice to Old Tom Morris at St Andrews; he had plenty of opportunity to play there before being recalled to Dornoch as professional-greenkeeper in 1895. He sailed to the

straight, and a remarkable putter. He had frequent duels with 'The Young Man', who had the similar-sounding name, Jerry Travers. The two first met in an invitation tournament in 1904, when the 17-year-old Travers won. Great respect grew up between the two, as both had the same fierce determination to win. As a result of all his hard-fought matches, Travers became the best match-player of the time. Travis retired from competitive golf in 1915. He continued to write with authority on golf until his death, at the age of 65, in 1927. Jerry Travers won the U.S. Amateur in 1907, 1908, 1912 and 1913; and he stamped his name as one of the great home-born American amateurs when he added the U.S. Open title to his collection in 1915. Like most top American amateurs of that time, he came from a well-to-do family and had started playing at an early age.

Left *Walter J. Travis, 'The Old Man', a massive figure in American golf. He won the U.S. Amateur three times in four years, and followed this with the British Amateur in 1904.*

Below *Jerry Travers, 'The Young Man': his record of four U.S. Amateurs and one U.S. Open speaks for itself.*

which was presented by the Curtis sisters.

In general, there was ample provision for lady players in the United States, and the country club facilities were available to all.

In 1911 there was a milestone in United States golf history when John McDermott became the first home-born American to win the U.S. Open, and he won again in the following year. In 1911 Harold Hilton became the only English player to win the U.S. Amateur. It was a nail-biting affair: Hilton was six up during the final round, but his opponent, Fred Herreshoff, a rather wild but hard-hitting golfer, staged a magnificent fight back, and the match was level after 36 holes. At the first extra hole, it was Hilton who hit a wild shot, but he had a fortunate bounce, and won the hole and championship.

At this time golf was still regarded with some suspicion by the average American as being a sport for the rich; further, it was seen as an occupation for the elderly and fairly infirm, and not worthy to be considered by the young and vigorous. True, there had been occasions when there had been young and good-looking winners – but they came from rich families and were an exception. Then came 1913.

In this year Harry Vardon and Ted Ray came again to the United States on tour;

Above *Francis Ouimet with his caddie, Eddie Lowery, in the 1913 U.S. Open, when he beat Vardon and Ray in a playoff.*

Right *Johnny McDermott was the first home-bred player to win the U.S. Open (1911).*

Meanwhile, ladies' golf had been making steady headway. The first heroine was Beatrix Hoyt who, at the age of 16, won the second U.S. Ladies' in 1896; she took the title in the following two years, then retired from competitive golf. Laurence Curtis, a vice-president of the original USGA, had two sisters, Harriot and Margaret, who both became winners of the U.S. Ladies', the former in 1906, the latter in 1907, 1911 and 1912. A group of ladies from the United States came to Britain in 1905 to play in the British Ladies' at Cromer; there were enough to form a team to play an unofficial match against a team of British ladies, and the home team won. It was an important step, for it led, albeit many years later – in 1932 – to the inauguration of a biennial match between American and British ladies for a cup

and as before it was a popular and very successful visit. At the U.S. Open at The Country Club, Brookline a young, little-known local amateur tied with the British pair – then won the play-off. Francis Ouimet, a modest, gentle person from an ordinary American home, had defeated the British giants, and at the same time had demonstrated to other ordinary Americans that golf was an all-American game. He did more that just win the tournament: he opened a door, and golf received a boost not only in the United States, but, ultimately, the world over. Ouimet remained a modest and gentle person, from an ordinary American home, and enjoyed a remarkably long career at the top of the amateur game.

Within a decade of Ouimet's Open triumph the number of players had rocketed, and the Americans had become the best in the world. Walter Hagen won the U.S. Open in 1914, while Ouimet won the U.S. Amateur; in 1916 'Chick' Evans, a frequent semi-finalist, was at last successful in winning not only the U.S. Amateur but the U.S. Open as well. Robert Gardner, youngest U.S. Amateur winner in 1909, won again in 1915. In 1916 the Professional Golfers' Association of America was formed, and the first U.S. PGA tournament – for long a matchplay event – was won by Jim Barnes, an American who came originally from Cornwall and would return to Britain to win the Open in 1925.

Tournaments were suspended in 1917 for the duration of the war. A number of Red Cross charity matches were played, and amongst those appearing was the young and prodigiously talented Robert Tyre Jones, who had played in the U.S. Amateur of 1916 at the age of 14 and had won his first open tournament in that

Above *Inverness Club, Ohio, a testing, tree-lined course, has hosted the U.S. Open four times since the First World War.*

Below *The 7th at Pebble Beach, the most photographed short hole in the United States.*

The beautiful and challenging Cypress Point, in California. After playing the course Bobby Jones invited its architect, Dr Alister Mackenzie, to design his own course at Augusta.

year. One important effect of these charity games was to enhance the position of the golf professional, who had hitherto been considered to be low on the social scale.

The full range of tournaments and championships resumed as soon as possible after the war. Golf was riding high, and Americans, looking for heroes in all their sports, soon found in the top professional golfers the kind they sought. It was the time of Walter Hagen, of Gene Sarazen, of Jock Hutchinson (American, though from Scotland); as the top players won their tournaments and filled the headlines, the youth of the nation looked on, and then tried to copy. At every level the game was approached with great determination.

In the United States there were so many players that you had to practice hard if you were to stand any chance in competitive events; and, if you wanted to reach the professional ranks, you needed to have done well as an amateur in college, district, state and national tournaments. Overall, golf was regarded as a stroke-play game and match-play was less common than in Britain; the foursome, with alternate shots, was rare. Only by keeping the score could you gauge your improvement, and lowering your handicap was an important part of the system; a lower

handicap could help socially, too. The game was taken very seriously, and little was seen of that useful shot, the conceded putt. Every round, therefore, was liable to produce a few 'character builders'; those who could not hole them slid quietly down the scale, to be replaced by those who had been hardened by relentless practice and the pressure of competition. And so was bred a generation of tough tournament amateurs; and it showed in, for example, the Walker Cup matches.

Then there was the continuous business of constructing new courses. Golf-course architecture is a science which has developed steadily through the 20th century. Whereas on the links in Scotland, the first courses evolved over the centuries, in the United States they were designed from scratch on a large variety of sites; hazards were, in many places, of necessity artificial, and there were many who preferred the artificial to the natural. There was a number of interesting courses constructed early in the century, amongst them the National Links on Long Island, Charles Blair Macdonald's dream translated into reality. He tried to reproduce a group of his favourite holes on British links, adapting them to the ground; the result, opened in 1909, was a striking course which captured the imagination, but never reached the top rank. One of the most difficult of the older courses is Oakmont; another popular for championships is Baltusrol Lower, which, however, has changed from its earlier form. Cypress Point (California), one of Alister Mackenzie's masterpieces, dates from the late 1920s, and Seminole (Florida), another of Donald Ross's, from the same time. Soon after the end of the First World War came Pine Valley (Pennsylvania), Pebble Beach (California), Winged Foot (New York), Medinah (Illinois), Merion (Pennsylvania) and many other superb courses.

Throughout the world there is always the problem of the over-zealous greens committee; there is always someone who wants to change a course, often from the best of motives. With balls getting more lively and clubs and shafts more powerful, there have been many cases of courses becoming as a result too short for the professional players, and changes have been necessary. Many of the best architects have managed to achieve the required alterations with sympathy and a feeling for the intentions of the original designer; others have been less successful.

The inter-war expansion

During the 1920s there were far-reaching changes in equipment. From the beginning of the century and the arrival of the

rubber-core ball, manufacturers had been experimenting with all sorts of different materials and designs; there was a vast choice of brand names of ball, and every one promised something particular to recommend it; most of them were more or less the same, however. With clubs it was quite another matter: the steel shaft brought a totally new conception of design, and soon clubs were made in matched sets, carefully graded and balanced. By

Above *Walter Hagen, never one to miss an opportunity for publicity, holds court at Sandwich in 1928.*

Left *At the Amateur at Muirfield in 1926, Bobby Jones made an unusually early exit, losing to Andrew Jamieson, who won the Scottish Amateur a year later.*

St. Andrews 1929: Joyce Wethered defeated Glenna Collett in the pulsating British Ladies' final. Miss Collett devoured the first nine holes of the final in 34 shots – described later by Miss Wethered as the finest golf she had ever seen by a woman player.

the middle of the 1930s some players were travelling round with a great armoury of assorted clubs; with 20 or 25 clubs to carry, you needed a big bag – and a big caddie; it was becoming ridiculous, and in the late 1930s legislation on both sides of the Atlantic restricted a player to 14 clubs.

Worldwide, was produced more and more ancillary equipment, which – the advertisements insisted – it became imperative for the keen golfer, of any standard, to have with him: an umbrella, of course; a set of waterproofs; a spare cap, in case your first one should get wet, or too hot, or failed to bring you any luck with your putting; a set of gadgets for putting new spikes in your shoes, with the appropriate gadget for getting them out again when they were piercing your feet; tees for all occasions; a ball washer; a scoring notebook; a tin of sticking plaster; some travel rations in case your round was slow; and so on. Most of this, as well as the basic equipment, came from the professional's shop, and the imaginative equipment manufacturer soon discovered further attractive items for the discerning golfer. It all became very big business, and every year as more and more played golf, so the marvellous superfluity of gadgets and gimmicks accumulated.

Money poured into the game, and as it did so, golf increased in prestige, and became the game which everyone must play. The social side was important to the aspiring family, and clubs became more and more exclusive. There were also many public courses, and a championship

was started in 1922 available only to amateurs who played all their golf on them; it met a growing need, and over the years has seen top-class winners. The idea of 'catching them young' led to junior competitions of all sorts, and the calendar was soon becoming crammed.

The status of the professional player rose gradually; it needed a great deal of work, but it was the top players, Walter Hagen in particular, who enhanced the image of the tournament player. Success at home and abroad was publicised, and crowds followed the top players wherever they went.

In 1923 Bobby Jones won the U.S. Open, and for the next seven years he dominated the championship scene. In the United States he was only once out of the top two in the U.S. Open (in the year when Tommy Armour won at Oakmont); he was almost invincible in the U.S. Amateur, the first round loss to Johnny Goodman by one hole in 1929 causing a major national shock. When Jones was in the field, there were many even in the professional ranks who had lost before they started, so much so that on one occasion Walter Hagen felt it necessary to give his fellow-pros a pep talk in the middle of a championship! Jones won the Open in Britain whenever he appeared in these years, but the Amateur proved more difficult for there was always the danger of meeting someone playing phenomenally well in 18-holes of matchplay. It happened in 1926, when he lost to Andrew Jamieson from Glasgow (who was Scottish champion in the following year); in

1930 he just managed to scrape through against Cyril Tolley, the holder, at the 19th in the 4th round – but it was a very close affair: on such threads does history hang.

There were many good lady golfers in the United States at this same time, but Glenna Collett stood out above them all, and the sobriquet 'the female Bobby Jones' was justified; there were as yet no professional championships for the lady golfer, but in the U.S. Ladies' Glenna Collett won four times between 1925 and 1930, and had two other wins, in 1922 and 1935; in four attempts at the British Ladies, she reached two finals, but could not win. Nonetheless, her epic match with Joyce Wethered in the 1929 final at St Andrews left no one in doubt of her supreme class.

When Bobby Jones retired from competitive golf in 1930, the public was shocked; he had become a national hero, and thousands followed his exploits. The top golf players, too, wondered who was going to fill his shoes, however inadequately. For the next few years there were a series of winners in both amateur and professional championships; but there was a different excitement, for now it was not just a question of 'who is going to be second'. Nevertheless, attendances fell.

Some part of this was due to the recession in the early 1930s; there was not so much money about and golf, like everything else, found the times hard. The storm was weathered, but it was not until 1936 that cash started to flow again. Gradually new heroes appeared, and crowds started to return. During the late 1930s, the Masters was taking its place amongst the major tournaments, and two great players started to make their mark: they were Sam Snead and Byron Nelson; and they were joined in the top echelon in the early 1940s by Ben Hogan.

The 1930s also saw significant changes in balls, and a new and large size of ball

Bobby Jones returns home to a ticker-tape welcome after his Grand Slam in 1930.

An 18-year-old Bobby Locke, who won many titles in his native South Africa before the Second World War and was successful all over the world after it.

became standard in the United States: a great deal of research went into the aerodynamic design, and it was found that the bigger ball gave more control, while backspin was easier to impart; it also sat up more in the fairway. The development of the flat-soled wedges made the pitch shot easier, and watered greens gave great scope to the player of the high shot with backspin; the running approach shot was used much less, and by some top players not at all. By the shortening or total removal of rough, courses were made less difficult, so that there was a premium on length, while direction from the tee was less important. Big hitters could play their high pitches to the receptive greens, and lower and lower scores were recorded: that was what the tournament sponsors liked, for it pleased the galleries.

Golf was taken seriously in all its aspects in the United States. By the time the war came, there was money to be earned in increasingly large quantities by the tournament players; press and radio coverage had made them well-known personalities and had given them prestige. It was eminently respectable to be a golf professional, and pictures in the newspapers of Walter Hagen and Gene Sarazen with royalty did the image no harm.

The American influence on the game had spread to the British Isles, and the big manufacturing companies were taking over the old clubmaking businesses; some remained, and it was still possible to have clubs made by a craftsman to fit the individual player; but too often clubs were mass-produced, and it was up to the player to fit the club.

British golfing societies were often as exclusive as their American counterparts, though for different reasons: money was not the only thing that mattered; long-seated tradition remained, and membership lists contained the names of families who had been connected with the society for generations. In the British Dominions and Colonies, too, the growth of golf had been as steady as in the home country, but there had not yet been much impact on the main championships from players in the southern hemisphere, although in the late 1930s a young man called Bobby Locke had been showing the kind of form which promised much for the future.

Left *Golf was beginning to realise its potential as a source of public entertainment in the late 1930s. Here Henry Cotton plays the best ball of Joyce Wethered, Enid Wilson and Mlle Simone Thion de la Chaume (Cathérine Lacoste's mother). He won with a 69.*

Below *On the 'Golden Track' in California in 1939: Jimmy Demaret (right), who won the Los Angeles Open, and Jimmy Thomson, a prodigiously long hitter, who originally hailed from near Edinburgh. By this time prize money in America was growing rapidly.*

Golf between the wars had made great strides; it had taken the United States by storm, and now the vast majority of the best golfers were there; in the British Isles it had also expanded to include many more players from many more clubs.

So came the Second World War. The championships went into abeyance. In Britain golf continued as best it could, but some courses – Turnberry, for instance – were used for military purpose, while others could not be maintained. The relaxing effect of golf on worn nerves was appreciated, and every effort was made to keep it going. In some places, there were special wartime rules: for example, if a bomb exploded just as you were playing your shot, you were allowed to replay it without penalty. Balls and clubs were, of course, in short supply, and every kind of antique piece appeared from the attic.

In America, a restricted tournament routine was maintained, though after 1941 many of the great American players were serving in the forces. Nevertheless, the therapeutic value of ordinary activities reported in the newspapers was realised. On both sides of the Atlantic there were Red Cross exhibition matches. Golf went on – even in some prisoner-of-war camps – but all golfers waited hopefully for the day when it could be resumed in full.

INTER-WAR STARS

In the years between the two world wars, giants such as Hagen, Sarazen, Cotton and Byron Nelson formed the link between the Great Triumvirate and the millionaire superstars of the decades since 1945. . . .

Walter Hagen

(1892–1969)

He was born in Rochester (New York), one of five children; his family was not well-off. Walter was a gifted player of all games, and very nearly became a professional base-ball player. His interest in golf started when he was working as a caddy; and, playing as often as he could, by 1912 he had become good enough to enter for the Cana-dian Open, in which he finished outside the top batch; a year later he entered for the U.S. Open, in which Harry Vardon and Ted Ray were playing: he was in contention till the last round, but finished fourth. In 1914 Hagen had his first success in a major competition: he won the U.S. Open, and he repe-ated this success in 1919. He came to Britain for the first time in the following year, and finished badly

in the Open at Deal; however, he won the French Open, in which many of the same players were involved. He won his first U.S. PGA title in 1921, and the following year won the Open at Sandwich. In the next seven years, he won three more Opens, had a sequence of four U.S. PGA wins from 1924 to 1927 (and was runner-up to Gene Sarazen in 1923); he won numer-ous other tournaments.

As a result of a fierce argument between their supporters, Hagen and Sarazen played a 72-hole chal-

Above *Walter Hagen, a supreme showman, and a shrewd golfer of immense ability. He was unquestionably the finest exponent of matchplay of his time.*

lenge match at two different courses for 'The World Golf Cham-pionship'; there was $3000 at stake – an enormous sum in those days. Hagen lost; but perhaps the main point of interest is in the money involved. At this time there were few tournaments, so that profes-sional golfers could not look for-ward to the kind of rewards which

Below *Nowadays a 'gallery charge' is taken for granted. It had started in the last years of the 19th century, but it was Walter Hagen who was responsible for improving the financial status of the golf professional.*

Right *In the 1920s Hagen won the British Open four times; his two U.S. Open wins were in 1914 and 1919; he won the U.S. PGA title five times.*

FINAL HALF
72 Hole
Worlds Golf Classic
WALTER HAGEN
BRITISH OPEN CHAMPION
vs.
GENE SARAZEN
AMERICAN OPEN CHAMPION
Westchester Biltmore Country Club
Rye, N. Y.
Saturday October 7th
10;00 A. M. and 2;00 P. M.
GALLERY CHARGE
$2.00

are taken for granted to-day. Hagen was fully aware of his own value; and in 1926 he played Bobby Jones in another 'World Championship'. This time he won and netted $7000.

Walter Hagen was a larger-than-life figure: he dressed in flashy clothes, drove large and expensive cars, and it was his ambition to live like a millionaire – which he did. He was well aware of his flamboyant image, and fostered it with relish to the huge delight of his devoted followers. The life style could hardly fail to be noticed, as he intended it should be; and it resulted in clubhouses being opened to professional players in a way that had been unheard of before. It is hard to avoid the feeling that there was gamesmanship involved in some of his matches, but it could have been largely inbuilt rather than carefully contrived. And he could play a bit, too; though never in a humdrum way. He delighted in playing to the gallery, making difficult shots look easy and easy ones difficult; he was a superb scrambler – which

Hagen, a brilliant scrambler, was famous for his ability to play recovery shots from almost any situation. Here (for once forsaking plus-fours) he escapes from a bunker.

was just as well in view of his occasional waywardness from the tee. Behind all this was a shrewd and capable businessman who knew what he wanted. He raised the whole status of the player, and was as much responsible as anyone for the rise in popularity of the game in the United States, which inevitably led to money being poured into tournaments in the way of sponsorship. Even after he had finished playing seriously in competitions, he remained a figure of influence and note in the world of golf.

Tommy Armour

(1895–1968)

Tommy Armour – the Silver Scot – was born in Edinburgh. Starting at an early age, he become a very successful school player. Fired by watching exhibition matches by Braid, Taylor and Vardon, he took lessons from Vardon and George Duncan. During the First World War Armour was a machine-gunner, but finished as a major in the Tank Corps; however, he had been injured, had lost the sight of one eye, and carried shrapnel in his shoulder for the rest of his life.

After the war, he became fully involved in competitive golf, and in 1920 won the French Amateur. His work took him to the United States, and while there he met Walter Hagen, who helped him to a job in America. He tied for first place in the 1920 Canadian Open, but lost to Douglas Edgar, from whom he subsequently took lessons; he reckoned that these were the most crucial in his career. Successful as an amateur, in 1924 he turned professional. He won his first title in 1925, and in 1927 the U.S. Open and the Canadian Open. In 1930 he took the Canadian Open again, and the U.S. PGA. Then, in 1931, he returned to Scotland to win the Open, the first at Carnoustie. Thus he held the Open, the U.S. PGA and the Canadian Open at the same time. His third Canadian Open came in 1934, and in 1935 he was runner-up in the U.S. PGA. To these impressive results could be added many lesser titles. The U.S. Tour started in 1929, and Armour, on the original committee, was heavily involved in its formation.

After the mid–1930s, he gave up serious competitive golf and concentrated on teaching. He gained a great reputation in this field, and also as a raconteur of note. A charismatic figure always, he carved himself a niche in United States golf, first, as one of the great

Right *Tommy Armour as an amateur, winning a tournament at Gleneagles in 1920.*

personalities of the inter-war years, and secondly as a teacher whom everyone wanted – despite his very high fees. Amongst many famous players who came to consult him was Bobby Jones. Armour was always looking for the perfect golf swing, and his book *How To Play Your Best Golf All The Time* was a best seller, and is still in demand.

He held a unique record: in 1921 he represented Great Britain as an amateur in a match against the United States, the forerunner of the Walker Cup matches which started in 1922; then, in 1926, he represented the United States as a professional against Great Britain in a match played a year before the start of the Ryder Cup series (the latter are for home-born professionals only, so that he could not participate in them as a member of the United States team).

Below *In 1931 Armour won the first-ever Open at Carnoustie.*

Gene Sarazen

(1902-

Gene Sarazen is a wee man with a big heart, masses of self-confidence, and oodles of personality. He hit the scene with a bang in 1922, and the reverberations have scarcely ceased yet. You can never tell what he is going to do next.

He left school early to help his father in the family business, but an illness followed and he was advised to get an outdoor job. His early days in golf were as a caddie, but he was lucky to get a job as an assistant professional, and in 1920 he had his first tilt at the U.S. Open. He finished down the field, and the next year saw no fireworks either. It was in 1922 that he won the U.S. Open, and in the same year he also took the U.S. PGA title at Oakmont – the first time the two had been won by the same man in the same year. Walter Hagen, the current top star, had missed the PGA in 1922. He was there in 1923 – but Sarazen won it again. A 'World Championship' challenge was then played between Sarazen and Hagen over 72 holes, and Sarazen won that one, too.

His passage through the next 10 years was somewhat marred by his experimenting with his swing and losing some of his natural effectiveness. He won a number of tournaments, played matches and exhibition golf, and remained in the top flight of players though not winning one of the majors. Then came 1932 and, first, a win in the Open at Sandwich; then came the U.S. Open title – he remains one of the few to have won the two titles in the same year. He followed this with another PGA win in 1933. Because he was touring, he did not play in the inaugural Masters at Augusta in 1934. In 1935 he did play: in the last round, he knew that he would need three birdies in the last four holes to catch Craig

Wood, who looked the likely winner: at the 15th, a par 5, he holed his second shot for a three-under-par albatross (or double-eagle), and went on to win. This shot ranks amongst the most celebrated of all time, and added further lustre to Sarazen's already glittering achievements. Moreover, his Augusta victory made him the first man to have won all four of the professional golfer's majors: the Open, the U.S. Open, the U.S. PGA and the Masters. Another claim to fame is that he was responsible for developing the sole profile of the modern sand wedge, which enables it to bounce off the sand rather than digging into it.

Sarazen played six times in the Ryder Cup team, his last appearance being in 1937. His final tilt at the majors came in 1940, when he lost to Lawson Little in a play-off for the U.S. Open. After the war, he entered only for odd events. The coming of the U.S. Seniors Tour stirred him into action again, and he was twice the Seniors' Champion, in 1954 and 1958. He is always to be seen at the Masters, and in 1973 was invited to take part in the Open at Troon – a full 50 years after his first major win. And once again he marked a big occasion with a sensational shot. He had a hole in one at the famed 8th hole, the Postage Stamp – and this time it was recorded on television.

Although only 5ft 4in tall, he is jaunty and decided in manner, and supremely aware of his own ability. He attacked whenever he played, and tried to play winning shots rather than just for safety. He rarely finished in the middle order

of a tournament – if he was not challenging, then he was right out of it. His cavalier attitude has won him many friends all over the world and in all walks of life.

Left and below *Gene Sarazen, whose natural skill and dedication during the lean years were rewarded by winning both the British and U.S. Opens in 1932. Here he displays the trophies.*

Henry Cotton

(1907–1987)

Henry Cotton is the only British player to have won the Open more than once since the time of the Triumvirate.

Born in 1907, he and his brother Leslie were encouraged to play golf by their father, a keen club player of modest standard. When the two boys were taken to play with J. H. Taylor, he wrote that Henry (then about 13) 'would be the better player as he had more determination and more power of concentration'. This insight does indeed go to the very core of Henry Cotton's success: he was always dedicated to playing the game to its highest level, and was prepared for all the hard work and practice needed. He probably practised harder than anyone, before or since, with the exception of Ben Hogan.

He became a professional when he was 16, and in 1926, after several jobs as assistant, was appointed as professional at Langley Park Golf Club at Beckenham (Kent). After two seasons, he felt it was time to find out more about American golf and, with the blessing of his club, he left in November 1928 to play in as much of the Winter Circuit as his finances would allow. It was at this time that United States players were having great success in the Open, and in general seemed much better and tougher players than their British counterparts; Cotton, determined to find the secret to their success, was lucky to get to know all the main players, in particular, perhaps, Walter Hagen and Tommy Armour, from whom he learnt much. The following winter he played in Argentina. All this was useful experience, and meantime he was steadily improving his game, though without great success at home.

In 1933 he decided to accept an appointment at the Waterloo Golf Club in Belgium, and he had four happy years there. Some questioned his going abroad, but he felt that the further experience would be a good thing; and so it turned out when, in 1934, he won his first Open Championship, at Sandwich. His life's ambition was achieved. He was the first home winner for over 10 years.

In 1937 he returned home as professional at Ashridge at Berkhampsted (Herts). When he came to this club, he insisted that he should be an honorary member of the club so that he could meet members on their own ground. It was an important innovation. From this club, he entered for the

1937 Open at Carnoustie, and won it again. This time the whole American Ryder Cup team was playing, so it was a particularly satisfying win.

During the Second World War he served in the Royal Air Force, and took part in many exhibition games in aid of the Red Cross. He resumed playing after the end of hostilities, and in 1948, at Muirfield, added his third Open title. This was to all intents and purposes the end of his competitive career.

In addition to these three major triumphs, he won many other tournaments, including the open championships of several Euro-

pean countries. But it was not just his titles that were important: he had shown that British golfers could hope to hold their own in any company, and particularly at that time with the Americans, who ruled the roast. He did much for the image of golf and for the image of professional golf and golfer in particular. He wrote with great authority and was the senior statesman of British golf for many years. He also designed and advised about courses, and was involved in every part of the golf scene. 'He was the man,' says Malcolm Campbell, 'who took professional golf out of the caddie shed and helped turn it into the "noble occupation" he always believed it to be.'

He died at the end of 1987, just before the publication of his knighthood in the New Year's Honours List – a richly deserved award, and one of which he had been aware.

Right *Byron Nelson in 1945,
when he won 18 tour events – 11 of
them in a row!*

Byron Nelson

(1912-

Two boys tied for the caddies' championship one year – and each won a new club: they were Byron Nelson and Ben Hogan.

John Byron Nelson, Jr was the son of a grain merchant who lived in a house adjoining the Glen Garden Country Club at Fort Worth, Texas. Nelson was caddying by the time he was 10, and soon there developed a friendly rivalry with Ben Hogan, who lived not far away. Competition between the two was destined to continue, though they never became close friends.

Nelson became a top-class amateur golfer in his teens, and in 1930 won the South-West Open. It was not long before he decided to turn professional. In the early 1930s there was not much money for a golfer and life was a hard grind; Nelson's first year produced a total of $12.50; and he gave up and went to work for an oil man, J. K. Wadley, in Texarkana. Wadley took an interest in the young man, and got him an appointment as professional to the local Country Club. With ample time for play, his confidence returned, and, after making a good showing in the San Antonio Open in 1934, he rejoined the circuit. Although he won no tournament that year, he netted $2000; furthermore, he caught the eye of George Jacobus, then president of the U.S. PGA, who took him on as assistant professional at Ridgewood (New Jersey). Here his opportunities were increased, and in 1936 he won the Metropolitan Open. In 1937 came the breakthrough into the top class when he won the Masters at Augusta. He was also selected for the Ryder Cup team, and assisted in the defeat of Great Britain for the first time on their own soil. He won his second major, the U.S. Open, after a tie in 1939, won the U.S. PGA in 1940, and the Masters again in 1942.

The war years were the great years for Byron Nelson: unfit for military service because of a blood condition, he and his friend, Harold (Jug) McSpaden, also unfit

for service, dominated the circuit. They became known as The Gold Dust Twins because, if one did not win, then almost invariably the other did. Nelson's greatest year was in 1945: he won the U.S. PGA, the Canadian Open and Canadian PGA as well as 15 other tournaments on the circuit; he had a spell of 11 wins in a row!

He was, however, finding tournament golf an undue strain, and after another season, moved gently out of the competitive spotlight to concentrate on teaching and commentating, and he was in constant demand as an elder statesman. In particular, he was Tom Watson's close adviser for many years.

There are those who suggest that much of Byron Nelson's success came at a time when others were away and when there was not a great deal of competition. This is

ungenerous, and seems to forget the pre-war successes. Moreover, in his great year of 1945 his average for the 120 tournament rounds was 68.3 shots per round – good enough to win anyone a hatful of tournaments against the greatest players in the world. Indeed, the case can be put even more strongly when one realises that, in that same magical season, his average for the *final* round in each of these tournaments was only a fraction over 67.

He was an efficient and almost mechanical player who aimed at lack of error. A tall man, pleasant and gentlemanly, his popularity in the United States was immense and deserved.

THE MODERN GAME

Golf worldwide

Since the 1950s, when television helped create a vast and enthusiastic worldwide interest in the game, golf has become an international business, catering to the growing army of ordinary golfers in every corner of the globe. . . .

By the Second World War golf had become well established throughout the English-speaking world. From 1945 it expanded, slowly at first, and then with a rush, to almost every part of the world. It is a game which can be played almost everywhere, by people of all ages, by players of all standards. As it has moved from country to country, each has given the game something new, with a difference of approach because of peculiar national characteristics, which are a question of temperament; and the phlegmatic attitude of some nationalities is matched by the fiery and excited dash of others.

Automation and the invention of new machines to do the jobs of many men have led to shorter working hours or unemployment, and the increased leisure time has meant that many have looked to sporting activities to spend the extra time they have available. Golf has been one of many such activities, and the large increase in the numbers playing has led to a huge increase in demand for playing facilities. Many clubs have added second

North Berwick has a magnificent situation on the southern shore of the Firth of Forth, east of Edinburgh. It has always been a popular holiday resort.

Preceding two pages
No inland course has captured public imagination as much as Bobby Jones's Augusta, one of the most beautiful places for golf in the world, and home every year of the U.S. Masters.

and third courses to their original one; and there have been many cases of nine-hole courses being extended to 18 holes; in addition, new courses are appearing; there was a time when much of the land in Britain was needed for agriculture or forestry, but with over-production of some commodities and limits now being set within the European Community, farming land may become more readily available for other uses. Country clubs proliferate, many with multi-sporting activities; the golf course is usually an integral part of the plans, and there may also be driving ranges and indoor facilities, all with instruction available. The increase in clubs, courses, facilities is matched by a bigger demand for every kind of golfing equipment, and many manufacturers sensibly plough back money into the game.

Television has been responsible for much of the growing interest in the game. People are able to follow the major tournaments at length, and recently there has been increasing coverage of the women's game as well as the men's. It does look an easy game, and many, seeing how easy the professional players make it look, are encouraged to try for themselves. Over many years the BBC has gathered experience of presenting golf, and they do it in a way which other channels, in Britain and abroad, so far have been unable to approach.

The commercial expansion

Golf today is big business. The sports shop and the professional's shop at the golf club are full of every kind of equipment; clubs have become more refined, with different materials used for shafts and heads; balls are designed to go further; golf bags, trolleys, buggies are available in all shapes and sizes. Clothing, too, is designed to be comfortable for playing and also to be attractive; this is nowhere better shown than in modern all-weather clothing: rainwear can now be not only fully waterproof, but also light and easy to wear. Money is poured into advertising, and every opportunity is taken to display the maker's or the sponsor's name. Big firms now dominate the market in golf equipment; the days of the small clubmaker are almost over.

Better and quicker travel has made it possible for people to reach other countries in much shorter times than before. Where the Americans, British and Japanese have gone, they have wanted their golf, and countries that attract warm-weather holiday-makers have been quick to realise the tourist possibilities. New courses, new hotels, new clubs have

British holiday-makers have helped to bring golf to Spanish resorts. In an ideal climate golf may be played all the year round. One of the best known courses is at La Manga, where the PGA European Tour holds its annual Qualifying School.

in, and the golf explosion for the tourist has continued all along and near the Iberian Atlantic and Mediterranean coasts. Visitors from northern continental European countries have taken their interest in golf back to their own countries, and fostered the demand there for new courses and club facilities.

The golf explosion in Europe over the past few years has been quite breathtaking: that there are more golfers in Sweden than anywhere else in continental Europe is an interesting fact, and does something to explain how Swedish players are com-

Above *The Flower Walk at Augusta, the most exclusive club in the world.*

Right *Pebble Beach, California: one of the spectacular Monterrey peninsula courses. U.S. Open winners here have been Jack Nicklaus (1972) and Tom Watson (1982).*

been spreading all over the world. One of the quickest growing of the associated ventures has been time-sharing. Large companies run time-share estates in all parts of the world, and there are few which do not have golf attachments; many such estates are built around a golf course. In these vast sport and leisure complexes there are facilities for all the family, and it is not surprising that such an easy way into golf has led to many complete families playing – it is not just father who departs to the course for the day; he is more than likely to be accompanied by mother and the children, even though all may be playing on different parts of the courses, driving ranges or practise grounds. Good time-share companies make it easy for owners of weeks or fortnights in one area to swap with those in other areas, and this means a healthy flow of ideas (and currency).

It was the British who started the movement into the Iberian peninsula: the Algarve of Portugal was an area which – like Florida for American northerners – lent itself particularly to golfers seeking the sun in the winter; at first it was only for the rich, but gradually, with more and more having holidays abroad, it became available to everyone; Spain soon joined

ing to the fore at both amateur and professional level; it is the more extraordinary as their courses are for the most part playable only for about half the year. There are many more German golfers now than there were a short while ago, and some of their courses in Bavaria have wonderful settings. In France the game is growing rapidly in popularity, and there is a massive programme of course construction which hopes to keep pace with the demand; France has its own winter playground near the Mediterranean coast, but there are courses coming in increasing numbers all over the country. In Denmark, the Netherlands, Belgium, Switzerland, Italy, Greece – everywhere there is the need for more courses and more clubs. And yet even in Spain, where large numbers of golfers go each year, golf is not a 'popular' game; in the areas near the courses, local boys caddy, and from their ranks have appeared some of the growing number of good Spanish professionals; but golf is still a game for the well-off; the average Spaniard is not interested in the game, and even the exploits of the top Spanish professionals, including Seve-

Shoal Creek, Alabama, was designed by Jack Nicklaus and opened in 1977. It makes full use of water, and has quickly taken its place amongst the top American courses. Here's a scene from the 1984 U.S. PGA Championship.

riano Ballesteros, do not attract as much notice in Spain as they do, for example, in Britain. However, the spread of the game continues: Madeira has courses; the Canaries are a popular haunt for winter golfers; on the north coast of Africa new courses entice the travelling golfer. Morocco has had courses for many years: did not the Pasha in his youth play *takoura*, a game with ball and stick, in the local hills? The course at Marrakesh is renowned; there are courses dating from the start of the century, while several new courses are planned.

Early golf courses, as we have seen, were designed largely by Mother Nature and given a few finishing touches by man. Later, golf architects radically altered the existing landscape, using machinery to create a variety of artificial features. Modern technology, from computers to the most sophisticated earth-moving equipment, allow designers to indulge a taste for an enormous range of designs. Many such designers, perhaps especially in the United States, have allowed passing fashion and gimmickry to influence their designs, or through failure of a genuinely golfing imagination have made their courses absurdly, indeed penally difficult.

At the same time, however, there has been something of renaissance in golf course architecture, headed by Robert Trent Jones (who has designed, altered or advised on courses the world over), Pete Dye and Dick Wilson; more recently, Jack Nicklaus has designed some testing and spectacular courses, in North America, Europe and elsewhere. Some amazing courses have been created, in every continent, in every kind of situation, climate, and geographical location. One opened in 1988 was the Emirates Golf Course in Dubai, in the middle of the desert: unlimited finance has made possible the piping of the million gallons of fresh water needed each day to maintain this green course amidst the sand. Australia, with a large sport-conscious population and excellent and varied climate, has over 1500 courses, many of which rank with any in the world. New Zealand, too, can point to magnificent courses which cater for the growing number of players; there is a population of only some three million, but there are several hundred courses. South Africa, another country where sport is taken very seriously, has many superb courses. Tourists have encouraged construction of courses in South and Central America and in the Caribbean, while in the Bahamas and Bermuda there are famous courses of long standing.

Nowhere has the golf explosion since 1945 been clearer than in Japan. The game started to grow in popularity in the 1950s, and now there are over 1500 courses in the country, and a great number of golfers – many of whom never play on one of the courses, which are expensive and very exclusive. Many Japanese visit other countries, mainly the United States, Australia and Britain, to play golf, and it is owing to them in particular, that Far East countries have been able to take advantage of the ever-growing desire to travel and to play golf.

There are two very large sections of the world's population which until now have not had any inclination towards golf. For many years the game was barred in Communist China. British communities had introduced the game at the end of the last century, and there was a Chinese Amateur tournament until 1940. After that, however, there was no golf until the mid-1980s, when the authorities decided to start training some youngsters, with proper tuition – available from the thriving golfing settlement in Hong Kong. The course at Chung Shan, with a totally foreign membership, was the place where a group of 18 promising games players was given golf tuition and instruction. It is a concentrated attempt to produce some

Above *The Chung Shan Hot Spring Club on the Chinese mainland near Canton: a portent of the future?*

good golfers by intensive methods, and eventually to show the way to other Chinese and start a golf boom in the country. It is in its infancy, but is going ahead as planned, and there seems no reason to doubt that there will be Chinese players amongst the world's best.

The other country where a modest start is in sight is the Soviet Union. Early in the century there were two courses in European Russia, but the Revolution put an immediate stop to any thought of further expansion. There were Russians abroad who played and enjoyed the game (the Grand Duke Michael, as we have seen, was one of them; though he was an exile), but there was no possibility of golf until the mid-1970s; even then, the political situation at the time prevented any firm plans. With the recent promotion of *glas-*

Left *St Irvine Bay course on the tropical paradise of Tobago, a few miles north of Trinidad.*

Above *Group-Captain Douglas Bader at the RAF meeting in 1945. With two artificial legs, he was an example and inspiration to others in overcoming a disability.*

Right *Boy champion in 1952, Michael Bonallack went on to become the most successful British amateur of the post-war years. He is now Secretary of the R&A.*

back a long way. There has been a One-Armed Championship since 1933, and there have been near scratch players amongst the winners. There are even blind people who play successfully, and there is a regular championship for them in the United States. Probably the best known handicapped golfer was Douglas Bader, who was able to play to a single-figure although he had two artificial legs. His story is famous; yet to play behind him and to find that he was not only able to keep his place on the course, but wanted to go, and was able to go, a good deal faster than the unfortunate modern amble which is so prevalent nowadays, made you realise just how much a disability can be overcome by determination.

The Golf Foundation, formed in 1952 in Britain, sets out to encourage youngsters to play, and to make it possible for everyone. Coaching is available in schools and clubs, and a large number of schools all over the British Isles take advantage of the scheme, which is funded by industry, golf clubs, and individuals. Lessons are available from local professionals, and a good part of the cost is borne by the Golf Foundation. Schools have been encouraged to take part in the competitions, and there is now an entry of over a thousand schools, who play in regional tournaments first, and then graduate by way of district to national, and then international level. Similar schemes in other countries have led to an international field beyond the original four home countries, and it is

nost at the top, there are now plans for a course to be opened in the early 1990s, and Robert Trent Jones, Jr is the designer. It will be interesting to see how this develops: in a country the size of Russia there are infinite opportunities.

Both China and the Soviet Union have shown that they understand the advantages of their athletes doing well on the world stage. In many sports they have shown the ability and dedication necessary to produce top-class performers. With this same approach, they may well make an impact at top level; but it will not be done overnight.

Golf at the grass-roots

Golf is a universal game; it can be played by almost anyone. In recent years there has been a large increase in the sporting activities of handicapped people, and their magnificent efforts have been widely applauded. Golf has been one such sport, and there have been those who have managed to play even in a wheelchair. However, golf for the handicapped goes

significant that the winners have twice come from Sweden. The event started in 1972, and since 1986 has been for a trophy presented by the Royal & Ancient. This event, however, is just the culmination of long years of practice and instruction. There are vivid memories of the sterling work done by the dedicated professionals: of one such standing for two hours in the freezing and biting cold of April in Perthshire while, one after another, pupils were carefully watched, instructed and encouraged; of another elderly ex-Ryder Cup player whose massive frame towered over the seven-year-old girl, and whose friendly advice never once faltered while for the first two minutes she failed entirely to make any contact with the ball; of another professional taking the same infinite pains with a handicapped child, and succeeding in making him realise that he, too, could enjoy golf. It is at this level that the work is being started; and if it ends with fame and fortune for some lucky few, yet it is in the increase of players at the ordinary standard that the Foundation is doing its most appreciated work.

Much has been done, too, for the young in junior sections of clubs; and the more far-sighted committees have ensured that their junior members are well-instructed in the etiquette of the game, and know how to behave on a course. International matches and championships are held at Boys and Youth levels, organised by the Royal & Ancient, and for Girls, organised by the LGU. Increasingly there are more entries from abroad – and the name of José-Maria Olazábal is inscribed on both the Boys' and Youths' trophies, whilst Marie-Laure de Lorenzi de Taya was the Girls' Champion in 1978. The Youths' trophy also bears the names of Sandy Lyle and Nick Faldo.

The United States is still ahead of other countries in its policy of encouraging competition from a young age, right through school and college levels. College golf offers scholarships to talented golfers, and there are many from Britain and from other countries who take advantage of them. It is causing some concern in the United States that now many of the top college golfers come from overseas, and there do not appear to be enough home American players of sufficient quality. It may be true that students who come from abroad have considerable incentive to

dedicate their time fully to their studies and to their golf; not all succeed, but many do. The new challenge from overseas will certainly be met in time, but meantime there is a school of thought in the United States which views with alarm the efforts of their colleges to produce top-class golfers from other nations. However, it is not all one way: for example, the Robert T. Jones Jr Memorial Trust has since 1974 awarded scholarships for a year's exchange between students from Emory University, Atlanta and the University of St Andrews; some hundred have so far benefited from these scholarships.

At the other end of the scale, there are now many events for senior golfers. There are many who do not have the chance of starting golf until later in life, and the weird contortions of P. G. Wodehouse's 'Wrecking Crew' are imitated daily on golf courses all round the world. Many clubs run seniors matches with other clubs, and also have their own seniors' events; with many more retired golfers about, these competitions can be held during the

Bing Crosby played in the Amateur Championship of 1950 at St Andrews, where his first round opponent was local player J. K. Wilson. The friendship which was formed between the two led to a competition for players over the age of 60 from local clubs in St. Andrews, now played annually in September.

At the Match-Play Championship at Wentworth in 1971 Jack Nicklaus wanted a 'free-drop' on the grounds of interference by an advertising hoarding. Referee Colonel Tony Duncan refused, and Nicklaus accepted the ruling.

week, so that clubhouses and courses are used more at times when otherwise they might be quiet. At the top end are the championships, with the British Seniors' and the Senior Ladies' British amateur championships proving just how long players can maintain a high standard.

The United States formed a seniors' society in 1905 for those over 55; a similar British Senior Golfers' Society was started in 1926, and there are other associated societies in various parts of the world. An international match is regularly played between British and American Seniors, and there are often visits to play against and with members of other societies.

Rules and standards

In itself golf is a very simple game: Rule 1–1 states:

'The game of Golf consists in playing
a ball from the *teeing ground* into
the hole by a *stroke* or successive
strokes in accordance with the
Rules.'

That is quite straightforward. It is the bit which comes after that which seems to make it more complicated! The Rules come under constant inspection, and the Royal & Ancient and the USGA have regular meetings, and not only are the same rules used worldwide, but the two committees publish their Decisions jointly, so that interpretations of the rules are the same. Conditions can vary enormously in different parts of the world, and what is appropriate in one place may be quite unsuitable in another. Large numbers of queries, some of them seeming strange, odd, or just funny, come to the Rules of Golf Committee every year, and are painstakingly considered and pronounced upon. It is an important function of the governing bodies of the game; in trying to cover every eventuality, the committees have evolved a very complicated document, and it is not surprising to find lawyers as committee members. Rule 1–4 is another which may be quoted:

'If any point in dispute is not covered
by the Rules, the decision shall be
made in accordance with equity.'

But what is equity? To help to define this, the Rules with all their sections and sub-sections, now go up to Rule 34, together with the associated local rules for particular clubs, courses and competitions. The meetings of the Rules Committees are the more important as golf becomes more widely spread; at international level it is vital for all taking part to know exactly where they stand. The detailed work done means that, although on the course there may be arguments and discussions, there are not the international incidents which could otherwise easily arise.

Golf has so far managed to preserve an overall image of the acceptance of fair play as a standard, of a lack of the grosser forms of gamesmanship, and of behaviour on the course which does the game credit. There are exceptions, as there must be to any generalisation, but the governing bodies set and expect high standards. More worrying, perhaps, is the behaviour of the spectators on occasions. Partisan support is to be expected in any contest, and in itself is healthy enough; it is when this descends into barracking the opponents, and even to applauding their mistakes, that is becomes quite unacceptable. It is no new phenomenon: in the last century Old Tom Morris refused to complete a match with Willie Park because the home crowd were actively interfering with his play; while Harry Vardon refused to play one leg of a match with Willie Park

Jr at Musselburgh because J.H. Taylor had had similar trouble there. None the less, this kind of incident had largely disappeared in Britain until recently, when there have been infrequent recurrences. These occasions are unfortunately the 'news', and are thus the focus of media attention. At a recent Dunhill Cup match, for instance, an incident when a player was barracked at one stage received a heavy coverage, and a good deal of sanctimonious comment, some of it from those who had not been on the spot; there was no comment in the Press about the generous applause given to the same player – and much deserved for his fine play – in a match where he had been playing against one of the local heroes. How to silence the unpleasantly noisy few is a matter which causes concern to many sporting authorities. Ultimately it is only by education that public opinion will ensure that such behaviour is eradicated from the golf course.

Nick Faldo stands his ground as the haar *sweeps in and obscures his view of the flag during the Dunhill Cup, 1988. He awaited a ruling, and eventually the PGA official accepted that the ball should be marked and play continued early the next day. It was a pity that a section of the crowd voiced its disapproval.*

GOLF IN JAPAN

The first Japanese golf course opened in 1901. Since the Second World War, Japanese in their millions have become enchanted by the game – yet only a fraction of them ever get to play regularly on a course in their native land.

There are now more than 12 million dedicated golfers in Japan: yet some 10 million of them rarely if ever see a golf course. The great majority play their golf at one of the country's 4,032 driving ranges, many of which have up to 150 bays mounted in tiers one above the other. For the minority there are 1,588 golf clubs, many on the slopes of mountains. Total membership at the last count was 1,680,000.

Golf seems to have become extremely important to the Japanese psyche. It now takes its place among the traditional 'artless arts' – archery, swordsmanship, dancing, painting, even flower-arranging – all of which provide for their masters a doorway to Zen, that aspect of Buddhism which is central to the aesthetic and even religious life of Japan.

Most Westerners find it difficult to understand this. 'Wrapped in impenetrable darkness, Zen must seem the strangest riddle which the spiritual life of the East has ever devised,' wrote the German philosopher Eugen Herrigel in *Zen in the Art of Archery* (1971). Perhaps the nearest any Westerner has come to expressing its essence in relation to golf has been a New York teacher, Phil Galvano:

'In swinging you should feel that your arms, hands and shoulders do not belong to you, that they do not exist and you have no control over the clubhead. The more attention

Right *Fujioka Golf Club, Nagoya, is a typical modern Japanese course, where great care is taken to make the game visually enchanting. In 1972 there were only 600 courses in Japan; today there are nearly 1,600.*

given to your swing, the lower the degree of skill. The true achievement of art is the concealment of art.' (*Secrets of the Perfect Golf Swing* by Phil Galvano.)

Golf in Japan therefore is not just a game; it is not just a social event; it is not just an exercise, or form of relaxation: it is an aesthetic, and for some even a spiritual, experience.

The first golf course there was opened in 1901. It was laid out by westerners on the slopes of Mount Rokko, near Kobe – just nine holes on a mountainside. Of the first 170 members all but seven were foreigners. But Japanese diplomats and businessmen working overseas became intrigued with the game and in 1914 the Tokyo Club was founded as a truly Japanese club. There were about 60 clubs operating before World War II. The war finished everything, of course, and it was not until the end of the Occupation in 1952 that things got going again. The big boom in Japanese golf started five years later when 'Pete' Nakamura and Koichi Ono won the Canada Cup (now the World Cup) and Nakamura took the individual title.

Flat land being extremely expensive in overcrowded and mountainous Japan, fees for membership in the country's private clubs are astronomical and besides their membership fees golfers also have to pay green fees. The price of entry alone at the Koganei club, whose course was designed by Walter Hagen, is the equivalent of £200,000.

A Japanese company director entertaining three British or American business acquaintances to lunch and a round of golf at a course near Tokyo may have to pay £1,500 for the privilege.

Besides stockbrokers Japan now has golfbrokers – merchants who collect information about club members who desire to sell their membership rights at a club and pass it along to a willing buyer who pays not only 2% commission but also a substantial extra fee for being allowed to join the club.

The stars

Until quite recently the life of Japanese professionals had not been easy. For a long time, with very few exceptions they were (and most remain) dedicated club pros and teachers. The first big name to be recognised in tournaments around the world and in Japan – and big is the right word – was Masashi 'Jumbo' Ozaki, who in 1971 left the world of bigtime baseball, where he was already a rising star, to try his hand at golf. With his two brothers 'Jet' and 'Joe' he dominates Japanese golf. Jumbo and Jet lost the World Cup in Melbourne, Australia, in 1988 by just one shot to the United States team and Tateo 'Jet' Ozaki lost the individual title by one shot to Ben Crenshaw. Jumbo won eight domestic events in 1988.

· BAND OF BROTHERS ·

Ten tournaments were won by three brothers in Japan in 1988:

Sapporo Tokyu: Naomichi 'Joe' Ozaki
Japan PGA: Tateo 'Jet' Ozaki
NST Niigata Open: Naomichi 'Joe' Ozaki
Nikkei Cup: Masashi 'Jumbo' Ozaki
Maruman Open: Masashi 'Jumbo' Ozaki
Suntory Open: Tateo 'Jet' Ozaki
ANA Sapporo Open: Naomichi 'Joe' Ozaki
Japan Open: Masashi 'Jumbo' Ozaki
Golf Digest Open: Masashi 'Jumbo' Ozaki
Bridgestone Open: Masashi 'Jumbo' Ozaki

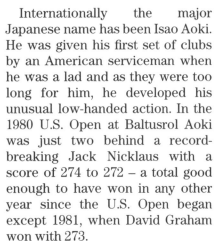

Internationally the major Japanese name has been Isao Aoki. He was given his first set of clubs by an American serviceman when he was a lad and as they were too long for him, he developed his unusual low-handed action. In the 1980 U.S. Open at Baltusrol Aoki was just two behind a record-breaking Jack Nicklaus with a score of 274 to 272 – a total good enough to have won in any other year since the U.S. Open began except 1981, when David Graham won with 273.

Aoki won the World Matchplay title at Wentworth, England, in 1978 and the European Open in 1983, the year when he also won the Hawaiian Open by one shot by pitching into the hole on the final green from a distance of 130 yards. The pre-eminent figure among Japanese women golfers is Ayako Okamoto, sixth in the U.S. women's money list in 1988, a year in which she won the Hawaiian, the San Diego Classic and the Greater Washington Open. Among the men Tsuneyuki 'Tommy' Naka-jima and Masahiro 'Massy' Kura-moto have also made names for themselves abroad.

At home in Japan now the pros are very highly paid, as might be expected. A good teacher will make the income of a company director and for this reason there is little incentive for most of them to travel abroad. This may how-ever change in the near future as Japanese companies buy up more

Left *A delightful golfer, Ayako Okamoto was Number 1 on the LPGA tour in the United States in 1987, 6th in 1988. She won the 1984 Ladies' British Open at Woburn by no less than 11 shots.*

Below *For most Japanese golfers the driving range is where they play most of their golf. Many ranges, like this one in Tokyo, have three tiers and are nearly always full. More than a million players manage only one round a year on an actual course.*

and more golf clubs overseas. They now own 18 of Hawaii's 47 golf clubs and a number of others in California, Florida and Georgia. Japanese interests own a number of clubs in Britain and are known to be looking for more.

Allying their obsession with golf to their technical genius, Japanese manufacturers now threaten to dominate the golf-equipment scene: Mizuno, Maruman, Daiwa, Yamaha, Bridgestone and Yonex sell golf clubs worldwide and have signed up many of the top professionals. Sony sponsors the World Rankings and Honda, Nissan, Panasonic and Isuzu are among Japanese companies sponsoring tournaments.

Japan's financial interest in golf no doubt derives from the fact that as a game on a golf course it is for businessmen and women only, or at least for the very rich and those sponsored by companies. Commercial companies own many of the golf courses, including foreign companies – until recently British Petroleum owned one of the finest courses near Tokyo.

But for the average Japanese golfer the game is played at one of the thousands of driving ranges, many of them multi-tiered so that one sees players swinging away from 150 bays one on top of the other in three tiers. It is usual for the ground-floor bays to be reserved for golfers with handicaps. The less experienced play from the mezzanine floor and beginners and long-handicappers are consigned to the top floor.

For most of them, method is of little importance: it is the joy of striking the little white globe, even of controlling it, that counts.

Writing of Zen and archery, Dr Daisetz Teitaro Suzuki wrote more than 25 years ago: 'If one really wishes to be master of an art, technical knowledge is not enough. One has to transcend technique so that the art becomes the 'artless art' growing out of the Unconscious.... Man is a thinking reed, but his great works are done when he is not calculating or thinking.'*

For the dedicated Japanese, perfection is reached when the player himself does nothing and 'It' strikes the ball unconsciously, perfectly to the target (whatever 'It' may be). It is the Inner Game of the West taken to an unfathomable extreme.

*Foreword to *Zen in the Art of Archery.*

The big time

Since the Second World War professional golf has been run on the basis of national or regional 'tours', which nowadays include the seniors and ladies tours. And, all over the world, sponsors swell the prize money for the big tournaments. . . .

The PGA started in 1901; the U.S. PGA in 1916. Tournaments at first began here and there, with no particular pattern. There were, of course, the national Open Championships which attracted most of the leading professional players, as well as the top amateurs. The 'bread-and-butter' tournaments depended on support and sponsorship, and to begin with most of this came from the newspapers. In the United States during the 1920s there were winter tournaments in the warmer areas – California, Florida,

Above *In 1924 in a 72-hole challenge match at St George's Hill & Oxhey, George Duncan and Abe Mitchell beat Walter Hagen (left) and Horton Smith (back to camera). Here the players shake hands at the end of the contest.*

Right *In 1936 rising young star Dai Rees beat Ernest Whitcombe to win the PGA Match-Play tournament at Oxhey. This earned him a top prize of £300.*

Texas. At this time of year there was less for the club professionals to do further north, and a series of winter tournaments became a regular feature of the calendar; this was really the tour in a rudimentary form. It developed during the 1930s, and by the start of World War II was getting far more organised. In 1937 Harry Cooper had become the first professional to win a five-figure amount – his total winnings as leading money winner for the year were $14,000; a year later, the total amount available for all the tournaments in the United States tour was $158,000.

A number of tournaments were played in Britain during the 1920s and 1930s; but club duties were still paramount for the professional, and tournaments took place during the week so that the professional could be at his home club at the week-end. The season revolved around the Open Championship and the Match-Play Tournament. The *Daily Mail* tournament in 1936 produced a record sum in prize money of £2000. By comparison, the total prize money in the 1946 Open Championship was £1000, with the winner taking £150. British professionals often went to play in the various European national open tournaments, too; but there was not a regular exchange of players across the Atlantic for tournaments other than the Open.

Sponsorship tended to provide limited

sums, and there was usually a percentage of gate money available after tournament expenses had been met. Gate money, taken originally as far back as 1892 in a challenge match between Jack White and Douglas Rolland at Cambridge, was not

Above *Dick Burton (left), the 1939 Open Champion, and Jimmy Demaret watch winner Byron Nelson drive in a $10,000 tournament in 1946 at Winged Foot.*

Left *Bobby Locke was successful in the United States after the war. In 1947 he was third in the U.S. Open and second top money-winner. Here's one of his big paydays. Vic Ghezzi is at left.*

taken at the Open until 1926 (at Lytham).

The main tournament golf in the 1930s was played in Britain and the United States, and there was not a great deal of coming and going with countries in the southern hemisphere, who had their own tournaments, or in the Far East. However, a young amateur from South Africa had done well in the Open; he had several South African amateur and open titles to his credit, and had turned professional in

Above *It is not always comfortable and warm in the commentary box. In the centre, at Turnberry in 1963, is Bert Stewart, TV stage manager, whilst at work on the commentaries are Bill Cox (right) and the inimitable Henry Longhurst, who set the standard for others to follow.*

Right *Helen Hicks, winner of the U.S. Ladies' Amateur in 1931, and runner-up two years later; she became a most successful professional golfer and toured extensively.*

1938. He was clearly a player who was going to make his mark at top level: his name was Bobby Locke.

A multi-million dollar enterprise

The war disrupted tournament golf throughout the world, but as soon as hostilities were over, it resumed. The American domination of the scene remained, and it was the heyday of Byron Nelson (who retired in 1946), Sam Snead, and, particularly, Ben Hogan. Prize money was soon up to some quarter of a million dollars; but the real expansion started towards the end of the 1950s. By 1958 professionals in the United States were competing for a share of a million dollars; by 1963, 2 million; by 1968, 5 million. There has been a steady increase every year, until the prize money has now reached some 35 million dollars. Even allowing for inflation, this represents an enormous increase. The British professional did not do as well financially after the war; many of the tournaments were now sponsored by the makers of golfing equipment, but as yet major commercial and industrial firms had not realised the advertising possibilities of sponsorship.

Television began to exert an influence soon after the end of the war. As equipment became more powerful and cameramen more skilful, outside broadcasts started to take a larger share of the programmes. Golf is a game which lends itself to television: although it is played over a large area, it takes place at a modest pace. In early days it was not easy to follow the ball, but the coming of colour pictures made an immense difference, and the growing expertise of the television teams made the game increasingly popular, and increased the stature of the players – now instantly recognisable to the viewing public; which means almost everyone. At first it was not easy to cover more than a few holes, but as time has gone by, the advance in cameras and techniques has made it easier to go to all parts of courses, though the tendency is still to concentrate on the last few holes, where the crunch action comes.

Not only has television brought competition golf to millions of homes – which has encouraged sponsors – but the fees paid by the television companies for the

filming and presentation rights have increased the prize money; so much of it has found its way to the professional.

The winning of a major championship is nowadays worth an enormous sum to the individual; the actual prize money won is often trivial compared to the vast sums which can come from sponsorship and other advertising; the major winner has a name which can be worth money in many ways: in addition to lending his name to every kind of golf equipment, he can command large fees for playing in matches or pro-am tournaments, for holding clinics, for appearing in tournaments. In addition, the top professionals are now increasingly involved in new clubs and course construction, for the name is enough to ensure success.

It would be easy for the top professional to commit himself to engagements for every day of the year; the pressure of tournament play is no less than it used to be – there were plenty of examples of players who took it out of themselves with a week of competitive tournament

'Babe' Zaharias, an astonishing all-round athlete and sportswoman. She won two golds and a silver at the 1932 Olympics; was first-class at any game she played. Starting golf only in her mid-twenties, she soon won many tournaments, including the U.S. Ladies' Amateur. She was the first American to win the British Ladies', in 1947. After she turned professional she won 10 majors in her short career.

Right *JoAnne Carner has had a most distinguished career both as amateur and professional.*

Below *Jan Stephenson, from Australia, has played in the LPGA tour since 1974. Winner of three major titles, she is seen here playing in the 1988 Mazda Champions at Tryall, Jamaica.*

golf; perhaps the most notable example was Bobby Jones, and his retirement at the age of 28 was largely a consequence of the strain imposed on him. The four major annual world tournaments – the Open, the U.S. Open, the U.S. PGA and the Masters – do not have to jockey for position in the golfing calendar: their standing is established the world over. Often the viability of other tournaments, however, depends on their being able to entice the top ranking players; if they do not come, a tournament will lose standing and, as a result, may lost its sponsors as well. As the number of willing sponsors grows, each wishes his tournament to be the biggest and best; and in the end it all comes down to money. The one event where, so far, money has not been all-important is the Ryder Cup. This for many years after the war seemed a dead duck, since the Americans demonstrated their superiority with discouraging regularity until the end of the 1970s. Since then, the

radical improvement of standards on the European tour, and the inclusion of continental Europeans in what before was a Great Britain and Ireland team, has transformed the situation. The Ryder Cup is approached with new keenness and determination by both sides, showing just how competitive it has become. Players try their hardest to qualify for the team.

The difference between the club professional and the tour professional was first highlighted in the United States in the late 1960s when there was almost a breakaway movement of those involved in the regular tour from the U.S. PGA. It led, fortunately without major ructions, to a Tournament Division of the U.S. PGA, which is responsible for the running of the tour, while maintaining close touch with the main association. A similar arrangement has been made in the European Tour, whose headquarters at Wentworth deal with all tour events, sponsorship, media coverage, and everything else connected with the tour professionals; the PGA, a separate organisation, works from The Belfry in Warwickshire, and is responsible for membership of the association and the club professionals.

The U.S. Women's Professional Golfers' Association was started in 1944 but made little headway until, in 1948, it became sponsored by Wilson, the sports-

equipment firm, and changed its name to the Ladies Professional Golf Association. Chartered in 1950, the LPGA soon had an organised tour. At first it did not arouse a great deal of public interest, but with a group of well-known players led by that supreme all-round athlete, Babe Didrikson Zaharias, it continued to prosper. In the early 1960s Mickey Wright arrived on the scene: she was a born winner, and a charismatic and dominant personality for a number of years. Amongst her 82 tour victories she included 13 'majors', and her four wins in the U.S. Women's Open and her winning of the U.S. Women's Open and the LPGA Championship in the same year on two occasions were milestones in a remarkable career.

The tour was now making great strides forward; indeed, by the early 1970s it was getting too big too quickly. It was at this stage that in 1975 Ray Volpe became the first Commissioner. Under his guidance for seven years, the LPGA was expanded to deal with greatly increased finances and responsibilities; television started to take an interest and, with the funds secured, the LPGA moved to a permanent headquarters and course at Sweetwater Country Club in Sugar Land, Texas. Throughout the years there have always been top stars, and the LPGA honours them in its Hall of Fame. There are now 11

Bobby Locke was first of the post-war generation of greatly gifted Commonwealth players to try their fortunes in Britain.

Above *Norman von Nida, a successful Australian pro, dominated the British golf scene in 1947 and 1948.*

Below, right *Flory van Donck, a Belgian pro who was twice runner-up in the British Open, in 1956 and 1959.*

names on the roll, recent additions being JoAnne Carner, who was a successful amateur before her equally successful run as a professional; and Nancy Lopez, the superstar of the present.

The Women's Professional Golfers' European Tour started in 1979, and in 10 short years has reached a position of eminence in golf. The WPGA is now running its own affairs, after a spell under

the guidance of the PGA. The number of tournaments on the tour has grown quickly during the years, as has the prize money; once again, television has helped to encourage sponsors. The leading money winner on the tour in 1979 amassed just under £5000. In 1988, the 60 players on the Woolmark Order of Merit all passed this figure, while the leader, Marie-Laure di Lorenzi de Taya, very nearly reached a six-figure sum. This was almost twice as much as that made by the 1987 winner, Dale Reid. The standing of the European Tour has been enhanced by the remarkable victories in the U.S. Women's Open of Laura Davies (1987) – who had also won the British Ladies' Open in 1986 – and Liselotte Neumann, from Sweden (1988).

It was after World War II that players from the Southern Hemisphere, who had been knocking on the door pre-war, started to make an impact. Bobby Locke had already been twice the leading amateur in the Open (1936, 1937) and had won the South African Open five times by 1940. After the war, he was very successful in the United States, taking many tournaments and finishing second in the money list of 1947, in which year he also won the Canadian Open. He did not

• AUSTRALIAN OPEN CHAMPIONSHIP •

RECENT WINNERS

Year	Location	Name	Score
1970	Kingston Heath	G. Player	280
1971	R. Hobart	J. Nicklaus	269
1972	Kooyonga	P. Thompson	281
1973	R. Queensland	J. Snead	280
1974	L. Karrinyup	G. Player	279
1975	Australian	J. Nicklaus	279
1976	Australian	J. Nicklaus	286
1977	Australian	D. Graham	284
1978	Australian	J. Nicklaus	284
1979	Metropolitan	J. Newton	288
1980	The Lakes	G. Norman	284
1981	R. Melbourne	B. Rogers	282
1982	Australian	R. Shearer	297
1983	Kingston Heath	P. Fowler	285
1984	R. Melbourne	T. Watson	281
1985	R. Melbourne	G. Norman	212*
1986	Metropolitan	R. Davis	278
1987	R. Melbourne	G. Norman	273
1988	R. Sydney	M. Calcavecchia	269

*Over 54 holes

manage a major American title, and in the end he concentrated on Europe, and took a host of titles there.

In the early years after the war, Norman von Nida was the first Australian to win in Britain – his seven successes in England in 1947 creating a record which has not been beaten; he was a prominent player for many seasons both at home and in Britain, but never managed an Open – he was third to Henry Cotton in 1948, and never too far away in his other attempts; his contemporary Ossie Pickworth, a prolific winner in Australia, never had equal success in Europe. After this came the years of Peter Thomson: he had four out of his five Opens in the five years from 1954; he also won tournaments all over the world, including two on the U.S. circuit. From his time, there have always been Australians in the top echelon of world players, with Kel Nagle, David Graham, Jack Newton (so unluckily injured), and more recently Greg Norman – so long at the top without recording the major titles which seemed his due – Graham Marsh and Rodger Davis. Bob Charles has been the most successful player to come from New Zealand, and he is the only left-handed player to have won the Open. The movement into the world scene of players from the Antipodes was not all in one direction, for the major world players' names feature in the winners of the Australian Open – Arnold Palmer, Jack Nicklaus (six times) and Gary Player (six times).

Above *Australian David Graham, a steady and tough competitor, has won all over the world, including the Piccadilly Match-Play (1976), the U.S. PGA (1979) and the U.S. Open (1981).*

Left *Harvie Ward was one of the best U.S. amateurs of his day. He won the Amateur Championship in 1952, and the U.S. Amateur in 1955 and 1956.*

The U.S. Amateur has remained the preserve of American players: Harold Hilton remains the only winner from outside North America, though there have been two Canadians – Charles Somerville in 1932 and Gary Cowan in 1966 and 1971. In a period when the world's major titles were dominated by the Americans, South African Gary Player was able to take them on on their own ground. He became the first non-American to win the U.S. Masters, in 1961. The U.S. PGA followed in 1962, and the U.S. Open in 1965; previously he had won the Open at Muirfield in 1959, and he was thus one of only four to capture all four of the major world tournaments. The U.S. Open was won by Tony Jacklin in 1970 to complete a magnificent double with his Open at Royal Lytham and St Anne's in 1969; he was the first British player to win the U.S. Open since Ted Ray in 1920. David Graham became the first Australian holder in 1981, and he also took the U.S. PGA (1979) to join Gary Player as the only non-Americans to succeed. The U.S. Masters, on the other hand, has seen five non-American winners in the last eleven years, with Seve Ballesteros as the first European to take the title, in 1980, and Sandy Lyle the first from Britain, in 1988.

The only player from South America to take a major so far is Roberto de Vicenzo from Argentina; he won many national titles, but his single major was in the 1967 Open at Hoylake, when at the age of 44 he beat off the challenge of the defending champion, Jack Nicklaus, who was then

Above *Gary Player is the most successful golfer to come from South Africa. His determination, astonishing fitness, and tidy swing have won him tournaments all over the world, including the Grand Slam of majors.*

Right *The lovely course at Serapong, with the harbour and skyline of the city of Singapore.*

reaching the height of his powers.

Golf winners of major tournaments are usually mature young men. It is becoming increasingly unlikely that there will be another winner of the Open as young as Tom Morris, Jr. who was only 17 at the time of his first title; one may yet emerge older than Tom Morris Sr was in 1867, when he was 46; but the greatest number of major winners have already served their apprenticeships, have won tournaments, and at last graduate to a major; they will usually be at least 25. One of the best things about the game of golf is that it can be played to any age: the idea of a Seniors Tour for those who had reached the age of 50 started in the United States, and has developed into a multi-million dollar circuit, offering large rewards to players who in other days would have thought their winning days were over; some find that they are earning in a few tournaments more than they had amassed before in their entire career. One notable winner – he has won all the Senior major championships, including in 1988 the British Seniors – is Gary Player, adding to an already glittering career. Peter Thomson and Bob Charles are others who have discovered that life may begin at 50. The

warning signs are already out, however: Jack Nicklaus reaches his fiftieth birthday in 1990.

The golf circuits

South Africa runs its own Sunshine Circuit, but there are few professionals from other countries willing to take part in view of the present isolation of South African sport. However, two from Zimbabwe who have reached world class by way of the Sunshine Circuit are Mark McNulty and Nick Price (who lost the magnificent duel for the Open at Lytham in 1988); while local player David Frost is another in the top rank.

The Safari Circuit gathers in the Opens of Nigeria, the Ivory Coast, Kenya, Zimbabwe and Zambia, and takes place early in the year, before the start of the European Tour, under whose aegis it is run. It does not generally attract many of the top players, so it gives an opportunity to the younger or less experienced players to make their mark; amongst former winners, however, are Seve Ballesteros, Sandy Lyle and Ian Woosnam, while Englishman Gordon J. Brand is the leading career money winner on this circuit.

Looking back from the 3rd green at the Emirates Golf Club in Dubai – a miraculous patch of green in the vast Arabian desert.

113

Tsuneyuki (Tommy) Nakajima was formerly rated amongst the world's top four. He was well in contention for the Open at Turnberry in 1986, but found trouble and lost his chance.

Opposite, above *Tony Jacklin, the young golfer who in 1969 became the first British player since 1951 to win the Open. Less than a year later he won the U.S. Open, and led the way for other European wins in the major championships.*

Opposite, below
Looking across the lake towards the 3rd green at the delightful Nom-de-la-Breteche course, venue for the Lancôme Trophy.

The Australia and New Zealand circuit, which runs from October to March, continues to grow in prestige, and attracts more of the top players each year. There is usually a number of winners from overseas, but they can be sure of some very healthy competition from the strong home contingent.

The Asia Circuit is fitted in at the beginning of the year, from February to April; it comprises Opens from the Philippines, Hong Kong, Thailand, India, Malaysia, Singapore, Korea and Taiwan, together with a tournament in Tokyo. The foundations of the tour were laid in 1959, and it has gradually developed to include the present events; other countries have wanted to join the circuit, but time has not been available for them. A number of players from this circuit have already made their mark, in particular in the United States, where Tze-Chung (T.C.) Chen from Taiwan had done well in several tournaments, including the U.S. Open, before his first win in 1988.

The Japanese tournament season is the same as the European, and starts towards the end of the Asian Circuit. There are huge prizes in Japan, where golf is expanding more rapidly perhaps than anywhere else. Japanese professionals have made their mark recently in both Europe and the United States; the most successful in the West has been Isao Aoki, whose titles include the World March-Play championship at Wentworth in 1978, and Tsuneyuki ('Tommy') Nakajima, at one time fourth on the world ranking list. Masashi ('Jumbo') Ozaki is another who has topped the Japanese lists and won many tournaments.

The European Tour

British and Irish golfers led the professional lists in Britain for many years, and even after World War II there were only a few from Europe to enter the tournaments. By far the most notable was Flory van Donck from Belgium, winner of many titles and tournaments, twice second in the Open, winner of the Harry Vardon trophy in 1953, when he won two tournaments in Britain and five of the European opens. Spanish professionals began to make their mark in the early 1960s, with the Miguel brothers and Ramon Sota often well up in the Open and other tournament results. They never quite reached the top class, but were followed in the mid-1970s by the first of a new batch who did reach the top: Manuel Pinero, José-Maria Canizares, José Rivero, and the greatest yet to come from Spain, Seve Ballesteros; then there is the youngster, José-Maria Olazábal, already launched into a brilliant career.

There is a growing crop of French professionals, with none yet in the top rank. Germany has not yet developed as much as other European countries, but has produced one of the world's leading players, Bernhard Langer, with a U.S. Masters title to his credit.

The Scandinavian countries began to show real interest in golf some time after the war, and efficient training schemes have led to a flow of good players, many of whom have now made a mark in the European Tour. Ove Sellberg, Mats Lanner and Anders Forsbrand have all won tournaments, and Magnus Persson has

Curtis Strange has been the U.S. player of the late 1980s. Twice running winner of the U.S. Open (1988, 1989), he had been knocking at the door of the majors while amassing an impressive list of tournament wins. He was leading money winner on the U.S. circuit in 1985, 1987, and 1988.

been very close; and there are many others on the way up. The Danes, too, though not so far advanced as the Swedes, have players who threaten soon to break through to the top.

The European Tour started in the early 1970s, when John Jacobs became the first Tournament Director; he was responsible for raising the status of the Tour and expanding it to include a number of new tournaments as well as many of the European national open competitions; with the full organisation came a large increase in prize money, with minimum sums guaranteed for every tournament by the sponsors. Tony Jacklin's wins in the Open (1969) and the U.S. Open (1970) had made him the leading British player of that time, while Peter Oosterhuis was another to attract sponsorship; and there were other big names, some of whom had played in the Ryder Cup match of 1969 which ended in a tie. During the 1970s and 1980s the standard has steadily risen, and British players of world class have emerged – Sandy Lyle and Nick Faldo have both won majors, while Ian Woosnam is well up the ranking list, and had a phenomenally good year in 1987.

With the Tour becoming ever more competitive, there is a rush to gain places, and a PGA Qualifying School was launched in 1976. Many young amateurs now saw a lucrative future in professional golf, and there has been a steady stream

of those who have done well as amateurs to join the ranks. Many who have gained recognition in the Walker Cup use this as a yardstick of their having reached the necessary standard, and try to qualify. Some have been spectacularly successful; but many others have not survived the cut and thrust of tournament golf. By the middle 1980s, the qualifications for entry into tournaments have been rationalised, so that players now know where they are, and do not have to play in numerous qualifying competitions. The pre-qualifying tournaments, followed by the six-round Qualifying School at La Manga (Spain) at the end of the season, is taxing and competitive, with only 50 places to be won for the following year's Tour. Players from many countries now take part, and the standard rises every year. For those unable to qualify, there are a number of satellite tournaments each year, played at the same time as Tour events, while the Tartan Tour also offers opportunities for further tournament play.

Golf rankings

Many modern ranking lists depend on the amounts of money won. While this is satisfactory within a tour, it is not at all reliable when considered between tours on a world scale, for it then depends on the money put into each tour, exchange rates, and other incompatible criteria. But, for the record, 19 players won more than half a million dollars on the U.S. PGA tour in 1988. The leading money winner, Curtis Strange, banked $1,147,644 (over £650,000) from official tournaments, many hundreds of thousands of dollars more from unofficial events – and probably as much again from 'endorsements'. The lowest ranked player, Billy Ray Brown, won $83,590 (about £48,000). Money was a great deal more valuable 50 or 60 years ago; but even so official prizes were tiny compared with today's. On the other hand Walter Hagen, whose official winnings would seem piffling by present standards, invariably stayed in a suite at the Ritz when he was in London, and ate his lunches beside his hired Rolls Royce outside the English clubhouses he was not allowed to enter because he was a professional. He said he did not yearn to be a millionaire – he just wanted to live like one.

The Sony World Ranking is a system devised to look at players' results in tournaments the world over; these are graded according to their relative importance, of which the size of the purse is only one element. Scoring points are awarded for the first few places in qualifying events, which may be increased if a sufficient number of high-ranking players are in the field. Thus, for example, a grade 4 tournament may have its winning points considerably enhanced if the participants include, say, seven of the first 10 players in the current Sony Ranking list. Furthermore, results are counted over a period of three years, with the current year's results worth double the previous year's, and four times those of the year before that. The system does produce an order which is credible and meaningful – even if there are those who do not like it, as it does not show their players suf-ficiently advanced. During 1988 European players dominated, with Ballesteros and Norman disputing top spot, Lyle threatening to overtake them, and Faldo and Woosnam up in the top 10.

It is certainly an interesting phase. In the very early days the Scots professionals dominated the scene; then came the English, and the Triumvirate, with Vardon, Taylor, and Braid sharing the honours. There followed a 60-year period of American domination; and even today the strength in depth of the American professional field is immeasurably greater than Europe's. The Australians are well to the fore. Will the Japanese dominate next? Or the Asian Tour? Perhaps there will soon be some new superstar who will carry all before him like the masters of the past. With the number of excellent players in the field always increasing, he will need to be very special indeed.

The superlative Jack Nicklaus course at Muirfield Village, Ohio, where the Ryder Cup was played in 1987. Nicklaus is perhaps the most distinguished of a number of great players who have turned their talents to golf architecture with conspicuous success.

MODERN SUPERSTARS

At the highest level, golf has become an immensely lucrative part of the entertainment industry, the great players treated as media stars. But, even among the top men, a few have stood out above the rest as the greatest of their time.

Sam Snead

SAMUEL JACKSON SNEAD: *born* Hot Springs, Virginia, 27 May 1912

One of a trio of great golfers born in the same year – Snead, Hogan and Nelson – Sam Snead has had the most natural, the most beautiful, the most powerful and the longest-lasting golf swing of any player in history.

'Sam don't know a dam' thing about the golf swing,' said Ben Hogan, 'but he does it better than anyone else.'

He is also a marvellous story-teller, so that by now it is hard to tell fact from fiction. But the facts are marvellous enough. He really was a barefoot boy from the mountain country; he really did once cut a 'club' out of the branch of a swamp maple and shoot 72 with it;

years ago, when he was told his picture was on the front page of the *New York Times,* he really did say, 'Must be a fake: I've never been to New York.' When he was 67 he really did 'break his age' with a round of 66 in the Quad Cities Open. He really has shot 25 holes-in-one.

Snead started with one huge advantage: he is a great natural athlete: from the start he had a superb eye for a ball; his coordination of hand and eye was – and is – as near perfect as makes no difference. He can still pick the ball out of the hole without bending his knees; and he has never lost either his rhythm or his competitive edge.

He loves taking money from golfing friends, these days usually playing $5 Nassaus. But he tells the story of how, with press bets, he ended up being owed something like $10,000 on one occasion. He told the boys to forget the money. But after changing they came in to the clubhouse and dumped the dollars on the table. He comments: 'I guess seeing all that greenery brought me back to my senses.'

He won his first big pro tournament in 1937 and by the time he reluctantly joined the Seniors was credited with 84 Tour wins and 135 in all. He won the Masters and the U.S. PGA thrice each, and The Open once. In Ryder Cup matches his singles record was superb – six wins out of seven. He won the Canada Cup (World Cup) indi-

Left *'Slammin' Sam in 1937. Already he was recognised as one of the most naturally gifted golfers in the history of the game.*

vidual title in 1961 and was in the winning team four times. He won the Greater Greensboro eight times and the Miami Open six. But he never could quite win the U.S. Open: in 1939, needing a par-5 on the 72nd hole to win, he took 8; in 1947 he made a birdie on the 72nd hole to tie Lew Worsham, but lost the play-off when he missed a 30-inch putt on the 18th.

Sam Snead's swing has always been beautiful to watch and must be beautiful to own. It seems to have come to him quite naturally. As Cary Middlecoff says, his greatest contribution to the game has been to give golfers a fuller

and better concept of swing tempo. Other players liked to be drawn to play with him because something of his grace and rhythm might rub off on them.

But apparently he was still learning at 70. He was watching a baseball game on TV and the commentator remarked that one batter was keeping his arms too close to his body. 'That's it,' he said to himself: *'extend!'* Next day, in a friendly at the Cascades, he shot a 60 (and missed a putt for 59!).

Swing back 'into the slot'; keep a good rhythm going; and *extend*, says Sam. That's really all there is to it.

Sam helped Ben Hogan win the World Cup for the United States at Wentworth in 1956 and Arnold Palmer at Portmarnock in 1960. In seven Ryder Cup appearances he won 10 of his 13 matches.

· MAJORS ·

The Open (St Andrews) 1946
The Masters (Augusta) 1949, 1952, 1954
U.S. PGA 1942 (Seaview, NJ), 1949 (Hermitage, Pa.), 1951 (Oakmont, Pa.)

Hogan (seen here in the 1951 U.S. Open) 'manufactured' this swing – and with it became the finest shot-maker golf has yet known. When he joined the U.S. tour in 1936 he hooked the ball all over the place. His first big win did not come until 1946: after that he was favourite in every tournament he entered.

Ben Hogan

BENJAMIN WILLIAM HOGAN: *born* **Dublin, Texas, 13 August 1912**

After an uncertain start Ben Hogan metaphorically shut himself away in a monk's cell of solitary concentration searching for the Truth. When he found it he became perhaps the purest striker of a golf ball in history; and this, combined with a relentlessly competitive edge, made him the one professional his fellow professionals held in awe.

The Welsh wizard Dai Rees said of him: 'He was the only golfer I have played alongside in the past half century who made me feel inadequate.' The Australian Peter Thomson wrote: 'He was our ideal. He set a standard to which we all aspired but none of us ever reached.'

It felt to the others that if his putting had not deserted him he could have won every tournament he entered up to the age of 60. Approaching that age he played in a tournament at Fort Worth and shot 281 for third place. Tee to green he took only 141 shots. Had he putted at all well he would have won quite easily.

He started as a caddie, along with Byron Nelson. But he did not have his first big win until the year Nelson retired, 1946. To continue winning he had to get rid of his damaging hook. He practised for hours on end, days on end. He found a 'secret', but only after he

too had retired did he reveal it in *Life* magazine. His secret, he said, lay in opening the clubface on the backswing and cupping his left wrist at the top. But the true secret, his peers said, lay in his long, lone, dedicated analysis of every shot he ever hit. In the end he could do whatever he wanted.

In 1949 he was terribly injured in a car accident – so badly, indeed, that it was thought at one time that he might never walk again, for both his legs were broken and his pelvis and collarbone smashed. His total determination proved the experts wrong: almost unbelievably, he won the U.S. Open at Merion

the very next year! He won again the following year at Oakland Hills. Then in 1953 he won not only the U.S. Open once again but the Masters and the Open into the bargain; doubtless he would have won the U.S. PGA that year too had it not been held too soon after our Open for him to enter it. As it is, he remains the only golfer ever to win three majors in one year.

That Open was held at Carnoustie. It involved a type of golf Hogan had never played before, using the smaller British ball with which he had never played before either. When he practised, his caddie Cecil Timms was often sent ahead to the

greens and told something like this: 'I will hit a 2-iron to the left with a fade, another to the right with draw, a third low and running and the fourth high. Tell me exactly what happens to each.'

In the Open he shot 73, 71, 70, 68 to win by four shots; his 68 is still regarded as one of the most perfect exhibitions in the last round of an Open. When he returned home via New York he was welcomed with a 'ticker-tape parade' like the one that had greeted Bobby Jones 23 years earlier.

Scots called him 'the wee ice mon', for he appeared cold, reserved sometimes to the point of rudeness. Gary Player once called him long-distance for advice. Hogan asked him whose clubs he played with. 'Dunlops,' replied Player. 'Then,' said Hogan, 'ask Mr Dunlop.' A warm and pleasant man in his home life, about golf he has always been really serious.

At his peak, Hogan's golf was of a quality that perhaps only Bobby Jones before him and Jack Nicklaus after him have aspired to. And yet, astonishingly, after his *annus mirabilis* of 1953, he never won another major. The cumulative effect of his putting, and the long-term consequences of his accident, blunted his game. Just occasionally, however, his putting would hold up for a few holes. For many in the crowd at Augusta for the 1967 Masters, the high point of the tournament was the 54-year-old Hogan's back nine in the third round. Hitting the ball with the magisterial splendour of old, he reduced Augusta's most difficult half to 30 shots.

· MAJORS ·

The Open 1953 (Carnoustie)
U.S. Open 1948 (St Louis), 1950 (Merion), 1951 (Oakland Hills), 1953 (Oakmont)
The Masters 1951, 1953
U.S. PGA 1946 (Portland, Or.), 1948 (Norwood Hills)

Bobby Locke

ARTHUR D'ARCY LOCKE:
born **Germiston, Transvaal, South Africa, 20 November, 1917;** *died* **9 March 1987**

When he was nine years old Bobby Locke was putting with a 2-iron on the practice green of the local golf club. A Mr Lightbody, who had just bought a new putter, asked the lad if he would like a real wand, and gave him his old hickory-shafted blade. Locke used it until the day he died.

Then when he was 13 his father gave him Bobby Jones's book on golf. 'A lot of people are going to try to help you,' his father said. 'Let it go in one ear and out the other. You just model your game on Bobby Jones.'

Although it never quite looked like that, Locke took his father's advice. With his rusty putter and his version of the earlier Bobby's swing, Locke became his country's Amateur champion three years later and both Amateur and Open champion four years later. Visiting Britain the following year (1936) he finished as leading amateur in the Open at Hoylake. Returning as a pro in 1938 he won the Irish championship. And then war intervened.

After serving as an RAF bomber pilot in the Middle East, Locke returned to golf a changed man. He had put on weight. And he had put on years, looking 10 years older than he was. He had also cast care

dispute with the U.S. authorities. He wasn't too upset – he was in any case more at home in Britain, and indeed he always referred to himself as British. He won the Open four times, the South African Open nine times and also the French, the Swiss, the New Zealand and the Egyptian Opens.

Bobby Locke was rarely if ever to be seen practicing. But he would play every day if he could, even if only nine holes, and with anyone of whatever handicap. He never hurried, never worried, always looked relaxed and calm. His American friends called him 'Ol' Muffin-face.'

Widely considered to have been the greatest putter of all time, he appeared to hook his putts just as he did his tee shots. In this way, he said, he put 'true topspin' on them. Assessing his overall game Cary Middlecoff, the American Open champion of 1949 and 1956, wrote: 'He was a master strategist. He never hit a foolish shot and rarely one that could be called unwise.... He extracted the absolute maximum from the talent he possessed.'

A few weeks before he died Bobby Locke, although very ill, fulfilled a promise he had made to play the local Boy's Champion. He lost, scoring 81 – but in that 81 there were only 27 putts.

aside: he had decided he would never worry again.

In 1946 Sam Snead visited South Africa to play Locke in a series of 16 matches: Locke won 12 of them. Then, encouraged by Snead, Locke visited the United States in 1947 to devastate the tour and its players. He wore baggy plus-fours and a tie which he always tucked under the third button of his white shirt. He had perfected a long, loose, looping swing with which he hooked every shot. Shorter off the tee than almost all the others, he didn't worry. Moving placidly at a leisurely pace he would hit his next shot onto or near the green – then putt the hope out of his opponents.

Sam Snead said, 'I wouldn't bet one red cent against him in any tournament.' Clayton Haefner not only made $4000 betting on the stranger from Africa but also is said to have won Lloyd Mangrum's Cadillac. Locke played only 12 tournaments, but won six of them and finished second in two others.

Later he was to win more tournaments in America, and also the Canadian Open; then he was banned for a year following a

· MAJORS ·
The Open 1949 (Sandwich), 1950 (Troon), 1952 (Lytham), 1957 (St Andrews)

Arnold Palmer

ARNOLD DANIEL PALMER:
born **Latrobe, Pennsylvania,**
10 September 1929

Arnold Palmer's story is boyhood fiction brought to life: son of a small-town greenkeeper-pro, strong as an ox, handsome as a Western movie star, broke to the wide, he wins the U.S. Amateur, borrows heavily to start out as a pro, wins the Canadian Open, the U.S. Open, the Open and the Masters and becomes a hero to millions through television. He raises the status of the game, is transformed into a multi-millionaire and remains exactly the same person that he always was – human, unaffected, approachable, solid.

His home is still in Latrobe. 'Everything I need to fill my life is there,' he says. 'Golf, family, friends and flying' (he is a first-class pilot). The best thing about his office, he says, is that 'it is 15 steps to the door leading downstairs and 17 steps down to my workshop.'

Conservative in so many other ways, in life as well as in golf he has always been prepared to gamble on an heroic scale. Getting engaged, he raised the cash for an extremely expensive ring by accepting an extremely hazardous challenge. He said he would break 72 on any course his boss liked to name, taking $200 for every stroke achieved below that target. The course his boss chose was Pine Valley, New Jersey. That course

had been open for 25 years before anyone broke 70, and has been called 'a 184-acre sand-trap'. Palmer bogeyed the first hole but finished with 68. As $800 wasn't quite enough to pay for the ring he borrowed the rest.

He borrowed more still to buy a second-hand trailer caravan and set out with his wife Winnie to make his name as a pro. Seven months later he had won the Canadian. Within three years he was top of the money list in the United States. He played electrifying golf. 'When I was young it never occurred to me that a shot couldn't be made,' he explains. He was fearless: his motto was 'If I can see it I can hit it, and if I can hit it I can hole it'. Such heroic golf was perfect for television, then in its first boom years, and the game took on a whole new meaning for the millions.

Palmer 'went for broke.' At Royal Birkdale a plaque marks the spot on the 16th (then the 15th) where he struck a fantastic, an impossible 6-iron shot out of deep, tangled scrub on his way to winning the 1961 Open. At the Rancho, Los Angeles, is another marking four successive tee shots he hit out-of-bounds into the ocean there.

Palmer's support for The Open in the 1960s restored it to its traditional status as the world's premier international tournament. Similarly his presence at the World Matchplay at Wentworth, which he won twice (1964–7), started that event off at the top. Palmer's power-golf ruled the world.

Between 1960 and 1964 he won 29 events on the U.S. tour. He

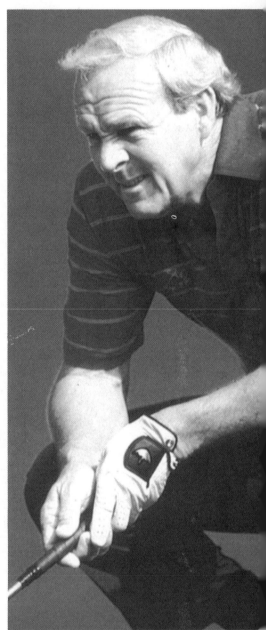

A study in concentration. You'll see exactly the same expression on Palmer's face at a dozen tournaments every year on the Seniors tour. He loves his golf.

Right *Palmer 'goes for broke' at Troon in 1962, where he won by six shots. The famous flourishing finish says it all.*

played in six Ryder Cups and six World Cups, taking the individual title in 1967. Fans were thrilled by his 'charges.' In the 1960 U.S. Open he picked up nine shots on the leaders in the final round to win the tournament.

He is also remembered, with equal affection, for the tournaments he all-too-humanly gave away. Needing a par on the 18th to win the 1961 Masters he took 6 and

let in Gary Player. Seven strokes ahead of Billy Casper in the 1966 U.S. Open with only 9 holes to play, he let Casper catch him while going for Hogan's tournament record score. Then Casper won the play-off.

Palmer entitled his autobiography *Go For Broke*. With this style of play and an engagingly human personality, he has won tournaments all around the world

– and the hearts and the respect of spectators and golfers everywhere.

· MAJORS ·
The Open 1961 (Birkdale), 1962 (Troon)
U.S. Open 1960 (Cherry Hills)
The Masters 1958, 1960, 1962, 1964

Gary Player

GARY JIM PLAYER: *born* **Johannesburg, South Africa, 1 November 1935**

Gary Player made himself into one of the most successful golfers ever and one of the greatest international star. *Made* himself because, although he parred the first three holes he ever played, he was not considered to have a natural talent for the game. He was small – 5ft 7in even when he grew up – and if he was going to keep up with others of his age he had to hit the ball with all his strength rather than to swing elegantly through it.

Bobby Locke was his first hero. So young Player adopted a four-knuckle hooker's grip and tried to emulate him. He did pretty well, and at 18 turned pro. Almost immediately he sailed for England to

seek his fortune and equally quickly realised he would have to change his method: too often he hooked into trouble. With the advice and example of the fine Welsh professional Dai Rees, who was also small in stature, he adopted a weaker grip and gained in accuracy. At 20 he won the Dunlop Masters and an invitation to the Masters at Augusta.

His early experience in America made him determined to make further changes to his method. He now studied Ben Hogan and exercised relentlessly to strengthen his legs. And in 1958 he came second to Tommy Bolt in the U.S. Open.

Since then Gary Player has won the U.S. Open once, the U.S. PGA Championship twice, the Masters three times, the South African Open 13 times, the Australian seven times, the World Matchplay five times, the World Cup individual title twice, the U.S. World Series three times, the Open three times; and when winning the Brazil-

ian Open his round of 59 made him the first golfer ever to break 60 in a national tournament.

He is only the fourth person, after Gene Sarazen, Ben Hogan and Jack Nicklaus, to achieve the pro 'Grand Slam' of winning all four majors – the Open, the U.S. Open, the Masters and the U.S. PGA. As a Senior he now claims a second Grand Slam – the U.S. Seniors Open, the British Seniors Open, the U.S. Seniors PGA and the U.S. Seniors TPC (Tournament Players' Championship).

In doing all this he reckons he has travelled 6.5 million miles, flown round the world 54 times and hit more than 7 million golf balls. He is one of the few people also who has won a personal victory over jet-lag.

A fitness fanatic, Gary Player often sleeps in the aisle of an airliner – lying flat is physically better than curling up. He does press-ups and knee-bends every day; he eats a lot of fruit and fibre and tops them up with vitamin-E. He believes implicitly in the Power of Positive Thinking.

As a practicer he rivals the legendary Ben Hogan. When young he would usually stay in a bunker until he had holed at least five shots: he has long been one of the greatest bunker players in history. Rather than practise a method, he thinks the average golfer should practise with each particular club continuously until it is mastered; then practise different shots with particular clubs one at a time until they too are mastered.

His first victory in the World Matchplay, at Wentworth in 1965, sums up his character. Seven-down to Tony Lema with 17 to play and still 5-down with 9 to play, he won the match and later the tournament. He is a little man with steel in his soul.

· MAJORS ·

The Open 1959 (Muirfield), 1968 (Carnoustie), 1974 (Royal Lytham)
U.S. Open 1965 (Bellerive, Mo.)
The Masters 1961, 1974, 1978
U.S. PGA 1962 (Aronomink, Pa.), 1972 (Oakland Hills)

Roberto de Vicenzo

ROBERTO DE VICENZO:
born **Buenos Aires, 14 April 1923**

One of nature's gentlemen, de Vicenzo started in humble circumstances, one of a large family which happened to live near a golf course. He and four of his brothers became caddies and all later turned professional. There was little scope in Argentina, however, when he was young; and five years after turning pro, when he had scraped together enough money, he set out for North America. He did well enough there in his first year to be able to take ship for Britain and the British Open, which for him was the tournament of tournaments.

De Vicenzo was equal third in his first Open and third again in 1949. In the next year, 1950, he was second. And so began an 18-year love affair with the oldest Open of them all. His eventual victory, at Hoylake in 1967, was cheered to the echo. The British fully returned his affection. As well as being a great shot-maker he was a trier (he had been third again in 1956, in 1960 and in 1964), and there was genuine delight throughout the British golfing fraternity that he had won at last.

Gentle by nature as so many big men are, de Vicenzo was blessed with a beautiful as well as a power-

Left *Portrait of a gentleman: Roberto de Vicenzo of Argentina, who had won the Open at Hoylake in 1967, lost his chance of winning the Masters the following year by signing for a last-round 66 when he had actually scored 65. He accepted the disaster with self-deprecating dignity.*

ful swing. He took it with him around the world, winning 20 national championships in some 14 different countries – everywhere in South America where golf was played, in Belgium, the Netherlands, France, West Germany, Spain.

He represented Argentina in 15 World Cups and was twice the individual winner. He won the World Pro Seniors in 1974, the Legends of Golf in 1979 and the U.S. Seniors in 1980. He is credited with more than 140 victories.

In 1968 he tied with Bob Goalby for the Masters at Augusta but was ruled out of a play-off on a technicality. He had not noticed that his partner Tommy Aaron had marked a 4 on his card for the 17th when, as everyone in the world who was watching television saw, he had made a birdie 3. In golf, rules are rules and if you sign your card wrongly you lose. Since that day the process of signing-off at the Masters, and in most other big tournaments, has been better regulated. At that time de Vicenzo took this unfortunate miscarriage of justice calmly and with typical dignity. 'I am a big stupid,' was about all he said.

In that tournament he had started breathtakingly well. His

pitch to the 1st green spun back into the hole. He tapped in at the next two holes. He turned in 31. He rounded Amen Corner safely and a birdie on the 15th took him to 7-under par. Goalby, playing behind him, eagled the 15th. De Vicenzo then birdied the 17th. The only blemish on the round was that be bogeyed the 18th.

In the 1967 British Open he had to fight U.S. Open champion Jack Nicklaus over the last few holes to gain the title he so desperately wanted to win. After three rounds he was just ahead. But Jack Nicklaus was close on his heels. Roberto finally settled the issue with a

splendidly brave 3-wood which cut the corner of the out-of-bounds on the 16th. A final round of 70 won him his treasured tournament.

De Vicenzo won his own national Open nine times and the Argentine Professional title seven times as well as the Chilean, Colombian, Brazilian and Panama Opens. His contribution not only to South American but to world golf has been outstanding.

· MAJORS ·
The Open (Hoylake) 1967

Right *De Vicenzo never gave up in his long pursuit of the Open title. Here, in 1953, he was sixth to Ben Hogan. In 1948 he had been third, in 1949 third again; in 1950 he had been runner-up to Bobby Locke. He was third again in 1956, 1960 and 1964. In 1967 he won, beating defending champion Nicklaus by two shots at Hoylake.*

Billy Casper was one of the steadiest putters the American game has known. He turned pro in 1954 and in the next 12 years won 33 tournaments. He won the Vardon Trophy for the lowest scoring average in 1960, 1963, 1965, 1966 and 1968.

Billy Casper

WILLIAM EARL CASPER, Jr: *born* San Diego, California, 24 June 1931

Billy Casper is a superstar who has received far less credit and much less attention than his golf deserves. He was to some a sort of anti-hero in the times of Palmer, Player and Nicklaus, but as a golfer he was right up there with them.

He was twice winner of the U.S. Open. He won the Masters. He won the Canadian Open. On the U.S. tour he won the Vardon Trophy five times for the year's best stroke average. He played eight times in the Ryder Cup, won 20 matches and lost only 10. He won 51 tournaments on the pro circuit and has since won several more on the Seniors tour.

The 1966 U.S. Open is usually remembered as the Open Palmer unaccountably lost. Seven shots ahead of Casper with nine holes to play Palmer allowed Casper to catch him. What is usually forgotten is that there was then a play-off, which Casper won with an excellent 68. In the same year at the finish of the Alcan tournament at Portland, Oregon, Casper made up seven shots on Lee Trevino over the last three holes to win by one stroke.

The press often paid more attention to his diet than to his golf. Severe food allergies caused him to put on too much weight and when he won the 1959 U.S. Open he tipped the scales at 212 pounds

– which is 50 pounds more than he ought to have weighed. By hook or by crook he had to slim down.

In one sense Casper was the Bobby Locke of the U.S. tour. He never hit a rash shot, stayed in the fairway and putted superbly. The big difference between them was that Casper has always been a fast a player, whereas Locke was slow. He never wasted a second. As for his putting, when he was second in the U.S. PGA championship in 1958 he needed only 112 putts – a steady average of 28 per round.

He was a 'rap' putter, not a stroker of the ball. His method is one which is very rarely used by others. The left wrist is close to the left thigh and is used as a vertical hinge. The right palm does the striking and is kept square to the line of the putt throughout the short stroke.

His swing on the tee and off the fairway has always been economical: a strong grip, a three-quarters backswing, the club dragged down with an early turn of the hips, and a firm left side at the finish.

A family man with strong Mormon convictions, Billy Casper has never put golf first. He and his wife Shirley have brought up 11 children, six of them adopted. Billy sometimes preaches at church meetings. He put a great deal of his money into fruit farming. This venture collapsed and with it went much of his wealth. Eleven children can be expensive, so he set out for the golf courses once more to restore his fortunes.

His first efforts were discouraging to say the least. In half a dozen

tournaments in 1980 he hit nearly 50 shots out-of-bounds. His routine seemed nervy, his swing forced, his putting uncertain. But he stuck with it and gradually put his old swing back together again after spending countless hours watching films of his earlier days on the Tour.

On the Seniors tour Billy Casper has already won back not only his lost wealth but his reputation as one of the superstars.

· MAJORS ·

U.S. Open 1959 (Winged Foot, NY), 1966 (Olympic, Cal)
The Masters 1970

Above *Casper has recouped his lost fortunes on the Seniors tour.*

Right *In 1961, when this picture was taken, Casper's economical swing took him to fourth in the U.S. money list. Five years later he made up seven shots in nine holes on Arnold Palmer to take the great man to a U.S. Open play-off, which Casper won by 69 to 73.*

Peter Thomson after winning the first of his five Opens in 1954 at Royal Birkdale. He won his last, again at Birkdale, in 1965, sealing his claim to be the best links player of modern times.

Peter Thomson

PETER WILLIAM THOMSON, MBE: *born* **Melbourne, Australia, 23 August 1929**

A sportsman with a simple view of golf and the golf swing but a sophisticated view of life and of society, Peter Thomson won the Open five times, matching J. H. Taylor and James Braid and being equalled later by Tom Watson. From 1952 through 1958 he was never worse than second. He also won the British Matchplay four times, the New Zealand Open eight times, the Australian three times, and with Kel Nagle won the Canada Cup (World Cup) twice.

It used to be said that he was the best small-ball player in the world – Great Britain did not go over to the larger sized American ball until 1974 – but it would probably have been truer to say that he was the best links-golf player. Since becoming a Senior he has shown that he has no difficulty playing the larger ball. In 1985, his second year on the U.S. Seniors circuit, he won nine events and pocketed $386,724.

If he did not play regularly on the American circuit when younger it was not the size of the ball that bothered him but rather the unreal life of a touring pro in the United States in the 1950s and 1960s. A music lover, an amateur artist, a writer and a man interested in politics, he has always wanted more out of life than con-

Some thought Peter Thomson was just a 'small-ball' player until he took the U.S. Seniors tour by storm in 1985, winning nine tournaments.

stant travel and continuous golf.

As a young man Peter Thomson says he learned a great deal from Bobby Locke, the fine South African who became his great rival in the Open. He played Locke head-to-head in South Africa, as Sam Snead had done, and, like Snead, looked like coming a cropper. But after losing a string of matches he suddenly realised why: he was trying to play Locke stroke-for-stroke and Locke was too imperturbable, too good on the greens for that. Thomson changed tack and played the course hole-by-hole and finished only one match behind.

In Britain from 1951 through 1958 Thomson and Locke won six of the Opens between them, Tommo winning three in-a-row, 1954, 1955 and 1956.

His view of the golf swing is essentially simple. Get aligned correctly. Get set-up correctly. Think how you want to be at impact. Have the left shoulder *up* and the right shoulder *down*. Then just 'draw the club back, gathering your power, and hit the ball precisely forward to the target.' Thomson, certainly, has proved the value of an uncomplicated swing.

The essential elements of golf, he says, are careful planning and calm and clear thinking. He stays relaxed, like Locke, and instead of always trying his utmost always keeps something in reserve in case adversity rears up before him.

A man with a strong social conscience, he has acted for a long time as Chairman of the James McGrath Foundation which set up Odyssey House in Melbourne to help solve the problems of drug addicts. In 1981 he stood for election to the Victorian State legislature as a Liberal (Conservative) candidate but lost by a few hundred votes.

He played occasionally in the first Legends of Golf tournaments in the United States but did not seriously attack the Seniors tour until 1984. He was immediately successful. After his big year in 1985 he has eased off a bit and now is turning more to course designing as well as to his writing and commentating.

· MAJORS ·

The Open 1954 (Birkdale), 1955 (St Andrews), 1956 (Hoylake), 1958 (Lytham), 1965 (Birkdale)

Right *A study in power: Jack Nicklaus on the tee in 1960. Still an amateur, he came second in the U.S. Open at Cherry Hills to Arnold Palmer.*

Jack Nicklaus

JACK WILLIAM NICKLAUS: born Columbus, Ohio, 21 January 1940

Many claim 'The Golden Bear' is the greatest golfer ever. Certainly his record is without equal: the only man to have won all four Majors three times; six times winner of the Masters; five times U.S. PGA champion; four times U.S. Open champion; thrice the Open champion; six times Australian Open champion; member of six winning U.S. World Cup teams and of six Ryder Cup teams; more than 70 victories on the U.S. tour and 58 second places. Who is ever going to match that?

This amazing golfer started to play when 10 years of age. His teacher Jack Grout reckoned he averaged 300 practice shots and 18 holes of play virtually every single day thereafter until he turned pro in 1962. He would play, in extreme heat, cold, wind, rain, even snow.

But he did more than merely hit golf shots. Grout reported that quite early he became fascinated with the courses he played on and the effect of trees, water, sand, rough and the shape and visual impact of the land itself. In short Jack Nicklaus became the complete professional golfer. He has never just played golf shots, he has always in a literal and totally understanding way played *golf courses*.

Blessed with a powerful physique – each of his thighs measured the same as the waist of his great friend and rival Gary Player – his masterly strategic approach to golf tournaments as much as his wide, upright swing and great strength made him the favourite in every tournament he entered over a span of almost 20 years. He won two U.S. Amateurs as a teenager, nearly won the U.S. Open the first time he entered it as an amateur; and *did* win it the first time he entered as a pro. And his last 'Grand Slam' of the four recognised Majors was achieved in eight years between the ages of 38 and 46.

During his heyday Nicklaus did relatively little practicing. In his off-duty time he was family man,

· MAJORS ·
The Open 1966 (Muirfield), 1970 (St Andrews), 1978 (St Andrews)
U.S. Open 1962 (Oakmont), 1967 (Baltusrol), 1972 (Pebble Beach), 1980 (Baltusrol)
The Masters 1963, 1965, 1966, 1972, 1975, 1986
U.S. PGA 1963 (Dallas), 1971 (PGA National, Fla), 1973 (Canterbury, Ohio), 1975 (Firestone), 1980 (Oak Hill, NY)

businessman, fisherman and course designer; and definitely family man first. For him it put the icing on the cake, the snowcap on the mountain, that his son Jackie caddied for him at Augusta when at the age of 46 he won the 50th Masters. This has sometimes been called the Masters that Ballesteros lost when, leading the pack, he put a 'soft 4-iron' into the water in front of the 15th green. But in fact Nicklaus made an irresistible charge. His final nine holes included six birdies and an eagle. He finished with 65. He won.

In 1988 Jack Nicklaus suffered a serious recurrence of a nagging back trouble and there were doubts whether he would ever be able to play seriously again. But if he doesn't he will probably make as big an impact as a course designer as he made as a player. Already his Muirfield Village course in Ohio, scene of the historic 1987 Ryder Cup match, is regarded as one of the half dozen finest courses in the United States. Jack Nicklaus has not only been the best golfer of his time but also the most complete man of golf.

Lee Trevino exhibits his highly individual action: the slicer's wide open stance; the hooker's closed clubface at the top; the good golfer's right leg buttress. What we cannot see is his ability to 'invent' shots to order.

Lee Trevino

LEE BUCK TREVINO: *born* **Dallas, Texas, 1 December 1939**

If any golfer ever fulfilled precisely the manly specifications set down by Rudyard Kipling – 'If you can meet with Triumph and Disaster and treat those two imposters just the same...' – it must surely be Lee Trevino.

A Mexican-American, he was

born into poverty on the edge of a city noted for its wealth. He had little formal education. But he let some golf clubs speak for him and by the time he was 30 had won the U.S. Open and pocketed half a million dollars. Most of the dollars, however, went into someone else's pocket, owing to a bad contract. So he started again. He won another U.S. Open and two Opens – but somehow lost a lot of money again. He was then struck by lightning on a golf course and quite seriously injured. Married for the third time at 44, he told his new wife he felt too old to try for the top again. 'Your clubs don't know how old you are,' she told him severely. So he went out and won the U.S. PGA championship!

Laughing, chattering, always ready with a wisecrack, you will never see Lee Trevino down-hearted and rarely even serious, except when just preparing for a delicate shot on the course.

But do not think he is just the Clown Prince of golf. When he had won the Hawaiian Open towards the end of 1986, he drew out $10,000 and handed them to the family of Ted Makalena, a fellow pro who had been his room-mate and had just been killed in a surfing accident.

Trevino made a bit of money as a caddie, did a stint at a local driving range, played a lot on the public course, taught himself a strangely consistent style of his own and did a little 'hustling'. His most famous hustle was when he bet someone he could beat him on the par-3 course using a 'Dr Pepper' soft-drinks bottle instead of a

Where it counts: as he comes through impact Trevino, still with his wide-open stance, shows the still head, the firm straight left wrist, the squared clubface and the lateral hip shift which makes it all come right.

golf club. What the victim didn't know was that Trevino had been practising with that bottle for a year. The bet was small but afterwards the soft drinks company signed him up to a four-year contract at $50,000 a year. The greatest hustler of all, Titanic Thompson, at the end of his career wanted Trevino to join him as his partner.

The swing he designed for himself is unique. His stance is wide open, his body aimed about 20 degrees left. His hand action is that of a hooker, with the left wrist bowed at the top and the clubface shut. At impact his hands are a long way in front of the clubhead. The result is a controlled, left-to-right fade which provides Trevino with pinpoint accuracy.

He was unsure of his own abilities at first and his wife pawned her few valuables to pay for his entry into the 1967 U.S. Open. He came 5th and was on his way. Next year at Oak Hill he won, breaking 70 in every round and beating Jack Nicklaus by four shots. He won again in 1971, beating Jack Nicklaus this time in a play-off. After that win Trevino flew to Britain and won that Open. Shortly afterwards he flew back to North America and won the Canadian. Next year he won the Open again.

Trevino won the Vardon Trophy for the lowest scoring average on the American tour five times. He played in six Ryder Cups, winning 17 matches and losing only 7, has won in Australia, France, Mexico and Morocco as well, and has career winnings of more than $3,500,000.

His gifts to golf have included not only his good-humoured chatter and his never-say-die attitude but also his repeated demonstration that golf, like life, is about individuality. A hugely gifted 'inventor' of shots for any occasion, Trevino is the very antithesis of the technically gifted, superbly coached but rather colourless young lions who feature in the money in the target-golf events that nowadays seem to dominate the U.S. Tour.

· MAJORS ·

The Open 1971 (Royal Birkdale), 1972 (Muirfield)
U.S. Open 1968 (Oak Hill, NY), 1971 (Merion, Penn.)
U.S. PGA 1974 (Tanglewood), 1984 (Shoal Creek)

Tony Jacklin

ANTHONY JACKLIN, OBE:
born **Scunthorpe, Lincs,**
7 July 1944

Tony Jacklin has been the shooting star, the brightest meteor that streaked across the sky, then disappeared, only to return in quite a different form a dozen years later.

Son of a lorry driver and a dressmaker he started with few advantages beyond a burning ambition to become the best golfer in the world and a millionaire.

He won the Lincolnshire Boys' Championship at 13, 14 and 15, breaking the course record on the last occasion. At 16 he won the Lincolnshire Open, nine shots ahead of the top pro. At 21 he won the Assistants' Championship. In his first year on the circuit Henry Cotton named him Rookie of the Year.

In 1968 he joined the U.S. tour and won the Jacksonville Open with a record score – 273, some 15 under par. Back in Britain the following year he won The Open at Royal Lytham and St Anne's, handsomely beating Bob Charles, Peter Thomson, Roberto de Vicenzo and Jack Nicklaus.

Then in 1970 at Hazeltine, Minnesota, Tony Jacklin won the U.S. Open. Not only was he the first British winner for 50 years – he won by the ridiculous margin of seven shots! He led all the way, only the fourth player in history to do so. He was also only the second

Left *Tony Jacklin, seen here driving fluently in the final round of the 1969 Open at Lytham, won with stoic steadiness, beating among others Bob Charles, Peter Thomson, Roberto de Vicenzo and Jack Nicklaus.*

Below *Jacklin will be remembered not only for holding the U.S. and British Open titles at the same time but for being the most successful (and most emotional) British Ryder Cup captain. Here he celebrates the first European win on American soil in 1987.*

player to record four sub-par rounds. So difficult was the course that Palmer had a round of 80 and Nicklaus an 81.

Although he was never to win another Open Jacklin had by far the best record in the tournament of any British player. He finished in the top five in four successive years. Twice he seemed to be robbed of victory by fate. In 1970 he played the first nine at St Andrews in 29 shots and seemed set for the record when a violent thunderstorm stopped play for the day. In 1972 at Muirfield he was right up there in contention when at the 17th Lee Trevino, who had mentally given the title up, casually chipped his fifth shot into the hole from the greenside rough to make his par. Jacklin, clearly unnerved, charged his first putt, went four feet past and missed the return to fall behind. Trevino won and Nicklaus charging up with a 66 strode into second place when Jacklin also bogeyed the 18th.

Jacklin won all around the world. In the Lancôme in Paris in 1970 he had put in a marvellous charge of his own, beating Arnold Palmer with an eagle, birdie finish; he won the Scandinavian Open by 11 shots; in Colombia he was 27 under par when he won that one. He was the youngest Briton ever to play in the World Cup. He played in seven Ryder Cups and in 1969 at Royal Birkdale he scored a total of 35 birdies and eagles and did not lose a match.

It was a tragedy then that, quite suddenly, he lost his touch on the greens and his appetite for travel. He tried everything, even the

bogus cult of 'Scientology'; but his putting nerves never recovered.

Jacklin's presence, however, was very important to the establishment of the European Tour; and it was fitting that, after the Ryder Cup was opened up to include Europeans, he was asked to captain the side for the first time in 1983. He proved an inspirational captain and his team lost in Florida by the narrowest of margins. In 1985 at the Belfry the European team won 16½ to 11½. Then came a greater triumph still. At Jack Nicklaus's own course, Muirfield Village, with Nicklaus himself the American captain Europe won for

the first time on American soil. The players did the winning of course but every single one of them acknowledged the great contribution made by their captain, Tony Jacklin.

· MAJORS ·

The Open 1969 (Lytham)
U.S. Open 1970 (Hazeltine, Minn.)
(Jacklin was the first British golfer to hold both titles at the same time since Harry Vardon, 70 years earlier.)

Right At Muirfield in 1980, when he beat Lee Trevino by four shots and Jack Nicklaus by nine for the Open championship, Tom Watson was at his best – consistent, relaxed, impregnable.

Tom Watson

THOMAS STURGIS WATSON: *born* **Kansas City, Missouri, 4 September 1949**

When he first joined the professional tour they called Tom Watson 'Huckleberry Finn'. But the name didn't and doesn't quite fit.

They classed him as a 'choker', because several times he got himself into a winning position but failed badly. That label proved wrong, too.

They assumed he was just another well-coached clone from the American college-golf system. That was another howler.

Watson is an intelligent, complex, thoughtful man with a university degree in psychology who sought to marry his knowledge of the mind with an understanding of the mechanically perfect golf swing. And for a span of eight or nine years he did just that.

He had made no great impact as an amateur. Maybe he was just doing too much practising, under the watchful eye of his instructor Stan Thirsk. Fellow pros claim to have seen him on the practice areas until his hands blistered.

He set out on the U.S. tour in 1971. Three years later he led the U.S. Open after three rounds... then shot a 79. The following year he began the Open with rounds of 67, 68 . . . then shot 78, 77. It did look as though the label 'choker' might be appropriate. However, the same year, 1975, he flew to Britain and won the Open at his first attempt, beating the Australian Jack Newton in a play-off.

That year the Open was at Carnoustie, a rough but subtle monster of a links course, and the field included Jack Nicklaus and Arnold Palmer. It was the first of five Open victories, putting him on a par with J. H. Taylor, James Braid and Peter Thomson. He has kept coming back year by year trying for that sixth Open championship which would put him equal in the record books with the great Harry Vardon.

Back home he won the Masters twice and the U.S. Open once. His golf, in its planning, execution and competitive spirit, has often looked close to perfection. He won two classic contests with Nicklaus, both in Open championships.

In the U.S. Open at Pebble Beach in 1982 Watson's approach to the 71st went into long greenside grass. His caddie urged him to play the downhill chip conservatively. 'Hell, I'm going to hole it', responded Watson – which he did, in one of the classic title-clinching moments of golf history.

Doubtless in Watson's mind was the memory of Turnberry in 1977. He and Nicklaus were out in front, both carding splendid 65s in the third round. In the final round Jack Nicklaus went ahead very early on. Tom Watson drew level with three birdies. Then he fell back again. He caught Nicklaus at the 15th, and at the 17th took the lead for the first time. At the 18th he split the fairway with a 1-iron. Nicklaus, trying for distance, drove into the right rough. Watson hit a superb 7-iron second to within two feet of the hole. Nicklaus responded by magically thrashing his second to the very edge of the green – and then to thunderous cheers sinking a monstrous putt that broke both ways before disappearing into the hole. Tom Watson nervelessly tapped in for his victory. He had scored a second 65. This was indeed links golf almost to perfection, for Nicklaus had scored a 66.

· MAJORS ·
The Open 1975 (Carnoustie), 1977 (Turnberry), 1980 (Muirfield), 1980 (Troon), 1985 (Royal Birkdale)
U.S. Open 1982 (Pebble Beach)
The Masters 1977, 1981

Left *Ballesteros with the Open trophy which he won for the first time at Royal Lytham and St Anne's in 1979.*

Severiano Ballesteros

SEVERIANO BALLESTEROS: *born* Santander, Spain, 9 April 1957

Intense, fiery, sometimes impetuous, often inspired, always charismatic, Severiano Ballesteros has taken European golf to new and almost unimagined heights.

He was born in a farmhouse in northern Spain overlooking the beach at Pedreña on the one hand and the Royal Golf Club of Pedreña on the other. When very young he practised golf shots using pebbles on the beach. Then he was given an old 3-iron with which he practised around the farmhouse and on the fringes of the golf course, where he later caddied. Playing every sort of shot with his one club – low, high, sliced, drawn, even sand-saves out of bunkers – young Ballesteros absorbed a basic truth: a golf ball will do exactly what the clubface tells it to and so the player can be, and should be, in control of the clubface at all times.

He set out as a professional aged 17. His stroke average in 1974 was 74.70. By 1981 he had brought it down below 70 – and had won the Open and Royal Lytham and the Masters at Augusta. He had also won the Dutch, Swiss, Spanish, German and Scandinavian Opens and the Lancôme Trophy in Paris. By 1986 his scoring average was down to 68.92 and he had won a second British Open and a second Masters as well as four World Matchplay Championships, three more French Opens, three more Irish, one more Spanish and one more Dutch.

He has won also in Japan, Australia, New Zealand, South Africa and Kenya and has been a major force in two Ryder Cup victories by Europe.

Although he won in Cannes, France, and was second in the British PGA, Ballesteros had for him a lean period toward the end of 1986 and through 1987. His confidence had received two shattering blows at Augusta in successive Masters. In 1986 he was leading by two shots and apparently cruising to victory again when, perfectly placed on the fairway at the 15th, he tried a soft 4-iron to the green and dumped the ball in the water in front of it. He took a bogey-6 and lost the tournament as Nicklaus charged through. In 1987 he might have won again. After 72 holes he was tied with Greg Norman and Larry Mize, but he three-putted the first extra hole in uncharacteristic fashion and was eliminated. (Larry Mize went on to win by chipping into the third extra hole from off the green.)

During 1988 Seve caught fire again. He won six tournaments, one in Japan and five in Europe, including both the German Open and, most importantly, the Open. At Royal Lytham there was a great

finish between him, Nick Faldo and Zimbabwean Nick Price. Faldo couldn't quite make it but Price fought to the very last putt.

Ballesteros took the lead at the 16th with a magnificent 9-iron approach shot to three inches. Then on the 18th, having run through the green into the rough while Price was safely on the green, he struck a perfect match-winning chip which lipped the hole, stopping only a few inches beyond. One cannot give higher praise than to say that his last-round 65 was fully comparable in quality with Tom Watson's culminating 65 at Turnberry in 1977.

Genuinely proud of the new stature of European golf, Severiano has been running a personal campaign to get the United States tour Commissioner Deane Beman to make it easier for overseas players to compete in America without committing themselves to most of the U.S. tour (which would reduce the European tour once again to second-class status).

On the golf course he is noted for making dramatic recovery shots – Ben Crenshaw said of him 'He is often in the woods, but he is never in trouble' – so perhaps he will one day win this point too. Meanwhile, his own rediscovered pleasure in the game makes him the greatest draw in world golf.

· MAJORS ·
The Open 1979 (Lytham), 1984 (St Andrews), 1988 (Lytham)
The Masters 1980, 1983

Right *Ray Floyd in action during the 1986 Masters, the year he became the oldest winner of the U.S. Open at Shinnecock Hills.*

STALWARTS OF THE TOUR

The professional tour in the United States produces an astonishingly high standard of play. In the top echelon is a group of golfers who have proved capable of winning one or more of the majors.

Raymond Floyd, born at Fort Bragg, North Carolina, in 1942 needs only to win the British Open to complete the professional Grand Slam: but his is perhaps the most up-and-down record of any top pro, and he has seldom achieved much in Europe.

He won his first tournament at 20 years of age. Then there were seven fallow years. In 1969 he won the U.S. PGA championship. Then he did little for another seven years. But in the 1976 Masters he started with a 65, led all the way and equalled Jack Nicklaus's record four-round total of 271. In 1982 he came back again, winning the PGA once more, and in 1986 at Shinnecock Hills he won the U.S.

Left *Johnny Miller lines up a putt during the 1974 Open at Lytham. Two years later he won at Birkdale, beating Nicklaus and Ballesteros by six shots.*

Open with a score of 279. In 1989 he captained the U.S. Ryder Cup team at The Belfry.

Johnny Miller, born in San Francisco in 1947, won the U.S. Open in 1973 at Oakmont with a superb final round of 63, breaking the Open record. In the following year he was the leading U.S. money winner. His winnings totalled $353,000, at that time a record too. In '74 and '75 he won 13 tournaments, in the latter year also taking the individual honours in the World Cup. And finally in 1976 at

Royal Birkdale he won the Open by six shots from Jack Nicklaus and Severiano Ballesteros, with Ray Floyd a further stroke behind. Then suddenly his name disappeared from the leader boards and even from the newspapers. He won a tournament here and there but from 1983 to 1987 nothing at all. In that latter year he won the Pebble Beach National Pro-Am; and once again his iron shots were things of beauty.

Ben Crenshaw, born in Austin, Texas, in 1952, has other golfers scratching their heads as to why he has not won more often. He had an outstanding amateur record, and when he joined the U.S. circuit in 1973 won the first event he played in, the San Antonio (Texas) Open. He was then second in the World Open. In 1976 he won the Irish Open and three events on the U.S. tour. In 1979 he tied with David Graham for the U.S. PGA but lost the play-off. In 1983 he was second in the Masters; and then at last, in 1984, he won the tournament.

A man in love with the history of golf, he is reckoned to be one of the world's best putters, with a lovely smooth stroke. Called 'gentle Ben' because of his quiet ways, he nevertheless broke his putter when it misbehaved in his 1987 Ryder Cup singles match against Eamonn Darcy at Muirfield Village. A man can stand so much . . . (besides, he putted more than competently with his 1-iron).

Bernhard Langer born at Anhausen, in West Germany, in 1957, is the finest golfer Germany has yet produced – and that in spite of recurring putting troubles. In 1981 he topped the European Order of Merit. In 1983 he won three tournaments and in 1984 four more. In 1985 he had two wins in Europe and two in the United States. One of those wins was the Masters. The 1986 Sony World rankings placed him second to Greg Norman, the Australian superstar.

In 1987 he won the British PGA at Wentworth and the Irish Open at Portmarnock and came second in the German Masters at Stuttgart;

Left *The perfect finish? Tom Weiskopf had one of the most elegant and powerful swings in golf. Nicklaus, a senior at Ohio State when Weiskopf was in his second year, thought he would overshadow everyone. But his need for perfection finally undermined his game: he took only one major – the Open of 1973 – and now turns his hand at broadcasting and golf-course design.*

and he was one of the linchpins of Europe's Ryder Cup victory. But his old putting troubles returned and in 1988 he had dropped to 30th in the Volvo European Order of Merit. A magnificent iron player, he comes close quite often even when not putting well; but, these days, if you can't putt you can't win.

Thomas Daniel Weiskopf, born at Massillon, Ohio, in 1942, is a golfer of extraordinary talent whose temperament got the better of his game. He won the Open at Troon in 1973, leading from the start, with a total (276) which equalled the then Open record set by Arnold Palmer in 1962.

Weiskopf won the Canadian and Argentine Opens and the South African PGA as well as the World Matchplay title, but he never quite won another Major. He was second in the Masters four times and second in the U.S. Open once. He also won two tournaments in his first year as a pro (1965) and was third in the U.S. money list three times in 10 years. His last win on the tour was the Western Open in 1982. After that he rather abruptly left the tour to go hunting, for long his second favourite sport and now his first.

Larry Gene Nelson, born at Fort Payne, Alabama, in 1947, took up golf at the age of 21 and in four years won a place on the U.S. Tour. The very next year he was second in the money list.

He won the U.S. PGA in 1981 at Atlanta and in 1987 at the PGA National and the U.S. Open in 1983 at Oakmont. Playing in the Ryder-Cup in 1979 and 1981 he achieved the record-breaking feat of win-

Right *In the 1981 U.S. Open at Merion, David Graham's final round of 67 was virtually without blemish.*

Below *Starting late, Larry Nelson learned his golf from books. He learned well: he's seen here winning the first of his two U.S. PGA titles, at Atlanta in 1981.*

Below right *One of the best long-iron players, twice U.S. Open winner Hale Irwin likes the long courses best.*

ning all his nine matches. In 1983 he also won the Dunlop International in Japan. A very consistent rather than a brilliant player, he maintains a high place on the money list year in year out.

Hale Irwin was born in Joplin, Missouri, in 1945. He has been another extremely consistent golfer, with a swing of classical elegance. He has won the U.S. Open twice, in 1974 at Winged Foot and 1979 at Inverness; and he won the World Matchplay at Wentworth in 1975. Between 1975 and 1980 he played 86 successive tournaments in the United States before missing

a 36-hole cut. This is still a record.

David Graham was the first Australian to win the U.S. Open. Born in Windsor, New South Wales, in 1946, he first picked up a golf club when 12 years old. The club happened to be left-handed and that is how he started. Already determined to become a golf pro, he quit school at 14 and became an apprentice at a local pro's shop. At 15 he was persuaded to switch to the right-handed game. He became head professional at a Tasmanian golf club when only 17. When 21 he won his first big tournament, the Queensland PGA. In 1969 he won six tournaments in Thailand, Japan, Australia and France, and with Bruce Devlin won the World Cup.

Invited to the Masters in 1971 he came 36th and finally decided he would have to make radical changes to his swing. Beset with

management difficulties, he took some years to get back in the groove; but in 1979 he won the U.S. PGA at Oakland Hills, and in 1981 the U.S. Open at Merion with a superlative 67 in the final round.

147

Right inset *Greg Norman holds the trophy aloft after winning the 1986 Open at Turnberry.*

Below *Norman plays a fairway shot on the 10th in the 1986 Open. The lighthouse is in the background.*

Near right *Sandy Lyle's victory in the Open at Sandwich in 1985 was the first by a home player since Tony Jacklin won in 1969.*

Far right *Lyle celebrates after his final birdie putt at Augusta in 1988 gave him a gloriously won Masters title.*

RISING STARS

Today the professional tours of Europe, Australia and Japan compete with the United States in producing young players capable of dominating world golf.

Greg Norman

GREG JOHN NORMAN: *born* **Mt Asa, Queensland, 10, February 1955**

Greg Norman started playing at 16, got hooked and decided that he would not join the Royal Australian Air Force after all. A tremendously powerful hitter and a striking personality – tall, tough, ash-blonde – he made his breakthrough at 25 when he won the Australian Open for the first time and also the Suntory World Matchplay title. In 1983 he won the World Matchplay again, and in 1984 he tied for first place with Fuzzy Zoeller in the U.S. Open at Winged Foot – though he lost the play-off by eight shots.

In 1986 Norman won the Open at Turnberry, might well have won both the U.S. Open and the Masters (though at Augusta he played an

Sandy Lyle

ALEXANDER WALTER BARR LYLE, MBE: *born* **Shrewsbury, Shropshire, 9 February 1958**

Born in England of Scottish parents – his father a well-known club professional and teacher – Sandy Lyle played with outstanding success in Youth Internationals as an Englishman. But when he turned pro he decided that he was really and truly a Scot.

As Seve Ballesteros has said, when Sandy is good he is the best, there is no-one to touch him; but when his is bad he is almost the worst. He is more an inspirational than a mechanical player. He seems always amiable, calm, even casual. But he hits the ball prodigious distances, his long-iron play can be breathtaking, and his putting seems to improve every season.

He has won in Europe, Africa, Japan, Hawaii and mainland United States. And he has won both the Open (at Royal St George's) in 1985 and the Masters, in 1988. In the Masters he lost his lead midway through the final round, then fashioned birdies at the 16th and 18th to win by one shot in one of Augusta's most rivetting occa-

astonishingly bad second shot at the 72nd hole), and was on the point of winning the U.S. PGA until Bob Tway's remarkable bunker shot snatched the title. A similar fate befell him in 1987 in the Masters play-off, when Larry Mize chipped in from well off the green.

With victories all round the world, from Australia to Canada via Hong Kong, Norman led the Sony World rankings for three years. He has twice been on the winning side in the Dunhill Cup and twice in the World Cup.

If 1988 proved to be a disappointment (he suffered a wrist injury in mid-season), nobody imagines he is anywhere near finished yet.

· MAJORS ·

The Open 1986
(Turnberry)

Below *This one for the Open: Nick Faldo sinks his putt on the 18th green at Muirfield to win the trophy in 1987. He joined Lyle in the superstar class with his 1989 Masters victory.*

sions. He also won three other tournaments in the United States that year and was only just edged out of the top spot by Curtis Strange. In Britain he won the World Matchplay title, beating his longtime rival Nick Faldo 2-and-1 – after disposing of Seve Ballesteros by the indecent margin of 7-and-6 in the semi-final.

Playing in the Ryder Cup from 1979 onwards, Sandy Lyle became an increasingly formidable matchplayer. In the 1985 European victory he won one, halved one and lost one. In 1987 he won three of four matches.

· MAJORS ·

The Open 1985 (Royal St George's, Sandwich)
The Masters 1988

Nick Faldo

NICHOLAS ALEXANDER FALDO: *born* **St Albans, Herts, 18 July 1957**

Nick Faldo took up golf only when he was 14 years old – but four years later he had become the youngest winner of English Amateur. He turned professional at the age of 19. Under Ian Connelly at Welwyn he had developed one of the most elegant, effortless swings in British golf. He was also an exceptionally gifted putter.

In 1977 he played in his first Ryder Cup, then the youngest player ever to do so – and beat Tom Watson in the singles! In 1985 he was completely off-form and lost

both matches he played in, but in 1987 he won three out of five, halved one and lost only one.

In Britain Nick Faldo won three PGA championships, in Europe in 1983 he won five tournaments and headed the money list. In America in 1984 he won the Sea Pines Heritage Classic. But he had come to the conclusion that his swing was not consistent enough for him to reach the top, particularly in the company of his great contemporaries Sandy Lyle, Seve Ballesteros and Curtis Strange. He sought out David Leadbetter, an English-born coach working in the United States. Together they tightened his elegant swing, improved its plane and stopped his occasional overswinging. After two years he came back to form and in 1987 won the Open at Muirfield, his final round being composed entirely of pars.

Below *Curtis Strange tees off at the 2nd at St Andrews during the 1987 Dunhill Cup, when he broke the Old Course record with a 62. He beat Faldo in a play-off to win the U.S. Open in 1988, then won it again in 1989.*

In 1988 he was in contention in almost every tournament he played in, was second in eight of them including the U.S. Open, won two, the French and the Volvo Spanish Masters, and had the best aggregate record of anyone in the four majors that year. Then in 1989 he won the Masters, beating Scott Hoch at the second hole of a sudden-death play-off.

· MAJORS ·

The Open 1987 (Muirfield).
Masters 1989

Curtis Strange

CURTIS NORTHRUP STRANGE: *born* Norfolk, Virginia, 20 January 1955

Curtis Strange finished 1988 in style. He won the Nabisco World Championship at Pebble Beach to become the first golfer to win $1 million on the U.S. PGA tour in a single season. He also won the Player of the Year award, his win in this tournament enabling him to step one pace ahead of Scotland's Sandy Lyle. The record he broke in earnings was his own.

He is known as 'the Grinder' in the United States. Not a spectacular golfer, he finds the fairway, hits the green, sinks many of the putts. In 1988 he became U.S. Open Champion, winning a play-off with England's Nick Faldo at the Brookline Country Club 71 to 75, having tied Faldo on the 72nd hole by getting up and down in two from a bunker. He would have stood a chance at the British Open had he not started with a 79.

Strange has not often played in The Open. 'Why should I take two

lower body and with hand action kept to a minimum.

He did not have an easy start. He left school at 16 and went to work as a greenkeeper. He spent four years trying to get his player's card for the European tour. When he had got it another four years went by before he made any real money. But in 1982 he won both the Swiss Open and the British Masters, in 1984 the Scandinavian Open, in 1985 the Zambian and in 1986 the Kenyan.

In 1987 he broke clear of the pack. He won six European events, including the World Matchplay title, the World Cup individual (taking Wales to its first ever win) and the Sun City Million Dollar Challenge. He also made a vital contribution to Europe's victory in the Ryder Cup, winning three matches. After signing a contract with a Japanese clubmaker, he had a dismal start to 1988 but came good again towards the end of the year; and while never quite scaling the peaks of 1987, he finished fourth on the European list.

A very aggressive player, he is now undeniably one of Europe's Big Four.

New Faces

Paul Azinger, born in Holyoke, Maryland, in 1969, went to the U.S. qualifying school three years running before he finally qualified for the tour. In 1987, not quite three years later, he was leading the Open in the final round at Muirfield when he bogeyed the 17th and 18th to finish second, one stroke behind

weeks out of my life to play in bad weather on some terrible course like Turnberry was in 1986?' he once remarked. But in 1987 he went to St Andrews for the Dunhill Cup and lowered the course record to 62. He's the Grinder, alright. But winning the U.S. Open may have strengthened his appetite for glory as well as for cash.

· MAJORS ·

U.S. Open 1988 (Country Club, Brookline), 1989 (Oak Hill)

Ian Woosnam

IAN HAROLD WOOSNAM: *born* **Oswestry, Wales 2 March 1958**

At 5ft 4½in Ian Woosnam is by far the smallest of the world's top golfers, but he is one of the longest hitters. Son of a farmer, he is a miniature powerhouse with very strong legs and forearms, and his method provides a perfect example of the modern swing – economical, on-plane, powered by the

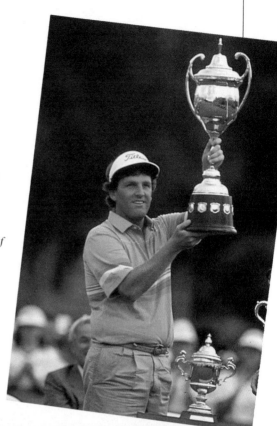

Nick Faldo. In 1986 he had made a quarter of a million dollars; and in 1988 almost $600,000.

Mark Calcavecchia, born at Laurel, Nebraska, in 1960, came good on the U.S. tour in 1986 after four fruitless years. In that year he won the South West Classic in Texas and next year the Honda Classic in Florida. In the Ryder Cup at Jack Nicklaus's Muirfield course in 1987 he won his single against Nick Faldo by 1 hole. In 1988 he won the Bank of Boston Classic. In 1989 he broke through to win The Open at Troon.

Right *Mark Calcavecchia holds up his Australian Open trophy, 1988. He was leading the U.S. Tour early in 1989, having won two of the first five events, and went on to win the British Open. His attacking style has made him one of the most exciting of the American players to watch.*

Below *Paul Azinger is a player with style. Technically his swing is nonconformist: his left wrist is bent back at the address and is still so at the top of his backswing. But it obviously suits him fine: he started 1989 in ninth place on the world rankings.*

THE SENIORS

The chance of rich pickings encourages many of the finest pros to switch to the Seniors' tour after their 50th birthday. The fans flock to see their old heroes in relaxed but highly competitive action.

Part of the glory of golf is that it is a game for all ages. Harry Vardon tied for second in the U.S. Open when he was 50. J. H. Taylor would have won the British Open at 53 had the two qualifying rounds also counted. Ben Hogan at 54 shot 66 in the third round of the Masters (he did the back nine in 30). At 67 Sam Snead 'broke his age' with a 66 in the Quad Cities Open on the American pro tour; when 70 he went round a full-sized course in Virginia in 60 shots. And when 71 Gene Sarazen competed in the British Open and, in view of the whole world's television cameras, scored a famous hole-in-one. So perhaps the rapid success of the Seniors Tour in the United States is not surprising.

The first U.S. PGA Seniors' Championship was held in 1937 and was won by Jock Hutchison (winner of the 1921 Open at St Andrews). After the Second World

Bob Charles became 50 in March 1986, and in the following 10 months won $570,000 on the Seniors tour. He did not quite make the half million the following year but in 1988 banked $533,929 in official prize money alone.

Thanks to more modern equipment, Charles hits the ball further than he used to but just as straight. Considered the best putter in the world in the 1960s, he lost his touch for several years but now on the tour it has returned in all its glory. When 40, he was preparing to retire to his farm back home in New Zealand where he had decided to start rearing deer and goats instead of sheep, selling venison and cashmere; but now he thinks he may stay on the golf course until he is 60. And he is actually playing more tournaments as a Senior than he did as a young man.

Arnold Palmer, now 60, remains a strong and successful supporter of the tour. So do his contemporaries like Don January, Miller Barber, Gene Littler, Billy Casper and Gay Brewer. But perhaps the most popular player, certainly among the children who turn out to watch him, is Chi Chi Rodriguez, the Puerto Rican.

Rodriquez was the magazine *Golf Digest*'s 'Senior Player of the Year' in 1988. In the previous year he, too, had won more than half a million dollars, a substantial proportion of which he gave away to charities, and had taken part in nearly 50 exhibitions and held some 20 'clinics'. In the meanwhile that year he won seven tournaments.

War a World Seniors was held in the United States from 1954 until 1978, the first winner being Gene Sarazen and the most frequent Sam Snead. In 1978 the first Legends of Golf tournament (a fourball) was played at Onion Creek, Texas, when Snead and Gardner Dickinson beat Peter Thomson and Kel Nagle by one shot. Considerable interest was shown by American TV channels, and when Arnold Palmer played in 1979 this became irresistible. Catching the tide of public opinion, the USGA launched a new Seniors' Open the very next year and simul-taneously the U.S. PGA inaugurated the Seniors Tour.

Since then several of the superstars of yesterday have done even better financially than they did when they were young.

Peter Thomson, winner of five British Opens, came out of retirement to head the Seniors' money list in 1984. Gary Player followed and not only won the top place on the list but (in his opinion, anyway) in 1988 completed the 'Seniors' Grand Slam' by winning the British Seniors' Open to add to his Seniors' PGA, TPC and Seniors' Open. New Zealand left-hander

Bottom *Chi Chi Rodriguez is the 'fun man' of the U.S. Seniors tour – but only the innocent would bet against him. Joining the Seniors in 1985, he had already won more than a million dollars by the beginning of 1989.*

Below *With a looping swing and a flying right elbow Miller Barber proves it's not how you do it that matters but how well. Barber does it very well indeed, winning the U.S. Seniors PGA in 1981, the Seniors Open the following year, and starting 1989 top of the Seniors money list.*

Chi Chi is a comedian, an artist with a golf club and something of a philosopher who has a special rapport with children. Even in serious competitions when he was younger he would sometimes raise a laugh from the spectators by covering the hole with his Panama hat after sinking an unlikely putt, as if to make sure the ball didn't jump out of the hole after all. For his clinics he writes his own patter, with sly digs at the foibles of his golfer friends – Gary Player's delight in making up his own list of 'majors', all of which he has won; Billy Casper's strange non-allergic diet; Lee Trevino's wide-open stance; Jack Nicklaus's deliberation. When instructing children Chi Chi explains that golf is like life:

you find out what's good and use it your own way.

Another colourful character who has struck it rich on the Seniors tour is Orville Moody – 'the Sarge' as he is known to everyone on tour – the man who came out of the United States army at 35, played a couple of years on the tour, won the U.S. Open in 1969 and, with Lee Trevino, the World Cup, played a few years more . . . then disappeared.

The Sarge earned quite a respectable amount during 14 years on the pro tour – around $390,000 – but he has trebled that in two years as a senior. Of course to get a realistic financial picture, one has to allow for inflation and yesterday's millions were worth far more than today's; but Sergeant Moody certainly doubled his real wealth in a matter of months.

Even when he was winning tournaments Orville Moody was an uncertain putter. Some days the putts went in, many days they didn't. His confidence evaporated. He tried every known method, cross-handed, sidesaddle, even putting backwards, but it was to no avail. He decided enough was enough: he left the tour to run his own golf course in Colorado.

The Sarge turned his game round in the 1987 Legends of Golf tournament and he did so by using the new long putter. The shaft of such a putter may be from 43 to 56 inches depending on the build of the player. The butt end of the grip is held firmly against the breastbone and the action is considered yip-free. Certainly if one looks at the statistics one sees that among

the seniors in 1988 the No. 1 in putting was Orville Moody. (The No. 1 in birdies was also Orville Moody; the No. 1 in eagles was Orville Moody, too.)

Other leaders in the Seniors money list are Harold Henning of South Africa, Bruce Crampton of Australia, Dave Hill, Dale Douglass, Bobby Nichols, Lou Graham, Don Massengale and Charles Coody – all famous names from the main tour's past. In the midst of them, and well up the list, is Walter Zembriski, a name unknown until a year or so ago. Zembriski ran a car-repair business until he was 50, when he qualified for the Senior Tour and now he is one of the golfing millionaires. He won two tournaments in 1988 and his scoring average was 71.19. He is described as 'short of stature and with a hand-made swing.'

Golf turns around the saying

Bottom, left *Billy Casper, still one of the canniest golfers around, has recouped all and more of the capital he lost after quitting the regular U.S. tour.*

Right *Orville Moody using the long pendulum putter with which he has restored his fortunes on the Seniors tour.*

Bottom, right *New Zealander Bob Charles is the best left-hander in golf history and, in the 1960s, was the finest putter in the world. Since becoming a Senior his all-round game has actually improved. He's seen here at the British Seniors Open at Turnberry in 1987.*

made famous in the old song so that it now runs this way: 'It *is* what you do, not the way that you do it.' The objective is to get the ball into 18 holes in the ground in as few strokes as possible.

The Seniors play slightly shorter courses than the youngsters and the pin positions are perhaps a shade easier; but their scoring averages show that this is still golf at a very high level. At the end of 1988 Bob Charles led with an average of exactly 70.00 per round; Gary Player was second with 70.41, Orville Moody third with 70.60.

In Britain, while there are a number of seniors' competitions, there is as yet no seniors tour. The country is by itself too small to sustain one, but a European Seniors Circuit is a possibility in a few years time. The best British and Irish seniors have been Christy O'Connor, Sr (known to the golfing Irish as 'Himself'), the great Scot John Panton and the consistent Englishman Neil Coles. In the opinion of many of his contemporaries Neil Coles would by now be renowned throughout the world did he not have an unconquerable aversion to flying. As it was, he played in eight Ryder Cup teams and in a record 40 matches, even though, when the matches were in America, he had to go by sea and then drive 1000 miles or more to the course. He was chosen as the first Chairman of the European circuit when it started in the 1970s.

As these great players demonstrate so conclusively, golf is a game not only for all ages but for a hundred different styles as well.

THE LADY CHAMPIONS

The U.S. LPGA tour and, more recently, the WPGA tour in Europe have transformed the standard of women's golf. As with the men's tours, the popular appeal of the ladies' game depends on the deeds of its superstars.

Babe Zaharias

MILDRED DIDRIKSON ZAHARIAS: *born* Port Arthur, Texas, in 1914.

She was a great athlete who took up golf quite late in her sporting life. Her first sport was basketball and two years after leaving school she made the American team. In 1932 she entered for seven events in the National Track and Field Championships and won six of them. These championships were part of America's preparation for the Olympic games and put the authorities in a bit of a quandary as no individual contestant could take part in more than three events in the Olympics. Which events should she enter? As it happened, she entered for the low hurdles,

the javelin and the high jump and won all three events. However her gold medal in the high jump was withdrawn because she used what was then an unorthodox method.

Everyone knew her as 'Babe', a nickname probably derived from the legendary American baseball star Babe Ruth (Mildred Didrikson had played pro baseball for a time as well!). She also reached professional standard at tennis. In 1938 she married an all-in wrestler George Zaharias and it was he who turned her attention to golf.

She had won the Texas Women's

Open in 1935 as an amateur but was subsequently banned from amateur events on account of her pro status in other sports. After her marriage, however, she was reinstated as an amateur and won the U.S. Women's Amateur in 1946. In those days it was a matchplay event and the Babe was never taken beyond the 15th hole in winning the tournament. In the following year she sailed for England and won the British Ladies'.

The great English ladies' amateur champion Enid Wilson wrote of her: 'Above average height but not abnormally tall, and of slender build, the "Babe" moved like a ballerina, as though she did not have a bone in her body'. It is a description that could hardly be bettered.

It was her ballerina's limbs which gave the Babe her extraordinary power at golf, just as they had powered her to success on the track and with the javelin. At

Muirfield it was said she never needed more than an 8-iron for her second shots and at nearby Gullane she was at the back of the green on the 540-yard 15th hole with a drive and a 4-iron.

It was at Gullane that she was sent in by the officials to change her attire, her red-and-white checked shorts she appeared in being considered 'inappropriate'.

After her experiences in Britain the Babe turned professional and her talent for showmanship as well as for golf brought new spectators to the women's tournaments in their thousands. She won the U.S. Women's Open in 1948, 1950 and 1954.

In 1951 she took a team of women golfers to Britain for a travelling circus of events. One of

them was a match against a team of scratch men golfers. Babe's women played the men level and won all their singles.

Tragically the Babe contracted a serious cancer and underwent surgery in 1953. This did not stop her. After convalescence she went out to win the U.S. Women's Open for her last time. And she won six more tournaments before she had so reluctantly to give the game up in 1955. A year later she died, mourned as a true heroine of sport.

Patty Berg

PATRICIA JANE BERG: *born* **Minneapolis, Minnesota, 13 February 1918**

Red-haired, blue-eyed, she had been a child prodigy long before the Second World War. She turned pro at the end of 1941; but it was only after the war that she had the chance to show her talent. She quickly became famous around the world.

She was the first President of the U.S. Ladies PGA. She won the 1946 Women's Open. She also won the Vare Trophy for lowest scoring average (named after the great American golf heroine Glenna Collett Vare) in 1953, 1955 and 1956. And she won the Women's World Championship three years running – 1953, 1954, 1955 – and then again in 1957.

Her last pro win was in 1962 and by that time she had gained 55 victories on the women's tour. One round of 64, at Richmond in California, stood as a competition record there for 12 years. However, her worldwide fame came from the clinics she gave in almost every golfing country. Her striking looks and vivid personality would have attracted attention anyway, but she added to those advantages an accurate and elegant golf game and a teacher's flair for communication.

Patty Berg became also a professional promoter and not only of golf but of other sports as well. This has kept her in the public eye to this day. The cause of women's golf has much to thank her for.

Patty Berg at 18, when she reached the final of the 1936 U.S. Ladies' Championship, losing to the great Glenna Collett Vare. Later Berg was to win the Vare Trophy three times.

Left *Mickey Wright, noted for her Henry Cotton-like hand action, shows in this early 1960s picture that there's a great deal, too, in a very full finish: she was the longest and straightest hitter of her day.*

Below *Wright, a legendary figure in women's golf, won her first U.S. Open in 1958 and stayed at the top for more than 20 years.*

Wright's was seen to derive from her active hands: she was, so to speak, the Henry Cotton of women's golf.

She won the Vare Trophy four years running as well as her other victories, and in 1966 won $40,000 (at that time an enormous sum of money for the women's tour). In 1979 she tied with Nancy Lopez in one tournament but lost the play-off – this more than 20 years after turning pro. Altogether she could claim 82 victories.

Mickey Wright

MARY KATHRYN WRIGHT: *born* San Diego, California, in 1935.

She followed Babe Zaharias at the very top of the game. Like Patty Berg she too was a child prodigy, winner of the U.S. Junior Girls' Championship in 1952. Two years later she was runner up in the U.S. Women's Amateur. She was always called Mickey, it is said, because her father had already decided before her birth that the baby would be a boy and would be named Michael. But she was anyway a bit of a tomboy. When only 15 she won a long-driving contest.

In 1958 Mickey Wright won the first of her four Opens and then from 1959 through 1968 won no fewer than 79 tournaments. She won the ladies' PGA four times during this period and remains the only player to win both Open and PGA titles four times each.

Her best year, if one can extract a best year from such a consistently excellent record, was 1961: she won 10 tournaments, four of them in a row. The Women's Open that year was played at Baltusrol over a severe course measuring 6,400 yards (5,850m) and Mickey Wright had a round of 69 which is still remembered as one of the best rounds of competitive golf ever played by a woman.

A very long, very straight hitter, she was particularly effective with long irons. And whereas Babe Zaharias's length was attributed to her athletic physique, Mickey

Below *Kathy Whitworth, Mickey Wright's rival and successor, shows the form that won her 88 tournaments.*

Below left *Although Whitworth won more tournaments than any other women golfer, she never managed to take the U.S. Women's Open title.*

Kathy Whitworth

KATHRYNNE ANNE WHITWORTH: *born* at **Monohans, Texas, in 1939.** She turned professional when she was 20, and in 1981 became the first player on the American women's tour to take home more than one million dollars in earnings from that tour. In terms of victories she has also been the most successful of America's lady champions, with 88 tournament wins. Yet she never won the U.S. Women's Open.

Tall and athletic, Kathy Whitworth began playing golf at 15 using clubs that had belonged to her grandfather. She quickly became something of a local celebrity, winning the New Mexico State Championship for amateurs and playing some exhibition matches with top women professionals when they were in the area. She even played in one or two pro tournaments when she was 17, although without success (she said

Right *'Big Momma' JoAnne Carner, a great competitor, sinks a long putt. She won her first U.S. Women's Open in 1971; 16 years later, in 1987, she lost in a three-way play-off to Britain's Laura Davies.*

afterwards that she was 'frightened out of her wits'). Even so she decide to become a pro herself and her father and some other local businessmen agreed to sponsor her. At 20 she joined the tour.

At first she had a hard time of it. For six months she did not earn a penny: she could not even break 80, and almost decided to quit. But her sponsors said that she should give herself three years before making her final decision.

In 1962 it suddenly happened: she won her first two tournaments and was second in eight others. In 1963 the record was almost exactly reversed: she won eight tournaments and was second in another. She was leading money winner in 1965, 1966, 1967, 1968, 1970, 1971, 1972 and 1973. In her best scoring year, 1968, she won 10 times, improving on the nine wins she had recorded the year before. She recorded eight victories in a season three times and won the Vare Trophy seven times.

Then in 1979 Kathy Whitworth's game fell apart and, winless in that year and in 1980, she very nearly decided to retire. However she was convinced the trouble was 'mechanical' and that as soon as she found out what it was she would be able to put it right again. She found out. In 1981 she scored her 81st victory and subsequently topped Mickey Wright's tally of 82.

Her advice to other ladies is to be realistic; to know what their ambitions are; to discover a stroke pattern that fits their style and to stick with it, altering a component here and there if necessary but not the basic pattern itself.

JoAnne Carner

JOANNE GUNDERSON CARNER: *born* Kirkland, Washington, 4 April 1939.

As JoAnne Gunderson she had a distinguished amateur career and did not turn professional until she was 30. She won her first pro tournament the following year.

While she was a schoolgirl she won the U.S. Junior Girls' title and the very next year the national Women's Amateur, a championship she was to win four more times before turning pro. In 1971 she won the U.S. Women's Open and again in 1976; she lost a play-off for the 1987 Open. Abroad, she won the Australian Ladies' Championship in 1975. On the U.S. tour she had 42 victories.

Sam Snead, who sometimes coached her, said in 1984 that she was the best woman player he had ever seen. This is interesting because her style was about as far

Left to right: Cathérine Lacoste (19) of France, Zelie Fallon of Ireland and Carol Sorenson of the United States preparing for the 1964-Women's World Amateur Team Championships. France won the team trophy, and Cathérine tied with Carol for the individual title.

from Snead's own as it is possible to get. Snead has always been a swinger with a long, flowing, elegant arc to his swing. JoAnne, a sturdy young woman with a great interest in physical training, has always had a relatively short swing and is a hitter rather than a swinger.

She has never been a great practicer. She always preferred to step onto the first tee and take it from there. She has never worried much about the mechanics of the swing. 'Keep it simple' has been her motto.

The basic elements of her swing were these: a short backswing but a big turn; a weight shift not *to* the right but rather *around on* the right; active use of the legs on the downswing and of the right forearm and the hands on the through-swing. It was a very different swing to those of her main American rivals; but it was equally effective, proving yet again that there is more than one way to swing a golf club victoriously.

Cathérine Lacoste

CATHÉRINE LACOSTE DE PRADO: *born* **Paris in 1945.**
She was the daughter of René Lacoste, the famous French tennis-player, and Simone Thion de la Chaume (until her marriage), a great golfer who had won the British Ladies' Open Amateur Championship of 1927. So she started with certain genetic advantages. And certainly she became

the greatest woman amateur since Joyce Wethered nearly 50 years before.

When she was 19 the first Women's World Amateur Team Championship (for the Esperito Santo Trophy) was held in Paris. She was chosen as a member of the team along with Brigitte Varangot and Claudine Cros and it was largely due to Cathérine that France won the trophy. She tied for first place in the individual scoring with that year's winner of the British Women's Championship, Carol Sorenson.

In 1966 she won the Astor Trophy in England at Prince's, Sandwich, scoring a record-breaking 66 in one of the rounds; in 1967 she won the French Open. But greater things were ahead. That same year she won the United States Women's Open against a strong field of professionals. It was a quite staggering triple triumph: she was the youngest player to win it, the first amateur to win it, and the first foreign player to win it. In 1969 she won both the Spanish and the French Women's opens and then went to Portrush in Northern Ire-

Right *Judy Rankin was leading amateur in the U.S. Women's Open when just 15 years old. With a strong grip and a full swing she hit the ball a prodigious distance for her size.*

land for the British Ladies' Championship which her mother had won over that very course nearly a quarter of a century earlier. Cathérine won too. Even then she wasn't finished. She went to the United States for the national Women's Amateur, played that year in Texas, and won that as well.

In 1970 Cathérine Lacoste married and withdrew from competitive golf, although she did play once more in the Espirito Santo for the sake of the side.

A sturdy athlete, rather like JoAnne Carner, she was a magnificent iron player and, unlike most women golfers, regularly used her 1-iron. She was thrilling to watch but devastating to play against, a true amateur but with a fierce pride in victory.

Judy Rankin

***Born* St Louis, Missouri, 1945.**
She too was a child prodigy. When 14 she won her State amateur title. When fully grown she was 5ft 3in and weighed 108lb. Bob Toski, the American teacher, claims she is the longest hitter pound-for-pound he has ever seen. When they first met Toski tried to get her to change her grip, which was and is very 'strong', but she refused. She likes to hit a draw on every shot if to do so is not actually crazy.

When only 15 Judy Rankin was leading amateur in the U.S. Ladies' Open. In 1962 she turned pro, but it was to be six years before she won her first professional tournament. Thereafter she won at least once a

year for the next 11 years, excepting only 1969. In 1976 she became the first woman to win more than $150,000 in a single season – almost twice as much as anyone had won in any previous year. She also became President of the LPGA.

The foundation of her success, she believes, lies in her grip – a four-knuckle grip (that is, at address she can see the knuckles of every finger of her left hand). She has always used it because it is natural to her and because it enables her to use the left wrist as a karate expert would use it. If the left hand is the guiding light, she insists, then it should be given every possible advantage. 'You would never grip a hammer so that the back of the hand was facing the target,' she says.

Left *Lacoste with the U.S. Women's Open trophy which she won as an amateur in 1967.*

Jan Stephenson

***Born* Sydney, Australia, 1951**.
Jan Stephenson is almost without question the best woman golfer Australia has yet produced. She first made her name as a junior. When still very young she won the Australian LPGA and Women's Open titles and at 22 set out to play the U.S. LPGA tour. From the start she was consistently well placed; in 1976 she won two tournaments, and at the end of the year she was 8th in the money list.

She won the Australian Women's Open again in 1977. But her greatest successes have been the 1982 U.S. LPGA and the 1983 U.S. Open.

She attracted most media attention thereafter by posing for a calendar, but it is likely that her most enduring claim to further fame will be as a golf course designer, possibly the first woman pro to enter that field.

A player of striking good looks, she has a fine, fluid swing which at its best is an object lesson in grace allied to power. She won two tournaments back-to-back in 1988, is consistently high on the earnings list, and is by no means finished yet on the Ladies tour.

Blessed with great good looks and a beautiful golf swing, Jan Stephenson has been called 'the Australian girl who has everything'. She has been consistently one of the top earners on the LPGA tour in the Eighties.

Nancy Lopez

NANCY LOPEZ KNIGHT: *born* Torrance, California, 6 January 1957.

A fine amateur, she started her professional career explosively in 1977 and in her first full season – 1978 – on the American women's tour won *nine* tournaments, five of them in a row! One of them was the U.S. LPGA championship; another was the European Women's Open at Sunningdale. In 1979 she won eight tournaments including, once again, the European Open. Everywhere Nancy Lopez played the crowds increased.

She was Rookie of The Year in 1977, Player of The Year in 1978 and 1979 and U.S. Sportswoman of The Year in 1978 as well. Marriage to pro baseball star Ray Knight and the birth of two children interrupted her career at various times, but her talent seemed undiminished each time she returned to the fray. In 1985 she had five victories. In 1986 she could play only four tournaments, but was highly placed in all of them and won nearly $70,000. In 1987 she won twice; and in 1988, although playing in fewer events than her rivals, won three tournaments, was second three times and third twice.

Although she was second in the U.S. Women's Open as an amateur and again in her first year as a pro, that most coveted title has so far escaped her. But she keeps after it; and, more significantly, week in, week out, she is regarded as the one to beat.

Purists say that her swing has several faults. She bows her left wrist, rather as Trevino does but without his wide-open stance; and her backswing goes 'out and around' rather than following the conventional arc.

But, with her record, why should she change?

It is as much Nancy Lopez's attractive personality as her powerful golf which has brought crowds flocking to American women's tournaments. With an action rather like that of Lee Trevino, her influence on the women's game has been as great as Arnold Palmer's on the men's.

167

THE NEW EUROPEANS

Laura Davies

LAURA DAVIES: *born* **Coventry 5 October 1964**, She has been called the 'Nancy Lopez' of Great Britain. She too started her career with a bang. She can hit the ball comfortably farther than any woman now playing, and possibly farther than any woman golfer in history.

She turned professional in 1985, borrowing a thousand pounds from her mother so that she could start off in the black. She was able to pay the loan back within a month. She won four times that amount in the Hennessy Cognac Cup in France. And in that rookie year she topped the WPGA Order of Merit. In 1986 she came top again and by that time had won the British Ladies' Open and come a creditable 11th in the U.S. Women's Open.

In 1987 she went one better and took the U.S. title – the most

Right *Laura Davies's power game has had a galvanic effect on women's golf throughout Europe. She's a natural, too, never having had a lesson in her life.*

Right, below *Liselotte Neumann proudly holds aloft the U.S. Women's Open trophy she won in 1988.*

prestigious prize in women's golf.

This victory completely floored the Americans. Earlier in the year the commissioner for the U.S. women's tour, John Laupheimer, had refused to allow Davies to play by invitation in an LPGA event, adding that women from Great Britain had not recently made any impact in the United States. Laura tied for the lead in the 1987 Open

after 72 holes and went into a play-off against JoAnne Carner and Japan's Ayako Okamoto. Birdies at the 14th and 15th holes put her in the lead and a round of 71 gave her the title. Flying home at once, she came second in the British Open.

Laura herself is 5ft 10in tall and sturdily built. Her long hitting is already legendary. In 1986 in a long-driving contest at Stoke Poges she beat former Amateur champion Peter McEvoy's best drive by eight yards – 282 yards against 274. Playing against her in America, LPGA star Betsy King remarked: 'Heaven help us if she reaches her full potential!'

Laura, who has never had a formal lesson in her life, pays little or no attention to the mechanics of

the swing. Although it is her big
hitting that gets all the attention,
she insists it is her short game that
wins her big tournaments. A cheerful and charming young woman
who likes to take an occasional
gamble on and off the course,
Davies was awarded the MBE in
October 1988.

The success of Miss Davies
seems to have raised the whole
level of European women's golf. It
cannot surely be coincidence.

Sweden's **Liselotte Neumann**,
now playing full-time on the American circuit, won the 1988 U.S.
Women's Open. She admits to
being inspired by Laura: after her
victory she said, 'I have played
many times with Laura and I

thought, if she can do it, so can I.'

In Europe the most exciting
newcomer has been **Marie-
Laure de Lorenzi de Taya**,
overwhelmingly the outstanding
player on the tour in 1988 winning
seven tournaments, some more
than comfortably. A Frenchwoman
married to a Spaniard, she is based
at Barcelona and intends to stay
there. She says she will not venture
yet onto the American circuit. 'My
family is my first passion,' she says.
(She has a daughter and hopes to
have another child).

Marie-Laure won the Hennessy
Cup at St-Germain, Paris, in 1988,
one stroke ahead of **Alison
Nicholas**, who is another European golfer of great promise. Scotland's **Dale Reid**, top of the Order
of Merit in Europe in 1987, is one
of the most consistent. She was the
first European player to top the
£100,000 mark in prize money.

THE GREAT EVENTS

THE MAJORS

The British Open

The oldest and most internationally representative of the major championships began, as it was to continue, 'open to all the world'. At the start and for many years afterwards, however, it was dominated by professionals from the home of golf....

The Open was first played on Wednesday 17 October 1860, at Prestwick, a small fishing village on the rough Ayrshire coast of Scotland, at the suggestion of the club Secretary, Major J.O. Fairlie. It was not strictly speaking an 'Open' at all, for the first tournament was confined to professionals. The top amateurs of the time were more than disappointed, and afterwards the committee resolved that in future it would be 'open to all the world' – whence its title.

Prestwick at that time was a 12-hole course and the championship was decided in three rounds played over the 12 holes. In the first tournament only eight professionals took part and the winner was Willie Park, Sr of Musselburgh who beat the local hero Tom Morris, Sr by two shots – 174 to 176. One pro, George Brown, came from as far afield as Blackheath, near London. Indeed, the concept of such a tournament was made practicable only with the completion of a national railway system.

We also have the completion of a national railway system to thank for national golf tournaments. And railway lines still play a part beside several Open courses. At St Andrews, home of the Royal and Ancient Golf Club, railway

Pages 170–1 *Tom Watson hits his tee shot on the short 11th on the Old Course at St Andrews in the 1984 Open.*

Opposite page *This is where Open Championships began – Prestwick on the Ayrshire coast of Scotland: rough, rugged, challenging. The Himalayas is a par-3 of only 176 yards, but it requires a disciplined tee shot. Unless you reach the green you can be in real trouble.*

Left *Musselburgh, the home of the Honourable Company of Edinburgh Golfers from 1836 until 1892, first hosted the Open in 1874 when local hero Mungo Park won. Here another local hero, Willie Park, Jr plays the Englishman J.H. Taylor in 1896.*

engineers built locomotive sheds at the elbow of the dogleg on the famous 17th hole of the Old Course. Long hitters had to drive the ball over the sheds, and still have to. When the actual sheds were demolished, other similar buildings were erected in their place so that to this day the tee shot is 'over the sheds,' preferably with a controlled fade.

In the earliest days of the Open, Willie Park, Sr and Old Tom Morris virtually fought out the championship between them for seven years. Then Young Tom Morris, took over. His first victory was as a lad of 17 in 1868. In those days the champion won a belt of Moroccan red leather and tradition had it that if you won such a thing thrice running it became your property. Young Tom did just that; the consequence was that there was no belt to play for in 1871 – and so no championship! However, the Honourable Company of Edinburgh Golfers and the R & A put up a trophy – the silver claret jug still used today. Young Tom Morris won that, too – making it four Open titles in succession.

Tragically Young Tom Morris, who was the first true golfing genius to appear since Open competition began, died at 24, of a broken heart it is said. His 36-holes score of 149 was never equalled while the Open was held at Prestwick.

At this time the Royal and Ancient Golf Club of St Andrews was also brought into the action. The championship was now divided between Prestwick, St Andrews and Musselburgh, where the Honourable Company then had its headquarters. For 10 years the tournament was dominated by Jamie Anderson of St Andrews and Bob Ferguson of Musselburgh, both of whom won the silver claret jug three times. The R & A meanwhile took over the running of the Open.

In 1890 came the first English and the first amateur winner, John Ball of the Royal Liverpool club at Hoylake. Two years later the Honourable Company of Edinburgh Golfers moved a few miles east from Musselburgh to Muirfield, and the championship was extended to 72 holes for the first time. Once again the trophy went to an amateur, Harold Hilton – also from the Royal Liverpool club; his friend John Ball was second and the top professional was James Kirkaldy of St Andrews.

Triumvirate triumphs

In 1894 the championship moved south to England for the first time – far south to Sandwich in Kent where there was, and still is, a long stretch of true linksland unique in the south-east of England. J. H. Taylor was the winner, the first English professional to win the title. A young man from the Channel Islands was sixth – Harry Vardon. He was to win next year up at Muirfield and again at Prestwick in 1898, then at Sandwich once more in 1899. J. H. Taylor won again in 1900 at St Andrews. Then in the following year came James Braid.

These three – 'The Great Triumvirate'

Above *J.H. Taylor receives the Open trophy at Hoylake in 1913.*

Below *Roger Wethered putting on the 18th green in his play-off against American winner Jock Hutchison in the 1921 Open at St Andrews.*

course. Burly Ted Ray – who habitually puffed at a pipe even while making his shots – also broke in at Muirfield in 1912.

By now so many golfers wanted to compete that qualifying rounds were introduced, limiting the field to 80 and ties. Harry Vardon's last victory was, fittingly, back at Prestwick. And then the World War brought play to a complete stop. It was not to be resumed until 1920. And in that year the quickfire Scot George Duncan (he entitled his autobiography *Golf at the Gallop*) won by making up 13 strokes on Abe Mitchell in a single day with rounds of 71 and 72. His 143 for the final 36 holes was not beaten for another 15 years.

The American conquest

Nineteen twenty-one was a year of seminal importance: the trophy went across the Atlantic to the United States for the first time. It was won by Jock Hutchison, a transplanted Scot from St Andrews, who beat the English amateur Roger Wethered (brother of the great Joyce Wethered) in a play-off after they had tied on 296. As many as four players broke the 300 barrier for the first time that year – a feat which was not to be bettered until 1926

(*see page* 39) – were to dominate the Open until the outbreak of the First World War in 1914. Vardon won six times (still a record), Taylor and Braid five times each. The courses at Hoylake (Liverpool) and Deal (near Sandwich) were now brought into play and the string of victories by the Triumvirate was interrupted first by Sandy Herd at Hoylake in 1902, then by the Frenchman Arnaud Massy on the same

and the era of the immortal Bobby Jones.

In 1922 Walter Hagen won at Sandwich. In 1920 he had been 53rd and promised, 'I'll be back. You'll see my name on that cup!' He was the first American-born golfer to take the trophy. He won after an amazing fight back by George Duncan. Hagen had finished early with a score of 300 and Duncan was out on the course in the gathering dusk seemingly out of it. Someone, possibly the great golf writer Bernard Darwin, told him he needed a 67 to win. Duncan became inspired: his play to the greens was magnificent, and if his putting had been half as good he must have won. He came to the 18th needing just a par-four to tie and take Walter Hagen into a play-off. He played to fade the ball into the green on his second shot but the ball went dead straight and he took a five.

Hagen was second the next year at Troon, but first again in 1924 at Hoylake. Victory was particularly sweet for him because earlier in the year he had played the Englishman Archie Compston in a match over 72 holes at Moor Park and lost 18-and–17. In the Hoylake Open J. H. Taylor, now 53 years old, came fifth.

By now the domination of American players had truly begun. From 1926 to 1930 Bobby Jones and Hagen shared the Open between them. In 1931 Tommy Armour – another Scottish-born American – intervened. In 1932 came Gene Sarazen and in 1933 Densmore Shute.

Bobby Jones' first win was over the

Leaders at Lytham, 1926.

Top *Walter Hagen (third); he won in 1922, 1924, 1928 and 1929.*

Above *Winner Bobby Jones (centre) waits to receive his first Open trophy; Hagen is on the left.*

Left *Al Watrous (second), pitches to the 6th hole; he was undermined by Jones's miraculous recovery shot on the 71st hole.*

Above *Henry Cotton won his first Open at Sandwich in 1934. Here he receives the trophy from Royal St George's captain, the Hon. Michael Scott, who had won the Amateur Championship in 1933.*

Right *Winner Cotton playing the 2nd hole at Carnoustie during the 1937 Open.*

Below *Fred Daly (right) and Sam King in the tense final phase of the 1947 Open at Hoylake. Daly won from King, Cotton, Arthur Lees and Norman von Nida.*

links at Royal Lytham and St Anne's, which was being used for the Open for the first time. He won with majestic and consistent golf with three other Americans, Al Watrous, Walter Hagen and George van Elm following him in that order. His third and last (1930) was at Hoylake with Leo Diegel and Macdonald Smith taking second and third places. Walter Hagen at Muirfield in 1929 was followed by Johnny Farrel and Diegel. When Shute won in 1933 at St Andrews there were four other Americans also in the first six: Craig Wood, Gene Sarazen, Leo Diegel and Olin Dutra.

The locals stem the tide

Then in 1934 at Sandwich the Americans were at last held at bay. Henry Cotton pulverised the rest of the field. His second round 65 was so perfect, so astounding that it gave a name to a golf ball still used to this day, the Dunlop 65. At the end of the day the nearest man, Alf Padgham, was nine shots adrift. A 72 in the third round made Cotton leader by 12. The start of the final round was delayed because a huge and uncontrolled crowd had turned up to watch him. He waited alone in a tent and felt sick. He started with a skied drive, then things got even worse. He looked as if he would have trouble breaking 90. But he sank a huge putt for a 4 on the 13th which pulled him together, and he played the remaining holes well for a 79. This still left him winner by five shots.

The nearest Americans that year, Mac Smith and Joe Kirkwood, were nine shots behind. And the next year (1935) at Muirfield a little known club pro from Leatherhead in Surrey, Alf Perry, won by four shots from Alf Padgham. The nearest American challengers, Lawson Little and Henry Picard, were six shots and nine shots behind respectively. In 1936 at Hoylake it was Alf Padgham's turn; Gene Sarazen that year was equal fourth. In 1937 at Carnoustie Henry Cotton won again, his final 71 in a fierce gale and lashing rain being hailed as one of the greatest rounds of golf ever seen in Scotland. Charles Lacey was third and Byron Nelson fiffth. Reg Whitccombe won next at Sandwich, with Henry Cotton third; and finally Dick Burton won the 1939 Open at St Andrews.

The Locke-and-Thomson benefit

The first Open after the war was was held, appropriately enough, at St Andrews in

Max Faulkner watches anxiously as his shot from the rough flies towards the 15th green at Portrush, Ireland, in the 1951 Open. But all ended well: six shots ahead at the start of the last round, Faulkner won by two shots from Antonio Cerda of Argentina, who had a last-round 70.

1946 and Sam Snead came over from the United States to take the title. Another American, Johnny Bulla, was equal second to a relative newcomer from South Africa, Bobby Locke (who had been leading amateur in 1937). The genial Irishman Fred Daly won in 1947 at

The 2nd green at St Andrews and the course beyond, a classic British Open vista, a links course with bumps and hollows, whin (gorse) and deep traps – many of them invisible from tee or fairway until the player is within a few yards of them.

Above *Ben Hogan is greeted by Charles Turcan, Chairman of the Championship Committee, after winning the 1953 Open at Carnoustie.*

Below *Hoylake, 1956: Australia's Peter Thomson pitches up confidently on the way to winning the Open title for a record three years in succession.*

Hoylake, with the American amateur Frank Stranahan equal second. Then Cotton won his third title at Muirfield in 1948.

After that the American challenge faded for more than a decade. Few bothered to come over from the United States, where the money was much better, although Ben Hogan took the trophy home from Carnoustie in 1953 at his one and only attempt. The field was left to Locke and the Australian Peter Thomson.

Locke and Thomson shared the Open over a period of 10 years, the only interventions being made by Max Faulkner in 1951, when the tournament was taken across the Irish Sea to Portrush, and by Hogan in 1953. In those 10 years Locke and Thomson won four Opens each (Thomson was to win a fifth title in 1965 at Royal Birkdale).

In 1949, at Sandwich, Locke defeated Harry Bradshaw in a play-off after the Irishman's drive at the 5th had finished in a broken bottle left in the rough. Being uncertain of the rule (he could have had a free drop) Bradshaw played it as it lay – that is, inside the bottle. Of course nobody can be sure Bradshaw would have won but for this incident, but it certainly robbed him of a good chance. In the play-off, however, Locke went round 67, 68 to win by 12 shots. Next year he lowered the record at Troon with a winning score of 279.

Bobby Locke was involved in another incident in 1957 at St Andrews when, on the 72nd green, he marked his ball a putter-head's length away from its spot. When he came to putt, he forgot to put it back and played it from the marker's spot. This was seen on television and the incident was reported to the Committee. It was agreed that as Locke was three shots ahead of Thomson the result should stand.

Television had started reporting the Open on 7 July 1955 at St Andrews, when Peter Thomson won his second Open. The following year he won his third in a row, this time at Hoylake. The gifted Belgian Flory van Donck was second, Roberto de Vicenzo of the Argentine third and the young Gary Player of South Africa fourth. Henry Cotton made one of his now rare appearances and finished a creditable sixth.

The American new wave

Player won his first Open in 1959 and again van Donck was second. And in 1960 – the Centenary Year – the American challenge began all over again. The great Arnold Palmer, who led the renewed transatlantic invasion, just lost the Centenary Open at St Andrews to Kel Nagle of Australia by one shot.

One whole day's play was lost in that Open because of a violent storm. The

same thing was to happen in 1961 at Royal Birkdale. In the second round, when the great storm was brewing, Palmer's 73 was rated one of the great rounds yet played there. A plaque on the 15th commemorates one particularly spectacular shot. Dai Rees of Wales, one of the finest golfers never to win an Open, was second and in that gale-swept second round he was only one shot behind the American.

At Troon in 1962 Palmer won again, defeating Kel Nagle this time by six shots, American Phil Rodgers by 13, and Sam Snead and Peter Thomson by 16. He set a record for the Open at Birkdale of 276. That was to be the last of Palmer's Open victories; but that year Jack Nicklaus made his first appearance at a British Open (he made little impression and had one round of 80).

This was quite a different Open for there had been weeks of drought and the fairways were rock hard. The small ball, which was then still played in Britain, was likely to bounce almost anywhere. But Arnold Palmer said, 'Well, it's the same for everyone' and driving furiously, like Jehu, striking enormous long-irons to the greens, and putting superbly in his knock-kneed fashion, murdered the course and left everyone else far, far behind.

There was a larger crowd at this Open than had ever before been experienced – 37,008 paid and probably 3,000 more wormed their way in free – and what was considered their 'grave discourtesy' to Palmer led to tighter crowd control in all future Opens. But in fact Palmer became a hero to the British as well (there has always been an Anglo-Scottish division of Arnie's Army) – and he remains one to this day. His loyalty to the Open brought it back from the shadows to its proper place in international golf. In the next few years players from New Zealand, Australia, Argentina and South Africa as well as the United States were to triumph – plus one lone Briton, Tony Jacklin.

At Royal Lytham in 1963 Bob Charles of New Zealand became the first and so far the only left-hander to win the trophy. He tied with Phil Rodgers but won the play-off by eight shots.

That year saw the beginning of several important changes. While qualifying rounds were played on nearby courses, a system of exemptions was introduced for former victors and other leading players. The number playing in the final 36 holes was reduced. In the following year the length of play-offs was reduced to 18 holes from 36. Two years later, in 1966,

Muirfield, 1966: Jack Nicklaus blasts out of a greenside bunker at the 11th under the confident eye of his caddie Jimmy Dickinson. Nicklaus beat David Thomas and Doug Sanders by a single shot. It was his first Open victory, owed in large part to his long-iron play in the final round.

play was spread over four days instead of three. Prize money for the first time topped £20,000.

In 1964 the American Tony Lema won at St Andrews after barely one day's preparation. Jack Nicklaus did the last two rounds in 134 shots but finished second five shots astern. In the next year Peter Thomson won his fifth Open and in 1966 Nicklaus won his first, playing superb long irons off tee and fairway at gusty Muirfield. Then (at Hoylake, for the last time) came the day of Roberto de Vicenzo's one and only victory – an extremely popular win, for the big Argentinian had tried and tried again, coming third four times and second once; this time Jack Nicklaus was second.

Nicklaus was to be second yet again in 1968 when over a tough, rough Carnoustie course, stretched to 7,252 yards, Gary Player won his second title after a superlative head-to-head tussle with the American. The scoring was exceptionally high: Player's total was 289 (the highest since 1947), and only Nicklaus and Billy Casper managed to break 70 in any round.

By now no British player had won the Open for 18 years, since the mercurial Max Faulkner at Portrush. So when Tony Jacklin won at Royal Lytham in 1969 it

was a cause of genuine national rejoicing. And it was indeed a sign that times were changing. Bob Charles of New Zealand was second, Peter Thomson of Australia third, Roberto de Vicenzo fourth and Christy O'Connor, Sr of Ireland fifth.

The Americans hit back, of course, and in the next nine years only Gary Player, this time at Royal Lytham in 1974, interrupted a string of successes by Nicklaus, Lee Trevino (twice), Tom Weiskopf, Tom Watson (twice) and Johnny Miller. Sever-

Above *The home hole at Royal Lytham & St Anne's, approaching the green and the clubhouse. Among many great transatlantic invaders, only the immortal Bobby Jones has prevailed here in the Open.*

Left *Tony Jacklin breaks the spell at Lytham, 1969. It was the first time in 18 years a British golfer had won the Open championship. And for the first time in 10 years there was no American golfer even in the first five: New Zealander Bob Charles was second, Australian Peter Thomson and Argentinian Roberto de Vicenzo equal third, and Christy O'Connor fifth. Defending champion Jack Nicklaus, who was placed sixth, is at left.*

iano Ballesteros intervened in 1979 but there was then another string of American victories, Tom Watson taking three more titles himself.

The Open of 1970 had been perhaps the most dramatic. Tony Jacklin, defending champion, had played the first nine holes at St Andrews in 29 shots and seemed to be cruising toward a record first round total when a thunderstorm broke over the course and on the 14th hole he had to mark his ball and wait until the next day to return and play it. He was not quite the same player again, although he finished that round in 67. On the 72nd hole the American Doug Sanders who had had to pre-qualify, needed only two putts to win but somehow contrived to take three. He had to play-off with Jack Nicklaus, and took the great man again to the 18th. But

after a tremendous tee shot of over 350 yards to the back of the green, Nicklaus scored a birdie to win.

In 1971 Lee Trevino, who had already won the U.S. Open, was victorious at Royal Birkdale. A couple of weeks later he was to win the Canadian Open, setting a unique record. In this Birkdale Open the Taiwanese golfer Lu Liang Huan – 'Mr. Lu', as Henry Longhurst called him – was second, only a shot behind Trevino; Tony Jacklin was third, two shots behind.

What happened in 1972 seemed to take the heart out of Jacklin; he was never again to finish prominently in a British Open. For at Muirfield Lee Trevino, who was not truly playing at his best, holed two unlikely chips and one magical bunker shot to steal the title. The clincher was on the 71st hole where Jacklin was leading and Trevino appeared to have lost his chance. But rather casually he chipped downhill into the hole from greenside rough. Tony Jacklin promptly charged his first putt and took two more to get down so that in effect three strokes changed hands and Trevino, playing the last hole carefully, won the title. What many people have forgotten is that if it can be said that Trevino stole it from Jacklin it can also be said, perhaps with even more force, that he stole it from Nicklaus – who was second for a fourth time, and by only one shot.

Nineteen seventy-three was notable for several reasons. In miserable conditions the tall American Tom Weiskopf, with his superb swing and magisterial long-iron play, took the trophy, having led from start to finish. His 276 tied Arnold Palmer's record set, also at Troon, in 1962. The great Gene Sarazen, playing once again in the Open at the age of 71 – he had been one of the most faithful transatlantic

supporters for almost 50 years – holed in one in front of the TV cameras at the short 8th. (The first televised hole-in-one in Britain had been scored by Tony Jacklin in the Dunlop Masters of 1967.)

In 1974 the larger American ball, legal for some time in Britain, was made compulsory. The tournament was held at Lytham and Gary Player almost walked away with the title, but for a stutter in the third round when he took 75. But he had started 69, 68 and a final 70 left him an easy winner, four shots ahead of Briton Peter Oosterhuis and five ahead of Nicklaus. Player thus became the first player of modern times to win the Open in three different decades. J. H. Taylor and Harry Vardon did so between 1893 and 1914.)

The Watson years

Carnoustie, which had been so difficult to play in 1968 when Player had won with 289, saw a spate of low scoring in 1975. It was a tournament anyone could have won, Watson, Nicklaus, Newton, Cole, Miller and Marsh finishing within two strokes of one another. In the end Watson and Jack Newton of Australia had to play-off, Watson winning by one shot to take his first major title.

From 1975 almost to 1985 Tom Watson was virtually unbeatable: he won at Carnoustie, Turnberry, Muirfield, Troon and Birkdale. His second victory, at Turnberry, in 1977 was perhaps the most celebrated. He and Nicklaus were tied in the first round with 68s. They were still tied in the second round, both with 70s. They were together again after the third round when both shot inspired 65s. Finally on the 72nd hole, where both had birdie-threes, Watson won having edged ahead for the first time on the 17th and carding another 65. So once again Jack was second after himself playing glorious golf. Watson's 268 was comfortably the lowest aggregate in Open history; third-placed

At Turnberry in 1977 Tom Watson and Jack Nicklaus fought out a classic head-to-head match, with the rest of the field toiling hopelessly in the rear. Nicklaus finished 65– 66, but Watson finished 65–65 to win by one shot and to lower the best Open aggregate by no less than eight shots.

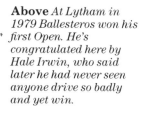

Above *At Lytham in 1979 Ballesteros won his first Open. He's congratulated here by Hale Irwin, who said later he had never seen anyone drive so badly and yet win.*

Above right *Tom Watson celebrates his fifth Open win, this time at Birkdale in 1983.*

Right *At Sandwich in 1985 Scotland's Sandy Lyle became the first Briton to win the Open since Jacklin in 1969.*

Hubert Green was 11 shots behind him.

Nicklaus won again at St Andrews in 1978, two strokes ahead of Simon Owen of New Zealand, Ben Crenshaw, Tom Kite and Raymond Floyd. Nicklaus was to take second place once again in 1979 when young Severiano Ballesteros from Spain startled the golf world by winning with a strangely inconsistent, not to say erratic, four rounds. One particular shot, on the 353-yards 16th in the final round, caused Americans to christen him the 'car-park champion.' Instead of taking the expected route down the left-hand side of the fairway, Seve hit the ball to the right in an area reserved for official cars, mainly belonging to BBC staff. From there he hit a wedge to the green – and sank the putt for a vital birdie!

Ballesteros was the first Spaniard to win the Open and the youngest player since Willie Auchterlonie in 1893. Lytham kept its own record, which was that no American professional had won there.

The golf world was now changing dramatically. Prize money was increasing rapidly. So were the crowds. At Lytham attendance had reached 134,000. Television began to reach around the world. Larger and faster jet liners made that world smaller. The number of international competitions grew.

Americans continued to dominate the Open for another four years, Tom Watson winning his fifth trophy in 1983 with Hale Irwin and Andy Bean tied for second place behind him and Lee Trevino fifth.

But the signs of change were more and more evident. Bernhard Langer of West Germany had been runner-up to Bill Rogers at Sandwich in 1981 with England's Mark James third.

Europe in the ascendant

In 1984 at St Andrews Severiano Ballesteros won for a second time. Langer was second, tied with Watson, who made a crucial error at the 71st hole; Nick Faldo and Greg Norman of Australia figured in the first seven places. Ballesteros's 276 was an Open record at St Andrews.

Nineteen eighty-five was to be Sandy Lyle's first big year. At stormy Sandwich he became the first home winner since Tony Jacklin in 1969 and the first Scot since James Braid in 1910 (if one does not count Tommy Armour, born in Scotland but a naturalised American).

The next year at Turnberry the Australian Greg Norman had what was almost a runaway victory after a superlative second-round 63, finishing five shots

Above *In 1986 Turnberry provided vile weather. Here winner Greg Norman finds deep trouble at the 9th in the third round.*

Below *Nick Faldo and Paul Azinger fight it out at the short 13th at Muirfield in 1987. Faldo, with his radically revised swing, finished with pars all the way, to take his first major championship.*

• BRITISH OPEN CHAMPIONSHIP •

YEAR	WINNER	VENUE	SCORE	YEAR	WINNER	VENUE	SCORE
1860	W. Park	Prestwick	174	1890	J. Ball (amateur)	Prestwick	164
1861	T. Morris, Sr	Prestwick	163	1891	H. Kirkaldy	St Andrews	166
1862	T. Morris, Sr	Prestwick	163	1892	H. Hilton (amateur)	Muirfield	305
1863	W. Park	Prestwick	168	1893	W. Auchterlonie	Prestwick	322
1864	T. Morris, Sr	Prestwick	167	1894	J.H. Taylor	Sandwich	326
1865	A. Strath	Prestwick	162	1895	J.H. Taylor	St Andrews	322
1866	W. Park	Prestwick	169	1896	H. Vardon	Muirfield	316
1867	T. Morris, Sr	Prestwick	170	1897	H. Hilton (amateur)	Hoylake	314
1868	T. Morris, Jr	Prestwick	157	1898	H. Vardon	Prestwick	307
1869	T. Morris, Jr	Prestwick	154	1899	H. Vardon	Sandwich	310
1870	T. Morris, Jr	Prestwick	149	1900	J.H. Taylor	St Andrews	309
1871	No Championship			1901	J. Braid	Muirfield	309
1872	T. Morris, Jr	Prestwick	166	1902	A. Herd	Hoylake	307
1873	T. Kidd	St Andrews	179	1903	H. Vardon	Prestwick	300
1874	M. Park	Musselburgh	159	1904	J. White	Sandwich	296
1875	W. Park	Prestwick	166	1905	J. Braid	St Andrews	318
1876	B. Martin	St Andrews	176	1906	J. Braid	Muirfield	300
1877	J. Anderson	Musselburgh	160	1907	A. Massy	Hoylake	312
1878	J. Anderson	Prestwick	157	1908	J. Braid	Prestwick	291
1879	J. Anderson	St Andrews	169	1909	J.H. Taylor	Deal	295
1880	B. Ferguson	Musselburgh	162	1910	J. Braid	St Andrews	299
1881	B. Ferguson	Prestwick	170	1911	H. Vardon	Sandwich	303
1882	B. Ferguson	St Andrews	171	1912	E. Ray	Muirfield	295
1883	W. Fernie	Musselburgh	159	1913	J.H. Taylor	Hoylake	304
1884	J. Simpson	Prestwick	160	1914	H. Vardon	Prestwick	306
1885	B. Martin	St Andrews	171	1915–1919	No Championship		
1886	D. Brown	Musselburgh	157	1920	G. Duncan	Deal	303
1887	W. Park, Jr	Prestwick	161	1921	J. Hutchison	St Andrews	296
1888	J. Burns	St Andrews	171	1922	W. Hagen	Sandwich	300
1889	W. Park, Jr	Musselburgh	155	1923	A.G. Havers	Troon	295

Mark Calcavecchia's superlative second shot from the right rough to the 18th green in the 1989 play-off. 'The best shot I've ever hit', he called it – and it finished 7 feet from the hole to set up his title-clinching birdie.

ahead of England's Gordon J. Brand and six ahead of Langer and the rising Welsh star Ian Woosnam; Nick Faldo was one shot further back.

Nick Faldo's turn came in 1987 at Muirfield. After making substantial changes to his swing, which kept him in or at least close to the wilderness for two years, he had become Mr Consistency. In the final round the young American Paul Azinger looked like winning. But as the pressure grew, Azinger stumbled. Nick Faldo kept his nerve and played a round of 18 pars to win by a shot.

Then at Lytham in 1988 Seve Ballesteros had another magical victory. It happened to be on Nick Faldo's birthday, but Faldo dropped behind to third place. Another Nick, Nick Price, chased an inspired Ballesteros all the way. But in the middle of the round the Spaniard had six successive birdies and on the 18th he hit

• BRITISH OPEN CHAMPIONSHIP •

YEAR	WINNER	VENUE	SCORE	YEAR	WINNER	VENUE	SCORE
1924	W. Hagen	Hoylake	301	1960	K. Nagle	St Andrews	278
1925	J. Barnes	Prestwick	300	1961	A. Palmer	Birkdale	284
1926	R. Jones (amateur)	Lytham	291	1962	A. Palmer	Troon	276
1927	R. Jones (amateur)	St Andrews	285	1963	R.J. Charles	Lytham	277
1928	W. Hagen	Sandwich	292	1964	A. Lema	St Andrews	279
1929	W. Hagen	Muirfield	292	1965	P. Thomson	Birkdale	285
1930	R. Jones (amateur)	Hoylake	291	1966	J. Nicklaus	Muirfield	282
1931	T. Armour	Carnoustie	296	1967	R. de Vicenzo	Hoylake	278
1932	G. Sarazen	Prince's, Sandwich	283	1968	G. Player	Carnoustie	289
1933	D. Shute	St Andrews	292	1969	A. Jacklin	Lytham	280
1934	T.H. Cotton	Sandwich	283	1970	J. Nicklaus	St Andrews	283
1935	A. Perry	Muirfield	283	1971	L. Trevino	Birkdale	278
1936	A.H. Padgham	Hoylake	287	1972	L. Trevino	Muirfield	278
1937	T.H. Cotton	Carnoustie	290	1973	T. Weiskopf	Troon	276
1938	R. Whitcombe	Sandwich	295	1974	G. Player	Lytham	282
1939	R. Burton	St Andrews	290	1975	T. Watson	Carnoustie	279
1940–1945 No Championship				1976	J. Miller	Birkdale	279
1946	S. Snead	St Andrews	290	1977	T. Watson	Turnberry	268
1947	F. Daly	Hoylake	293	1978	J. Nicklaus	St Andrews	281
1948	T.H. Cotton	Muirfield	284	1979	S. Ballesteros	Lytham	283
1949	A.D. Locke	Sandwich	283	1980	T. Watson	Muirfield	271
1950	A.D. Locke	Troon	279	1981	W. Rogers	Sandwich	276
1951	M. Faulkner	Portrush	285	1982	T. Watson	Troon	284
1952	A.D. Locke	Lytham	287	1983	T. Watson	Birkdale	275
1953	B. Hogan	Carnoustie	282	1984	S. Ballesteros	St Andrews	276
1954	P. Thomson	Birkdale	283	1985	S. Lyle	Sandwich	282
1955	P. Thomson	St Andrews	281	1986	G. Norman	Turnberry	280
1956	P. Thomson	Hoylake	286	1987	N. Faldo	Muirfield	279
1957	A.D. Locke	St Andrews	279	1988	S. Ballesteros	Lytham	273
1958	P. Thomson	Hoylake	278	1989	M. Calcavecchia	Troon	275
1959	G. Player	Muirfield	284				

an astonishing chip from off the edge of the green which lipped the cup and stopped a few inches away to give him his third Open victory.

Troon in 1989 provided a useful corrective to the tiresome 'Europeans are best' jingoism of the British tabloids, with five of the American Ryder Cup team in the first 10 places and the European superstars nowhere. It was also unique in featuring a three-man play-off over four holes of strokeplay, in which Mark Calcavecchia outplayed Australians Wayne Grady (who had led from the second round) and Greg Norman (whose wonderful closing 64 was not quite enough). Calcavecchia had enjoyed a couple of lucky breaks on the last day in carding his third 68, but his breathtaking second shot to set up his birdie at the 18th in the play-off was the stroke of a true champion.

MOST WINS
6: Harry Vardon 1896, 1898, 1899, 1903, 1911, 1914
5: J.H. Taylor 1894, 1895, 1900, 1903, 1911, 1914
James Braid 1901, 1905, 1906, 1909, 1913
Peter Thomson 1954, 1955, 1956, 1910
Tom Watson 1975, 1977, 1980, 1958, 1965
1982, 1983

OLDEST WINNER
Old Tom Morris: **46** in 1867

YOUNGEST WINNER
Young Tom Morris: **17** in 1868

LOWEST WINNING SCORE
268: Tom Watson, Turnberry, 1977

FIRST EUROPEAN WINNER
Arnaud Massy of France, 1907

FIRST AMERICAN-BORN WINNER
Walter Hagen, 1922

MOST SECOND-PLACE FINISHES
7: Jack Nicklaus

The United States Open

The largest and richest of the major championships is played over courses whose difficulty is deliberately increased by the USGA. Since the first official championship in 1895 the U.S. Open has rarely failed to produce a true champion....

Willie Dunn, first U.S. Open Champion, but an unofficial one. The 1894 'championship' was played at the St Andrews Club, New York. The first official championship was held in 1895 at Newport, Rhode Island.

'Tall oaks from little acorns grow'. In 1894 an unofficial U.S. Open was held at The St Andrews Club in Yonkers, New York. Only four professionals competed. In the following year the United States Golf Association was formed and the first official Open was played at Newport, Rhode Island, home for the ocean-sailing set. One amateur and ten pros took part. Today the U.S. Open is the largest, richest, most highly competitive championship of all.

Some 5000 golfers now enter for the U.S. Open every year. Only some 150 survive the qualifying rounds. Only 50 are exempt from qualifying because of their recent tournament records. Although the field is not as international as in the British Open the American tournament must surely be considered the toughest.

It is played over a number of the most difficult courses in America, most of which the pros do not see in the course of their annual Tour. Then for the Open these courses are rendered more difficult than usual by the USGA, which masterminds the tournament: fairways are narrowed, rough is thickened, carries are lengthened, greens are quickened. To win in these circumstances and under such pressure is to secure a place among the best; to win twice puts a player among the greatest; to win three or four times confers golfing immortality.

For the first 14 years the winners were all expatriate Britons. In the 1880s golf was beginning to take hold in the States, particularly in New England. Several British golfers were tempted to sail there in search of a new and richer life. Most were Scots, although the winner of the first official U.S. Open in 1895 was an Englishman from the Isle of Wight, Horace Rawlins.

In the unofficial Open the previous year, Willie Dunn beat Willie Campbell, both from Musselburgh, by two holes in a matchplay contest. Dunn, much to his surprise and annoyance, then lost to Rawlins by two shots – 175 against 173 – in the first official Open, which was at strokeplay like the British Open. Many had hoped that Willie Park, Jr would play, for he toured parts of America that year; but he sailed for home too soon.

The second U.S. Open was played at Shinnecock Hills on Long Island, New York, over the shortest course in history – only 4,423 yards – and this was won by another expatriate Scot, Jim Foulis.

In 1898 at the Myopia Hunt Club in Massachusetts Fred Herd, also from Scotland, won. For the first time the tournament was played over 72 holes. Golf was now spreading its influence and in 1899 the Open was held at Baltimore, Maryland, where Willie Smith won by the record margin of 11 shots. Then in 1900 something happened which fired the imagination of the American sports public.

The Vardon tours

In that year Harry Vardon and J.H. Taylor were both in North America, Vardon sponsored by Spalding for a series of exhibition matches that took him from

coast to coast and into Canada, and Taylor by a new clubmaking firm in which he was a partner. Their golf, Vardon's particularly, was an eye-opener to the Americans. In a pro match Vardon beat Willie Dunn 16-and-15; but most of the time he played club members two-at-a-time and won. When they both entered the U.S. Open at Chicago they became odd-on favourites. And in the event Vardon beat Taylor by two shots; Willie Smith was 15 shots behind.

Vardon caught the imagination of the American public. His swing was so graceful, so effective that it seemed like magic. Even Jerry Travers, a great American amateur, spoke in terms of 'poetry' and of a man 'making the game so easy a child could play it.' From that year on golf exploded as a sport in the United States.

The next five years, however, belonged to Willie Anderson, originally from North Berwick. He won four Opens out of five and three in a row (1903-4-5). He had been persuaded to emigrate at the age of 14 by a member of the Slazenger family and became a golfer of exceptional talent. Tragically, he died at 30.

In 1911 the United States at last produced its own home-bred champion,

Shinnecock Hills, on Long Island, where the second official United States Open championship was held in 1896. Jim Foulis, a Scottish pro, won over 36 holes.

Above left *Johnny McDermott, first native-born American to win the U.S. Open in 1911.*

Above right *Charles 'Chick' Evans, who won the U.S. Open in 1916, the third amateur to do so. One of the most accomplished Americans of his day, amateur or pro, his total of 286 was not bettered for 20 years. He followed up by winning the U.S. Amateur the same year – the only man other than Bobby Jones to achieve this feat.*

Right *20-year-old amateur Francis Ouimet beat Ted Ray and Harry Vardon in a play-off for the 1913 Open at Brookline, Boston.*

Opposite page, above *Ted Ray stuffs Walter Hagen into his pocket after winning the 1920 Open (Hagen had belittled British golfers earlier at Deal).*

Opposite page, below *Bobby Jones takes his first U.S. Open title, at Inwood in 1923.*

Johnny McDermott of Philadelphia, son of a postman. He was only 19 when he won at Chicago, the youngest player ever to do so. He won again the next year at the Buffalo Country Club in a match that produced two amazing bursts of low scoring. His main rival, Tom McNamara, another American-born player, broke 70 in two of his rounds, something unheard of in those days, but McDermott was steadier and won by two shots. Tragedy, however, was to strike down this accomplished player, too. He lost money on the stock market, faced ruin, was involved in a shipwreck in the English Channel after failing to get into the British Open, and was finished as a golfer at 23. He lived to be 80, but never played in a tournament after 1914.

Meanwhile a new American hero appeared unexpectedly on the scene – Francis Ouimet, at 20 the Amateur Champion of Massachusetts. Harry Vardon was on tour again and had with him this time the big-hitting Ted Ray. It was assumed that one or other of them was pretty well bound to win the 1913 Open, held at The Country Club in the Boston suburb of Brookline. But young Ouimet had other ideas. In the pouring rain he went round in 74 to tie the English pair on 304. Then in almost equally bad weather he scored a 72 next day to win the title by five shots from Vardon and six from Ray. A young golfer called Walter Hagen, by the way, had tied for third place over the 72 holes.

Ouimet's victory made this modest young man the hero of America. Henry Leach writing in the magazine *The American Golfer* wrote: 'Nothing can dim the merit and the glory of Mr Ouimet's victory; no British golfer would ever wish for an instant to injure the imperishability of the honour that was achieved on that dripping day in Massachusetts.' Hyperbole could be forgiven, for this did indeed mark the end of an era and the beginning of another. Ouimet opened the way for Walter Hagen, Gene Sarazen, Bobby Jones and indeed all the many truly great American golfers who have followed. American golf became supreme. (Ouimet remained an amateur; he took his second U.S. Amateur championship 18 years later, in 1931.)

Walter Hagen won the first of his two U.S. Opens in 1914, leading in each round. Jerry Travers, the second amateur to win, came next; Chick Evans, another amateur, followed in 1916, before the entry of the United States into the First World War put a stop to championships.

The Jones era

In 1920 the English returned: Ted Ray beat old Harry Vardon by one shot for the prestigious title. But it was to be 50 years before a Briton took that title again – although it is true that Jim Barnes, who won by nine strokes in 1921, was born in Cornwall. But Gene Sarazen won in 1922. And then it was time for Bobby Jones.

Jones had been second to Sarazen at the Skokie Country Club. He needed an eagle two to tie on the 18th: he got a birdie three. Next year he won. And he, the perfect amateur, was to win three more times.

Bobby Jones learned his golf from Stewart Maiden, the Scottish pro at his father's club. He was also heavily influenced by Harry Vardon, whom he partnered in a qualifying round in 1920. He too developed a swing of classic grace. Around him things were changing. Many American golfers were doing their own thing. They became hitters rather than swingers, a trend that was to come to full fruition in Arnold Palmer and Jack Nicklaus. But while he shared the elegant style of the best of British golfers, Bobby Jones personified the particularly American trait of tough competitiveness. He intended to win, however gentlemanly he might be and was.

And of course he did win – in 1926 he won both British and American Opens; in 1929 he won the U.S. Open for a third time; and in 1930 he did the Grand Slam, winning both Opens and both Amateurs in the same year. Then he retired from competitive golf.

That year, 1930, marked another milestone. For the first time entries for the U.S. Open topped the 1,000 mark. Competition got tougher. In 1932 Gene Sarazen won both the British and the U.S. Opens. He returned from Britain feeling worn out. He dragged himself to the Fresh Meadow course in Flushing, N.Y. 'feeling like a business-man who had slaved for weeks so he could take a short vacation and then had been called back to his office from the Maine woods.' He decided on safety-play.

Right *Bobby Jones on the final green of the 1926 Championship at Scioto, Ohio, when he became the first player to win the British and U.S. Opens in the same year. He made this putt to win by a single shot from Joe Turnesa, member of a family of distinguished golfers.*

Below *Gene Sarazen plays a delicate bunker shot in front of a huge and appreciative crowd on the 18th green to win the 1932 U.S. Open at Fresh Meadow, New York. He had a final round of 66, then a record, and famously played the last 28 holes of the championship in exactly 100 shots. Two weeks before, he had won the British Open.*

He shot two poor rounds, and in the third round he bogeyed four of the first eight holes. On the ninth tee he decided to live dangerously instead of playing for safety. He came home in 32. After lunch with Bobby Jones, Sarazen went out for the final round in the last flight. He went for every shot, however difficult, was round in 66 and won the Open. He had done the final 28 holes in exactly 100 strokes. Jones called it 'the finest competitive exhibition on record.'

The next few years saw a sequence of surprise wins, although Ralph Guldahl won two Opens in successive years, but the next superstar was not to appear until 1939 – Byron Nelson. Yet Nelson won only one single Open. His impact on American golf, however, was sensational. He developed a method of his own that enabled him to set scoring records and tournament records that have never been equalled. It was almost certainly these successes that drove his Texan contemporary Ben Hogan to make his own unrelenting search for perfection. In 1946 Byron Nelson tied for the Open once more but was defeated by Lloyd Mangrum in a three-way play-off. At the age of 34 he retired with dignity, his nerves burned out by the pressures.

Hogan's triumphs

Ben Hogan won his first U.S. Open in 1948; his 276 total set a new record. Then, on 2 February 1949, he was involved in a terrible car accident. He broke both legs, his pelvis, a rib and his collarbone, and was fortunate to be alive.

But in 1950, after a try-out in the Los Angeles Open – where he only just lost to Sam Snead in a play-off – Hogan again entered the Open. That year it was at Merion in Pennsylvania, one of his favourite courses. Although his left leg was still bandaged and he could barely drag himself over the last few holes of each 18, he won the title again, having had to go through another play-off to do so.

In 1951 the Open went to Oakland Hills, Michigan, a long course which had been redesigned to make it hideously difficult. None of the pros liked it, particularly not Ben Hogan. The fairways had been so narrowed on many of the long holes that

there was no choice but to hit the centre of the fairways off the tee. For two rounds almost everyone, including Hogan, played safe. Then he decided to attack. In the final round he played magical golf, so magical that enormous crowds rushed from all parts of the course to see him. He finished the winner again with a record 67. 'I'm glad I brought this course, this monster, to its knees,' he commented.

He was to win his fourth U.S. Open in 1953 after his once-for-all raid on the British Open, which he also won. He beat Sam Snead by six shots, playing Oakmont's horribly challenging last four holes like the supreme master he was. It looked as though he had won his fifth in 1955 until an unknown municipal-course pro,

Jack Fleck, birded the last two holes to tie him. Then the unlikely Fleck won the play-off 69 to 72, proving that any golfer good enough to qualify is good enough to win if on the day he has the nerves and the inspiration for it.

In 1959 Billy Casper's putter won the Open for him. Hogan, still trying for the elusive record fifth win, played superbly from tee to green, was second after three rounds, but never stood a chance. Casper, who had needed only 27 putts in the third round, did take one more than that in the fourth but Hogan faded from the scene. Bob Rosburg, another great putter, might have tied if he had sunk a 30 footer on the 18th green but he failed. At Winged Foot nobody sank 30 footers except Casper.

Below *Ben Hogan sinks a birdie putt on the final hole of the 1951 U.S. Open at Oakland Hills. This was his third Open victory in three starts (his near-fatal injury in 1949 interrupting the 1948, 1950 and 1951 sequence). Two years later he won for a fourth time at Oakmont, leading after every round and finishing six shots ahead of Sam Snead.*

Left *Oakland Hills, the course Ben Hogan called 'this monster'. He scored 76 in his first round in 1951, but he tamed it with a closing 67.*

Arnie arrives

Came 1960 and Arnold Palmer. Palmer attacked every golf course as if his irons were rifles. He loved firing at the flag. And he believed in himself. He had just won the Masters, birdieing the last two holes. At Cherry Hills in Denver he was however extra-wild off the tees and after three rounds was 15th, seemingly with no chance. Over lunch two of his colleagues

told him so. 'I might shoot 65,' said Palmer. He then shot 30 over the first nine and 35 over the second, becoming a mite conservative over the last two holes.

In that Open the great Ben Hogan partnered a young amateur named Jack Nicklaus. 'The kid ought to have won the thing by 10 strokes,' Hogan said afterwards. Two years later the kid beat Arnold Palmer in a play-off to win the first of his four titles.

In 1960 Arnold Palmer made his most famous charge. After 54 holes of the U.S. Open at Cherry Hills, Colorado, he was seven shots adrift. In the last round he scored six birdies in the first seven holes and won by two shots from young amateur Jack Nicklaus.

Except that Jack Nicklaus came along every five years to win 'the thing' yet again, the next decade or so was wide open. Julius Boros won for a second time in his relaxed way. Ken Venturi, so exhausted that a doctor had to be called, somehow won the title at the Congressional, Washington, DC. Gary Player won a play-off with Kel Nagle at Bellerive, St Louis – the first non-British foreigner to win – and gave $25,000 of his prize money back to the USGA, $5,000 for cancer relief and $20,000 to promote junior golf.

In 1966 at the Olympic, San Francisco, Arnold Palmer, shooting to beat Hogan's record score, let Billy Casper make up seven shots on him in nine holes and then lost the play-off. It was Nicklaus who was to beat Hogan's record. He did so the very next year at Baltusrol, New Jersey, scoring 275. And the year after that a newcomer on the tour, Lee Trevino, equalled that record at Oak Hill, New York.

Trevino was the first player to beat par in every round. In the same tournament Bert Yancey beat the record for 54 holes with 205 but was four strokes behind at the end. For the first time the total entry for the Open topped the 3,000 mark. And as the scoring showed the golf was getting better and better and the competition tougher and tougher.

A determined Tony Jacklin watches another putt go in at Hazeltine, Minnesota, in 1970. He led the U.S. Open after every round, was the only player to beat par and eventually won by 7 shots. Hazeltine was the second longest course ever to host a USGA championship.

In 1969 a recently demobbed sergeant in the United States army, Orville Moody, won the Open at the Champions Club, Houston, with 281. But the biggest surprise of all was to shatter Americans the very next year. At Hazeltine National at Minneapolis, on a course with a number of blind holes and several severe doglegs, Jack Nicklaus and Bert Yancey both had one round of 81, Gary Player and Tommy Bolt had 80s, Arnold Palmer had a 79 and Deane Beman shot an 82. But Britain's Open Champion Tony Jacklin breezed round the course 71–70–70–70 to win by seven shots. He was also seven under par, a record. Dave Hill, who was second, got into trouble with the authorities for saying that all the course lacked was 'Eighty acres of corn and a few cows.'

Next year Jacklin was to fail to make the cut and although he won once again on the American tour the pressures of this kind of golf at this level before long reduced him almost to a nervous wreck. His confidence on the greens deserted him entirely. There are many other players who know exactly how he feels. The entry for the U.S. Open in 1971 topped the

Right *Lee Trevino gives the clenched fist salute to a putt at Merion in 1971, when he won his second U.S. Open. He had tied with Jack Nicklaus, but won the play-off 68 to 71.*

Below *In 1974 Winged Foot, New York, was particularly difficult. Hale Irwin won by two shots from Forest Fezler with a score of 287.*

4,000 mark for the first time. Every good golfer stood a chance.

It was to be the happy-go-lucky Lee Trevino who was to challenge Nicklaus. That year, 1971, the Open went back to Merion, Jack's favourite course where as an amateur he had once shot a 269. It was a course now that demanded precise planning. Nicklaus planned to use his driver on only three holes. He was long enough with his 1-iron and even more accurate.

After the third round Nicklaus was lying second, Trevino fourth. An amateur, Jim Simons, was leading. The second nine at Merion was very, very difficult. The pressure was enormous. Simons gave way. Both Nicklaus and Trevino were always on the edge of trouble. Trevino pushed a 3-wood into the crowd on the 18th, Nicklaus missed a 14-foot putt on the same hole. They tied on 280. Trevino won the play-off with a 68. Next year however Nicklaus won his third Open at Pebble Beach.

Johnny Miller threatened as the new superstar. He won at Oakmont, scoring a record 63 in the final round, hitting every green in regulation putting like a demon

and making up six shots on leader John Schlee to win by one stroke. Hale Irwin won twice, at the horribly testing Winged Foot, New York, and at Inverness, Ohio. Lou Graham, Jerry Pate, Andy North and Hubert Green all won. But the golf world was waiting once again for Jack Nicklaus.

Nicklaus clinches his fourth title

In 1980, back at Baltusrol, Jack in the very first round just missed a putt for a 62. A 71 and a 70 gave him a three round record of 204. Isao Aoki of Japan with three 68s tied with him on that score. In the third round Hubert Green had eight threes in a row

Top *Fuzzy Zoeller and Greg Norman after their duel in the sun at Winged Foot. Zoeller thought Norman had won with a spectacular putt and (literally) threw in a towel, only to find that he had tied the Australian. In the play-off Zoeller won easily, by 68 to 75.*

Left *In 1986 at Shinnecock Hills, Ray Floyd became the oldest winner of the U.S. Open. His 279 beat Lanny Wadkins by two shots; his age beat old Ted Ray's by five months.*

Curtis Strange makes a brilliant recovery from the sand on the 72nd hole of the 1988 U.S. Open, enabling him to tie Britain's Nick Faldo. Strange was always in command of the play-off. He successfully defended his title at Oak Hill in 1989.

but could not stay in contention. Then Nicklaus compiled a 68 in the final round to set another record with 272 and win his fourth Open by two strokes from the gallant Aoki.

More drama was to come. In 1981 David Graham became the first Australian to win the title. Tom Watson won at Pebble Beach, chipping into the hole at the 17th and robbing Nicklaus of that fifth title. At Winged Foot in 1984 Australian star Greg Norman tied with the white-towel-waving Fuzzy Zoeller after holing out from at least 40 feet on the final hole – but Zoeller played relentlessly accurate golf in the play-off to win by eight shots.

Andy North won for a second time when it looked almost certain that Tze-Chung Chen of Taiwan was bound to win. (He faded after hitting the ball twice on the 5th in the final round and took 8.) Ray Floyd made light of his almost-44 years at Shinnecock Hills and won with a final round of 66. Scott Simpson won with 277 at San Francisco, keeping a happily resurgent Tom Watson at bay with superb putting in the last round.

In 1988, in a very exciting tournament, Curtis Strange successfully turned aside the challenge of England's Nick Faldo, 1987 winner of the British Open. Faldo, after two years in the wilderness while he tightened his technique, had become Europe's most consistent striker. He confirmed that reputation at the Brookline Country Club, Mass. He scarcely missed a fairway and looked quite likely to win

MOST WINS
4: Willie Anderson, Bobby Jones, Ben Hogan, Jack Nicklaus

OLDEST WINNER
Raymond Floyd at 43 years and 9 months (1986); Ted Ray (1920) and Julius Boros (1963) were also over 43

YOUNGEST WINNER
Johnny McDermott at 19 (1911)

LOWEST WINNING SCORE
272: Jack Nicklaus at Baltrusol (1980)

FIRST AMERICAN-BORN WINNER
Johnny McDermott (1911)

MOST SECOND PLACE FINISHES
4: Bobby Jones, Sam Snead, Arnold Palmer, Jack Nicklaus

• U.S. OPEN CHAMPIONSHIP •

YEAR	WINNER	VENUE	SCORE	YEAR	WINNER	VENUE	SCORE
1895	H. Rawlins	Newport, RI	173	1942–1945 No Championship			
1896	J. Foulis	Shinnecock Hills, NY	152	1946	L. Mangrum	Canterbury, Ohio	284
1897	J. Lloyd	Chicago	162	1947	L. Worsham	St. Louis, Mo	282
1898	F. Herd	Myopia, Mass	328	1948	B. Hogan	Riviera, Cal	276
1899	W. Smith	Baltimore, Md	315	1949	C. Middlecoff	Medinah, Ill	286
1900	H. Vardon	Chicago	313	1950	B. Hogan	Merion, Pa	287
1901	W. Anderson	Myopia, Mass	331	1951	B. Hogan	Oakland Hills, Mi	287
1902	L. Auchterlonie	Garden City, NY	307	1952	J. Boros	Northwood, Tex	281
1903	W. Anderson	Baltrusol, NY	307	1953	B. Hogan	Oakmont, Pa	283
1904	W. Anderson	Glen View, Ill	303	1954	E. Furgol	Baltusrol, NJ	284
1905	W. Anderson	Myopia, Mass	314	1955	J. Fleck	Olympic, Cal	287
1906	A. Smith	Onwentsia, Ill	295	1956	C. Middlecoff	Oak Hill, NY	281
1907	A. Ross	Philadelphia, PA	302	1957	D. Mayer	Inverness, Ohio	282
1908	F. McLeod	Myopia, Mass	322	1958	T. Bolt	Southern Hills, Okla	283
1909	G. Sargent	Englewood, NY	290	1959	B. Casper	Winged Foot, NY	282
1910	A. Smith	Philadelphia, PA	298	1960	A. Palmer	Cherry Hills, Col	280
1911	J. McDermott	Chicago	307	1961	G. Littler	Oakland Hills, Mi	281
1912	J. McDermott	Buffalo, NY	294	1962	J. Nicklaus	Oakmont, Pa	283
1913	F. Ouimet (am)	Brookline, Mass	304	1963	J. Boros	Brookline, Mass	293
1914	W. Hagen	Midlothian, Ill	290	1964	K. Venturi	Congressional, Md	278
1915	J. Travers (am)	Baltursol, NJ	297	1965	G. Player	Bellerive, Mo	282
1916	C. Evans Jr (am)	Minikahda, Minn	286	1966	B. Casper	Olympic, Cal	278
1917–1918 No Championship				1967	J. Nicklaus	Baltusrol, NJ	275
1919	W. Hagen	Brae Burn, Mass	301	1968	L. Trevino	Oak Hill, NY	275
1920	T. Ray	Inverness, Ohio	295	1969	O. Moody	Champions, Tex	281
1921	J. Barnes	Columbia, Md.	289	1970	T. Jacklin	Hazeltine, Minn	281
1922	G. Sarazen	Skokie, Ill	288	1971	L. Trevino	Merion, Pa	280
1923	R. Jones (am)	Inwood, NY	296	1972	J. Nicklaus	Pebble Beach, Cal	290
1924	C. Walker	Oakland Hills, Mi	297	1973	J. Miller	Oakmont, Pa	279
1925	W. MacFarlane	Worcester, Mass	291	1974	H. Irwin	Winged Foot, NY	287
1926	R. Jones (am)	Scioto, Ohio	293	1975	L. Graham	Medinah, Ill	287
1927	T. Armour	Oakmont, Pa	301	1976	J. Pate	Atlanta Athletic, Ga	277
1928	J. Farrell	Olympia Flds. Ill	294	1977	H. Green	Southern Hills, Okla	278
1929	R. Jones (am)	Winged Foot, NY	294	1978	A. North	Cherry Hills, Col	285
1930	R. Jones (am)	Interlachen, Min	287	1979	H. Irwin	Inverness, Ohio	284
1931	B. Burke	Inverness, Ohio	292	1980	J. Nicklaus	Baltusrol, NJ	272
1932	G. Sarazen	Fresh Meadow, NY	286	1981	D. Graham	Merion, Pa	273
1933	J. Goodman (am)	North Shore, Ill	287	1982	T. Watson	Pebble Beach, Cal	282
1934	O. Dutra	Merion, PA	293	1983	L. Nelson	Oakmont, Pa	280
1935	S. Parks, Jr	Oakmont, PA	299	1984	F. Zoeller	Winged Foot, NY	276
1936	T. Manero	Baltusrol, NJ	282	1985	A. North	Oakland Hills, Mi	279
1937	R. Guldahl	Oakland Hills, Mi	281	1986	R. Floyd	Shinnecock Hills, NY	279
1938	R. Guldahl	Cherry Hills, Colo	284	1987	S. Simpson	San Francisco	277
1939	B. Nelson	Philadelphia, PA	284	1988	C. Strange	Brookline, Mass	278
1940	L. Little	Canterbury, Ohio	287	1989	C. Strange	Oak Hill, NY	278
1941	C. Wood	Colonial, Texas	284				

when Curtis Strange wedged out of a greenside bunker on the 72nd hole to tie.

In 1989 Curtis Strange ground out a level-par final round at Oak Hill while third-round leaders Tom Kite and Scott Simpson pushed the self-destruct button. Ian Woosnam had his best U.S. tournament so far, taking joint second place. In successfully defending his title, Strange emulated the feat of Ben Hogan in 1950 and 1951.

Strange may not be the most exciting player on tour, but his relentless concentration on risk-free essentials would undoubtedly have earned a nod of approval from the great Texan.

The U.S. PGA championship

Although intended primarily for native American pros, the U.S. PGA has earned its status as one of the world's majors. And, for its first 42 years, it had the distinction of being the only championship to be decided by matchplay. . . .

The United States Professional Golfers Association championship, considered the fourth 'Major', is actually third in seniority. It was first held in 1916 when the U.S. PGA was founded just before America's entry into World War I. Jim Barnes, the Cornish-American, defeated Jock Hutchison, the Scottish-American, by one hole. For the PGA was a matchplay event until 1958.

The championship was and remains essentially for American professional golfers and visitors playing the American circuit or qualifying through victories in nominated American tournaments. Victory in this event gives a player a lifetime exemption from pre-qualifying in any and every PGA event thereafter. In 1968 the tournament players formed their own division of the PGA and started their own championship, leaving the PGA to run mainly the affairs of club professionals and teachers and to arrange the tour.

Hagen and Sarazen

The first hero was the flamboyant Walter Hagen, who did for American professionals what Henry Cotton was to do for British pros a decade or more later. He raised the status of the golf pro. While doing this he won the PGA matchplay championship five times.

He very nearly won six PGAs, for in 1923 his match with his friend and rival Gene Sarazen went into extra holes. On the 38th hole Sarazen tried to cut a dogleg and hooked abruptly into the woods where his ball seemed to hit the roof of a cottage. His caddie found it however with a clear path between two trees; and taking his niblick he hit the ball onto the green two feet from the hole. Hagen fluffed his pitch. He was ever afterwards convinced that the owner of the cottage threw Sarazen's ball back onto the course.

Hagen was without argument the greatest of all match players. From 1924 through 1927 he won four PGA championships running. At French Lick, Indiana, he beat Jim Barnes by two holes. At

Walter Hagen, seen here driving off, was reckoned to be the best match-player in America. The U.S. PGA championship was at matchplay until 1958; Hagen won it five times between 1921 and 1927.

Olympia Field, Illinois, he beat 'Wild Bill' Mehlhorn 6-and-5. At Salisbury, New York, he beat Leo Diegel 5-and-3. Then in 1927 at Cedar Crest, Texas, he beat Joe Turnesa on the final hole.

Sarazen had three wins, Sam Snead three, Ben Hogan and Byron Nelson two each. Another two-time winner was Paul Runyan who in 1938 beat the great Sam Snead 8-and-7.

The PGA goes to strokeplay

In 1957 the last professional matchplay championship was won by Lionel Hebert at Miami Valley, Ohio.

First winner in the new strokeplay format was the very man who had been runner-up to Hebert in the final matchplay event, Dow Finsterwald. He shot a last round 67 to defeat Billy Casper by two strokes and Sam Snead by four.

Arnold Palmer was never to win the PGA, but perhaps his best chance came in 1960. He was Open Champion and he opened with a powerful 67 over the Firestone course in Ohio. But a third round 75 killed his chances and the title went to Jay Hebert, Lionel Hebert's brother. In 1964 Palmer shot 68, 68, 69, 69 and still lost to Bobby Nichols. In 1968 at Pecan Valley, Texas, he tied with left-hander Bob Charles for second place by one shot from Julius Boros.

Nineteen sixty-one was Jerry Barber's year. A slight figure, only 5ft 5in, Barber could be a magical putter. He tied the elegant Don January with 277 at Olympia Fields, Illinois, and then won the play-off.

In 1962 Gary Player won the third trick in his eventual international Grand Slam at Aronimink, Pennsylvania. It was the first time he had played in the PGA and he won by a stroke from Bob Goalby. Jack Nicklaus, in his first year as a pro, was equal third with George Bayer. Player was to win again in 1972 at Oakland Hills, Michigan, but the next 17 years were to belong to Jack Nicklaus. Starting in 1963 at Dallas, he won five PGAs.

Nicklaus's second win was at the new PGA National course in Florida in 1971, two shots ahead of Billy Casper. Two years later at the Canterbury Club, Ohio, he won by four shots over the Australian Bruce Crampton. This win gave him his 14th major title, putting him one ahead of Bobby Jones.

Left *Leo Diegel's elbows-out putting style inspired Bernard Darwin to invent the verb 'to diegel'. Here he is, diegeling away to crushing effect in the 1928 PGA at Five Farms, Baltimore. He beat Hagen in the third round, then slaughtered Gene Sarazen 9-and-8, and finally beat Al Espinosa 6-and-5 to win the title.*

Below *Gene Sarazen recovering from a bunker in the 1933 final against Willie Goggin at Blue Mound, Milwaukee, to win his third PGA title.*

Above Ben Hogan holds
the PGA cup after his
victory over Mike
Turnesa in 1948. This
was his second win, but
what made the year
specially memorable
was that he went on to
win his first U.S. Open.

Right Lanny Wadkins
made up five shots in
nine holes to catch Gene
Littler in the 1977
Championship at Pebble
Beach, California,
holing from 20 feet to
tie. In the first sudden-
death play-off Lanny
beat Gene on the third
extra hole.

Nicklaus's fourth win came back at
Firestone, where once again he was
chased all the way by Bruce Crampton,
who fired a record 63 in the second round.
His fifth win came in 1980 when he won
by seven shots at Oak Hill, New York.

At Oakland Hills in 1979 David Graham
became the first Australian to win the
PGA. He had a tremendous tussle with
Ben Crenshaw. They tied over 72 holes on
272 and went into a play-off.

In 1984 Lee Trevino, who had just
pipped Jack Nicklaus by one shot 10 years
earlier at Tanglewood, North Carolina,
beat 70 in all four rounds, as he had also
done in the U.S. Open in 1968. Trevino
was 44; and tying for second place in this
championship was old Gary Player, 48.
Trevino's win gave him, too, a major
championship in each of three decades.

But also on the leader board were a
number of younger names who were beginning to make their mark – Scott Simpson,
Hal Sutton, Larry Mize and a little lower
down Fred Couples and Nick Faldo.

At Cherry Hills in 1985 Hubert Green
won and he was 39. Lee Trevino came
second. The Taiwanese golfer Tze-Chung
Chen was third.

1986 a classic head-to-head

The Championship at Inverness, Ohio, in

1986 was astonishing in many ways. It is
chiefly famous for the bunker shot which
Bob Tway holed on the 72nd green to win
over Greg Norman of Australia, the 'Great
White Shark.' But in strokeplay every shot
counts one and there had been many
extraordinary shots even before that one.
Norman, holder of the British Open title,
started with a course record 65. He
followed that with a 68. Bob Tway who
had started 72, 70 then lowered Norman's
record with a record of his own, 64. It was
Greg Norman who chipped into the hole
in this round, and in total he did so three
times during the tournament.

In the final round the championship
almost turned back again to matchplay. At
the 17th Tway hit his second shot into
deep rough beside the green and seemed
certain to lose a shot to the Australian.
But he somehow manufactured a superb
sand-iron shot which saved him his par.
This was possibly a better shot than the
one he holed out of the bunker on the
18th to win. He was round in 70 to
Norman's 76 and for that he deserved to
prevail.

Larry Nelson won for the second time
in 1987. He tied with Lanny Wadkins over
the 72 holes but won the play-off at the
first extra hole. His previous win had been
at Atlanta, Georgia, in 1981. Nelson is an

Left *In 1980, Having won the Open, Jack Nicklaus notched up his fifth PGA title at Oak Hill, New York, beating second-placed Andy Bean by the record margin of seven shots.*

Below *Lee Trevino confers with caddie Herman at Shoal Creek, Alabama, in 1984. He won with a score of 273 at the age of 44; joint second was Gary Player at the age of 48. Trevino had four rounds under 70, a record he also holds for the U.S. Open.*

Left *While defending champion Trevino watches from the other side of the green, Hubert Green putts up with plenty of shots to spare. This is Cherry Hills, Denver, in 1985, and Green won by two shots.*

Near right *Bob Tway holes from a bunker at the 72nd hole at Inverness, Toledo, to snatch victory from the Australian Greg Norman.*

Far right *Jeff Sluman pitches to the final green at Edmond, Oklahoma, to win the 1988 title. His was a steady rather than spectacular game; his superlative last-round 65 depended greatly on pitching and putting.*

exceptional golfer in that he did not start playing until he was 21 years of age and when he did he taught himself the game by studying Ben Hogan's classic *Modern Fundamentals of Golf*. He was 14th in the U.S. money list in 1987 and won more than half a million dollars. (Curtis Strange won $925,941.)

The 1988 championship produced another surprise. Journeyman pro Jeff Sluman won in searing heat at Edmond, Oklahoma with a final round of 65, as good a final round as anyone had seen in the tournament for many years. But from tee to green the best player in the tournament had been Great Britain's Nick Faldo, as he had been earlier in the U.S. Open.

Mike Reid was 1989's walking disaster, suffering last-round collapses when on the brink of victory in both the Masters and the U.S. PGA. At Kemper Lakes Payne Stewart, a hugely accomplished player who had also found it hard to win, this time hung tough to the end, carding a final 67 which included a brilliantly frugal 31 on the back nine to edge out Curtis Strange, Andy Bean and the luckless Reid.

Right *Payne Stewart, masquerading as a Chicago Bear, sinks his putt on the 72nd at Kemper Lakes to take his first major title.*

MOST WINS
5: Walter Hagen (at matchplay); Jack Nicklaus (at strokeplay)

OLDEST WINNER
Julius Boros at 48 (1968)

YOUNGEST WINNER
Gene Sarazan at 20 (1922)
Tom Creavy was also 20 (1931) but four months older.

LOWEST WINNING SCORE
271: Bobby Nichols (1964)

FIRST AMERICAN-BORN WINNER
Walter Hagen (1921)

FIRST OVERSEAS WINNER AT STROKEPLAY
Gary Player (1962)

MOST SECOND PLACE FINISHES
4: Jack Nicklaus

• U.S. PGA CHAMPIONSHIP •

YEAR	WINNER	VENUE	SCORE	YEAR	WINNER	VENUE	SCORE
1916	Jim Barnes bt. Jock Hutchison	Siwanoy, NY	1-hole	1949	Sam Snead bt. Johnny Palmer	Hermitage, Pa	3 & 2
1917–1918 No Championship				1950	Chandler Harper bt. Henry Williams	Scioto, Ohio	4 & 3
1919	Jim Barnes bt. Fred McLeod	Engineers, NY	6 & 5	1951	Sam Snead bt. Walter Burkemo	Oakmont, Pa	7 & 6
1920	Jock Hutchison bt. J.D. Edgar	Flossmoor, Ill	1-hole	1952	Jim Turnesa bt. Chick Harbert	Big Spring, Ky.	1-hole
1921	Walter Hagen bt. Jim Barnes	Inwood CC, NY	3 & 2	1953	Walter Burkemo bt. Felice Torza	Birmingham, Mich	2 & 1
1922	Gene Sarazen bt. Emmet French	Oakmont, Pa	4 & 3	1954	Chick Harbert bt. Walter Burkemo	Keller CC, Minn	4 & 3
1923	Gene Sarazen bt. Walter Hagen	Pelham, NY	38th	1955	Doug Ford bt. Cary Middlecoff	Meadowbrook, Mich	4 & 3
1924	Walter Hagen bt. Jim Barnes	French Lick, Ind	2-holes	1956	Jack Burke bt. Ted Kroll	Blue Hill CC, Mass	3 & 2
1925	Walter Hagen bt. Bill Mehlhorn	Olympia Fields, Ill	6 & 5	1957	Lionel Hebert bt. Dow Finsterwald	Miami Valley, Ohio	2 & 1
1926	Walter Hagen bt. Leo Diegel	Salisbury, NY	5 & 3	1958	Dow Finsterwald	Llanerch, Pa	276
1927	Walter Hagen bt. Joe Turnesa	Cedar Crest, Tex	1-hole	1959	Bob Rosburg	Minneapolis	277
1928	Leo Diegel bt. Al Espinosa	Five Farms, Md.	6 & 5	1960	Jay Hebert	Firestone, Ohio	281
1929	Leo Diegel bt. Johnny Farrell	Hill Crest, Cal	6 & 4	1961	Jerry Barber	Olympia Fields, Ill	277
1930	Tommy Armour bt. Gene Sarazen	Fresh Meadow, NY	1-hole	1962	Gary Player	Aronimink, Pa	278
1931	Tom Creavy bt Denny Shute	Wannamoisett, R.I.	2 & 1	1963	Jack Nicklaus	Dallas, Tex	279
1932	Olin Dutra bt. Frank Walsh	Keller, Minn	4 & 3	1964	Bobby Nichols	Columbus, Ohio	271
1933	Gene Sarazen bt. Willie Goggin	Blue Mound, Wis.	5 & 4	1965	Dave Marr	Laurel Valley, Pa	280
1934	Paul Runyan bt. Craig Wood	Park, NY	38th	1966	Al Geiberger	Firestone, Ohio	280
1935	John Revolta bt. Tommy Armour	Twin Hills, Okla	5 & 4	1967	Don January	Columbine, Colo	281
1936	Denny Shute bt. Jimmy Thomson	Pinehurst, NC	3 & 2	1968	Julius Boros	Pecan Valley, Tex	281
1937	Denny Shute bt. Harold McSpaden	Pittsburgh, Pa	37th	1969	Ray Floyd	Dayton, Ohio	276
1938	Paul Runyan bt. Sam Snead	Shawnee, Pa	8 & 7	1970	Dave Stockton	Southern Hills, Okla	279
1939	Henry Picard bt. Byron Nelson	Pomonok, NY	37th	1971	Jack Nicklaus	PGA National, Fla	281
1940	Byron Nelson bt. Sam Snead	Hershey, Pa	1-hole	1972	Gary Player	Oakland Hills, Mi	281
1941	Vic Ghezzi bt. Byron Nelson	Cherry Hills, Colo	38th	1973	Jack Nicklaus	Canterbury, Ohio	277
1942	Sam Snead bt. Jim Turnesa	Seaview, NJ	2 & 1	1974	Lee Trevino	Tanglewood, NC	276
1943 No Championship				1975	Jack Nicklaus	Firestone, Ohio	276
1944	Bob Hamilton bt. Byron Nelson	Manito, Wash	1-hole	1976	Dave Stockton	Congressional, Md	281
1945	Byron Nelson bt. Sam Byrd	Morraine, Ohio	4 & 3	1977	Lanny Wadkins	Pebble Beach, Cal	282
1946	Ben Hogan bt. Porky Oliver	Portland GC, Ore	6 & 4	1978	John Mahaffey	Oakmont, Pa	276
1947	Jim Ferrier bt. Chick Harbert	Plum Hollow, Mich	2 & 1	1979	David Graham	Oakland Hills, Mi	272
1948	Ben Hogan bt. Mike Turnesa	Norwood Hills, Mo	7 & 6	1980	Jack Nicklaus	Oak Hill, NY	274
				1981	Larry Nelson	Atlanta AC, Ga	273
				1982	Ray Floyd	Southern Hills, Okla	272
				1983	Hal Sutton	Riviera CC, Cal.	274
				1984	Lee Trevino	Shoal Creek, Al.	273
				1985	Hubert Green	Cherry Hills, Col	278
				1986	Bob Tway	Inverness, Ohio	276
				1987	Larry Nelson	PGA National Fla	287
				1988	Jeff Sluman	Oaktree, Okla	272
				1989	Payne Stewart	Kemper Lakes, Ill	276

The Masters

The Masters, played on the breathtakingly beautiful Augusta National course, is the youngest and most exclusive of the four majors: entry is 'by invitation' only. Yet it unfailingly produces a tournament of rare quality and excitement. . . .

Horton Smith on his way to winning the very first Masters at Augusta in 1934. He birdied the 17th and parred the 18th to beat Craig Wood by a stroke.

The youngest of the Majors is unique in that it is played on the same course every year. And what a course! Augusta National, in Georgia, ablaze with flowering shrubs when the tournament is played there in the spring, was the realised dream of Bobby Jones when he retired from tournament golf after his golden year of 1930. His intention was to hold an informal event to which he would invite the most distinguished of his golfer friends, professional and amateur.

The Masters remains an invitational event: if you haven't been invited, you don't get to play – though nowadays success on the pro tours 'qualifies' players for an invitation, which is also extended to certain leading amateurs and to past winners of the tournament.

The first Invitational Tournament was held in 1934 and was won by Horton Smith with a score of 284, four under par. Bobby Jones himself played, though not very seriously, and came thirteenth. The story goes that Jones's father, 'The Colonel', officiating on the course in that inaugural year, was asked at the 12th by a senior golfer to give a ruling on a free drop. 'How are you doing, old-timer?' enquired the Colonel. 'I'm 17 over,' he was told. 'In that case, as far as I'm concerned,' said the Colonel, 'you can do what the hell you like!'

Horton Smith was a considerable player. He had won eight tournaments in 1929 and was the only American to win a singles match that year in the Ryder Cup.

He was to win the Masters for a second time in 1936. Like all winners of this tournament he was a very fine putter, the great Bernard Darwin describing his putting as 'easy, elegant and of a horrid certainty'.

The shot heard around the world

It was the second year at Augusta, however, that made the headlines. On the long 15th hole, a par-5 protected securely at the front by water, Gene Sarazen hit the shot of a lifetime. He was trying to catch Craig Wood, who seemed to be coasting to victory. Three behind when he stood on the 15th tee, Sarazen hit a good drive of perhaps 250 yards, which left him about 235 yards from the pin – an ideal distance for a full shot with his favourite club, a 4-wood which he often used instead of long irons, especially if he needed height as well as length. He made perfect contact with the ball, which flew high over the pond, landed on the front edge of the green – and ambled slowly into the hole for an albatross or double-eagle. He was now level with Wood; and he parred the last three holes. The following day he beat

Wood by five shots in the 36-hole play-off, in the course of which he carded 24 consecutive pars.

The unfortunate Craig Wood had been runner-up the previous year; he had lost a play-off to Densmore Shute in The Open of 1933; he lost the (matchplay) final of the U.S. PGA Championship of 1934 at the 38th hole; and he would lose a play-off to Byron Nelson in the 1939 U.S. Open. However, he kept plugging away and in 1941 won both Masters and U.S. Open.

In 1936 Wood ruined his chances with an 88 in the first round. Harry Cooper took up the lead after two rounds, six ahead of Horton Smith. But Smith caught him and, playing spectacular golf over the last nine holes, won by a single shot. The very next year Byron Nelson made up six shots on the then leader Ralph Guldahl in

Above *Water and vast expanses of lawn-like fairways lend a distinctive character to Augusta's magical setting of flowering shrubs and trees. Here in 1987 Greg Norman and Ben Crenshaw make for the green after hitting over the water on the short 16th.*

Above, right *Henry Cotton (left) chats with Bobby Jones on the verandah of Bobby's cottage by the 10th tee. It is 1957 and Bobby is partly paralysed, his slow but relentless degenerative disease already taking effect.*

just two holes, making a birdie at the 12th (the most famous and perhaps most difficult par 3 in the major championships) and an astonishing eagle at the par-5 13th by holing a delicate chip – with a 3-iron! – from almost 50 feet.

In 1939 Sam Snead looked every inch a winner. But Ralph Guldahl, the runner-up in 1937, fulfilled Bob Jones' specifications for his 'winner's course' – charging over the back nine in 33 shots to win by a single stroke. Augusta is the hardest course in the world on which to protect your lead.

The following year Jimmy Demaret covered the back nine in 30 in the first round, while Lloyd Mangrum shot 64 – a score not equalled for another quarter of a century. After three more rounds of tense competition Demaret beat Mangrum for the title by four strokes, 283 to 287. Demaret had been a nightclub singer until he decided to play golf professionally. In 1940 he won six tournaments in succes-

Left *The crowd rises! Arnold Palmer, their favourite, has won his fourth Masters title in seven years and by a margin of six strokes. The year is 1964 – and the great man is never to win another Major.*

Opposite page, below *Amateur Billy Joe Patton receives his cup from Bobby Jones as 1954 lowest amateur. He very nearly won: with six holes to play he led Ben Hogan (centre) by one and Sam Snead (in hat) by three. But then he wrecked his card with a seven. Hogan and Snead tied and Sam went on to win by a shot.*

Below *Charles Coody plays a fairway shot on his way to victory in the 1971 Masters. He beat Jack Nicklaus and Johnny Miller by two shots.*

Seve Ballesteros playing up to the 13th green in 1983, when he won by four shots.

Below *Ben Crenshaw sinks another long putt on his way to his first victory in a major in 1984. He won by two shots from Tom Watson.*

sion, including the Masters; and he was to become the first golfer to win three times at Augusta (1940, 1947, 1950).

Nineteen forty-one was Craig Wood's year. Caught by Byron Nelson in the final round he finished the second nine in 34 and won by three strokes. The next year saw the first 18-hole play-off. This time Nelson gained five shots on his fellow Texan, the great Ben Hogan, in the space of 11 holes in spite of Hogan playing the holes excellently in one-under par.

The postwar giants

In 1947, when Jimmy Demaret won for the second time, Gene Sarazen and George Fazio, who were off first in the final round, completed the course in three minutes under two hours. They knew they were not going to win, but they played not only fast but well; Sarazen came in with a 70. In 1948 Claude Harmon won by five shots and had a record-equalling total of 279 – and he was only an occasional tour player.

The Masters often brings out the best in the best. In 1949 there were gale-force winds which lasted for two days and sent most scores into the 80s. When the winds abated Sam Snead shot 67, 67 to win with a respectable 282, making eight birdies in the final round. His rival Ben Hogan won his first Masters in 1951 with a final round of 68 and a total of 280. Then in the next year the gales blew again, but in the final two days rather than in the first. Only one player broke 70 on the final day, Jack Burke. But Sam Snead, thanks mainly to a second round 67 and some steady play thereafter, beat Burke by four strokes in spite of a finishing 72.

In 1953 Ben Hogan was unbeatable. Over the last three rounds he shot 69, 66, 69 to finish with a record 274 and win by five shots. (He then went on to win the U.S. Open and the Open.) He believed then, and he believes now, that his Masters win that year produced his best play ever.

The following year a remarkable amateur, Billy Joe Patton, very nearly won the Masters, with Snead and Hogan trailing. He led after to rounds, dropped back in the third, but in the fourth had a hole-in-one at the 190-yard 6th and shot into the lead again. But Bob Jones' second nine defeated him. Trying to protect his

lead, he took seven on the 13th and six on the 15th (both par-5 holes), leaving Snead to win by one shot from Hogan.

Palmer, Player and Nicklaus

Art Wall had five birdies in the last six holes in 1959. Naturally he won – but only after Arnold Palmer hit a 7-iron tee shot into the creek at the 12th. Palmer had had his first Masters win in 1958 after making an eagle at the 13th. In 1960 he led the field in every round; but he had slipped behind Ken Venturi in the final round and won – in typically Palmer-esque style – by getting birdies on both the 17th and 18th. That year saw the fast-round record of Sarazen and Fazio beaten. George Beyer, the big hitter, and Jack Fleck, surprise conqueror of Hogan in the 1955 U.S. Open play-off, got around the course in 1 hour 52 minutes.

The first overseas winner of the Masters arrived in 1961 – Gary Player. He won by managing a par four on the 18th after bunkering his approach, while Arnold Palmer, who found himself in the same bunker, took six. But the true surprise of the tournament that year was Charlie Coe, who produced a record score for an amateur and finished only one shot behind Player.

The next five years were dominated by the Big Three of the period – Palmer, Jack Nicklaus and Player. Palmer beat Player in a three-man play-off in 1962; Nicklaus won for the first time in 1963; and Palmer won his fourth and final Masters title by six strokes over Nicklaus in 1964. Nicklaus lowered the record to 271 (17 under par) in 1965, when Palmer and Player tied for second place nine shots adrift. The following year Nicklaus became the first champion to defend the title successfully – but with a near-record *high* score of 288. Again there was a three-man play-off, this time between Nicklaus, Gay Brewer and Tommy Jacobs. Brewer was rewarded with a win the following year by one stroke over Bobby Nichols.

Golf, like life, is not fair. (Only the golf course is fair.) And in 1968 came the saddest conclusion in Masters history. The popular Argentinian Roberto de Vicenzo – a man who truly embodied Jones's ideal of golfing chivalry – started his final round by playing the first three holes in four-under par, holing a 9-iron for

West Germany's Bernhard Langer plays out of the sand on the 72nd hole of the 1985 Masters to score a second 68 and take the title by two shots from Curtis Strange, Seve Ballesteros and Ray Floyd.

Jack Nicklaus put in a Palmeresque charge up the last nine holes of the 1986 Masters, making magic with his outsize putter. It had looked as though either Tom Kite or Greg Norman must win. But Greg faltered at the very end, while Jack surged through with a superb round of 65 to take his sixth Masters and become at 46 the oldest winner.

Opposite below *Lyle's putt for a birdie and the 1988 title is just about to drop.*

an eagle at the 1st. He continued to play magical golf and finished the round with a 65, which theoretically tied him with Bob Goalby and should have led to a play-off. Unfortunately, his playing partner had marked him down for a four at the 17th when, as everyone watching on television knew, he had actually made a birdie three. In his excitement de Vicenzo did not notice and signed the card as it was. His score now *had* to be entered as a 66, and so Goalby had won. There was a great deal of heart-searching about this. The committee even asked Jones to arbitrate. But Jones knew the decision was not in his hands: he could 'correct' de Vicenzo's score only by flouting one of the rules of golf – and to him such an action was unthinkable. Roberto de Vicenzo accepted the ruling with grace and dignity. It was, incidentally, his 45th birthday.

Jack Nicklaus equalled Arnold Palmer's record of four championships in 1972.

Next year, when Tommy Aaron won, Peter Oosterhuis of Great Britain, a 24-year-old, led after three rounds; but once again the final nine holes proved just too much of a test and he finished equal third.

Gary Player won his second title in 1974 and Nicklaus his fifth (after brilliantly sustained challenges by Johnny Miller and Tom Weiskopf) the following year; and then in 1976 Ray Floyd set new aggregate records for the first two rounds (65, 66) and first three, and finally equalled Nicklaus's record total of 271.

The following year is significant in marking Tom Watson's breakthrough to victory in a major American championship – his last-round 67, including a crucial birdie three on the 17th, edging out Nicklaus.

Player won his third green jacket in 1978, when he was 42 years old. He started the final round seven shots behind Hubert Green but scored seven birdies over the final 10 holes and posted a winner's record final round of 64. The 'Eighties opened with Severiano Ballesteros taking his second major championship at the age of 23. After three superlative rounds (66, 69, 68) and a brilliant first half on day four, he stood at 16 under par – but the relentless challenge on the back nine nearly undid him. He three-putted the 10th, suffered a double bogey on the 12th and took six on the 13th. Then he steadied himself, played the last five holes in one under par and finished as the youngest-ever winner – and the first European Master. He won again in 1983, by four shots, and this time his brilliance on the first nine won him the title. He opened his final round with two birdies and an eagle in the first four holes.

The following year saw a hugely popular victory when Ben Crenshaw, seemingly destined never to win a major (he had been second in the Masters three times in eight years), kept his nerve and let his magical putter do its work.

Now the foreign challenge was strengthening. In 1985 Bernhard Langer of West Germany won the green jacket. Curtis Strange had overtaken him with nine holes to play but that second nine, and specifically Rae's Creek, again took its toll. Langer finished steadily with a 68 to win. Next year it looked as though there would be another European victory: coming to the par-5 15th Ballesteros was nine

under and leading by two. He had hit the perfect drive and waited 210 yards out for Nicklaus and Watson to clear the green. He looked certain of at least a birdie-four. Astonishingly, he fluffed a 4-iron and dumped the ball in the pond before the green. Nicklaus meanwhile had eagled the hole. He played the famous last nine with six birdies, one eagle, one par and one bogey – sinking putts from all distances – to finish with 65 and win his historic sixth Masters at the age of 46.

Next year Ballesteros was in a three-man play-off with Greg Norman of Australia and local hero Larry Mize. Ballesteros dropped out on the first extra hole (the 10th), three-putting – then, on the next, Mize chipped into the hole from 40 yards to defeat Norman.

True grit from Lyle

The Masters rarely lets the fans down in either excitement or the sheer quality of

play shown by the winner at the crunch, and 1988 was no exception. Scotland's Sandy Lyle began the last round two shots clear of Ben Crenshaw (his partner on the final day) and Mark Calcavecchia. After the first nine holes it seemed clear that

Above *Sandy Lyle's Masters-winning 7-iron bunker shot on the 72nd hole, 1988, which finished 10 feet from the flag.*

victory lay between Lyle and Cal-cavecchia, both of whom are brave shot-makers who dislike playing defensively. For Lyle the crisis and, seemingly, disaster, came at the short 12th when, going for the flag, he saw his tee shot hit the right front of the green and spin back into Rae's Creek; he had to be satisfied with a double-bogey five. Obviously upset by this reverse, Lyle failed to pick up shots on either of the two remaining long holes (13th and 15th), and stood on the tee of the short 16th, with its sloping, horrendously slick green, one down to Calcavecchia. And it was here that he retrieved one of his dropped shots, unerringly sinking a 12-foot, curling, downhill putt for a birdie.

Lyle came to the 405-yard 18th level with Calcavecchia, who was playing ahead of him and who now safely carded a par four. The American had sustained a relentless challenge right to the end, and when Lyle put his 1-iron tee shot into the bunker on the left of the fairway, Calcavecchia must have been convinced that victory was his. Lyle was some 140 yards from the hole, the ball in a reasonable lie but within three feet of the lip of the bunker. Taking his 7-iron, Lyle played what Herbert Warren Wind, the *New*

Nick Faldo of England wins the 1989 Masters in a play-off with Scott Hoch. This is the 11th hole and Faldo sinks a 25ft birdie putt in the gloom to win the hole and the tournament.

Yorker's distinguished golf correspondent, called 'the greatest bunker shot in the history of the game'. It soared over the bunker fronting the green, landed about 20 feet past the pin, then spun back down the slope to within 10 feet of the hole. Lyle wasted little time on the putt, and his ball dropped into the middle of the cup for a birdie three and victory.

Bob Jones conceived the Masters as a tournament that would not only bring out the best in the world's greatest golfers but would be played in a spirit of chivalry and high sportsmanship. Nothing better exemplified this spirit than the grace with which Calcavecchia acknowledged Lyle's achievement in snatching the title from under his very nose. And Ben Crenshaw, who has steeped himself in the game's history, spoke for many of the golfing fraternity around the world when remarking on how pleased Bobby Jones – a Freeman of St Andrews and a folk hero to countless thousands of Scotsmen – would have been that a Scot had at last earned the right to wear the Green Jacket.

Britain broke through again in 1989 when Nick Faldo, having endured a disastrous, rain-interrupted third round, changed putters and shot a superlative seven-under-par 65 in the fourth. One by

• U.S. MASTERS TOURNAMENT •

ALWAYS PLAYED AT AUGUSTA NATIONAL

YEAR	WINNER	SCORE
1934	Horton Smith	284
1935	Gene Sarazen	282
1936	Horton Smith	285
1937	Byron Nelson	283
1938	Henry Picard	285
1939	Ralph Guldahl	279
1940	Jimmy Demaret	280
1941	Craig Wood	280
1942	Byron Nelson	280
1943–5 No Tournament		
1946	Herman Keiser	282
1947	Jimmy Demaret	281
1948	Claude Harmon	279
1949	Sam Snead	282
1950	Jimmy Demaret	283
1951	Ben Hogan	280
1952	Sam Snead	286
1953	Ben Hogan	274
1954	Sam Snead	289
1955	Cary Middlecoff	279
1956	Jack Burke Jr.	289
1957	Doug Ford	282
1958	Arnold Palmer	284
1959	Art Wall Jr.	284
1960	Arnold Palmer	282
1961	Gary Player	280
1962	Arnold Palmer	280

YEAR	WINNER	SCORE
1963	Jack Nicklaus	286
1964	Arnold Palmer	276
1965	Jack Nicklaus	271
1966	Jack Nicklaus	288
1967	Gay Brewer	280
1968	Bob Goalby	277
1969	George Archer	281
1970	Billy Casper	279
1971	Charles Coody	279
1972	Jack Nicklaus	286
1973	Tommy Aaron	283
1974	Gary Player	278
1975	Jack Nicklaus	276
1976	Ray Floyd	271
1977	Tom Watson	276
1978	Gary Player	277
1979	Fuzzy Zoeller	280
1980	Seve Ballesteros	275
1981	Tom Watson	280
1982	Craig Stadler	284
1983	Seve Ballesteros	280
1984	Ben Crenshaw	277
1985	Bernhard Langer	282
1986	Jack Nicklaus	279
1987	Larry Mize	285
1988	Sandy Lyle	281
1989	Nick Faldo	283

one his main rivals fell away: Seve Ballesteros, who had taken the first half apart in 31 shots and looked every inch the champion, unaccountably cooled off on the back nine; Greg Norman once again contrived to bungle the 18th with a poor approach and a worse pitch; Ben Crenshaw hit his approach to the 18th into the bunker fronting of the green. Scott Hoch, however, kept his game together, surviving numerous crises over the last three holes to force a play-off in swiftly gathering darkness.

They began at the downhill, par-4 10th hole, where Faldo played a poor greenside bunker shot, and Hoch seemed certain to win. But he dwelt fatally long over a curly 2-foot putt. At the next hole, the 11th, Faldo fired a wonderfully brave 3-iron approach into the green (Hoch landing in Larry Mize country to the right), then sank a 25-foot putt to take the title in the grand manner. It was the fifth time in 10 years that the Masters had been won by a European.

MOST WINS
6: Jack Nicklaus

OLDEST WINNER
Jack Nicklaus at 46 (1986)

YOUNGEST WINNER
Severiano Ballesteros at 23 and four days (1980); Jack Nicklaus was also 23 (1963) but was older by two months

LOWEST WINNING SCORE
271: by Jack Nicklaus (1965) and Raymond Floyd (1976)

FIRST OVERSEAS WINNER
Gary Player (1961)

MOST SECOND PLACE FINISHES
4: Ben Hogan, Tom Weiskopf, Jack Nicklaus

THE TEAM MATCHES

The Ryder Cup

The greatest of all professional team matches in golf, the Ryder Cup was dominated by the Americans for much of its first 50 years. Today the strength of the game in Europe has restored the prestige and excitement of this great event. . . .

Samuel Ryder made his fortune selling flower-seeds in penny packets in the days when a penny was really worth something. In the 1920s he decided to take up golf and hired England's top professional, Abe Mitchell, as his private tutor. So it came about that in the first week of June 1926 Ryder attended a golf match between the British and United States Professional Golfers' Associations at Wentworth, Surrey, in which Mitchell played a prominent part. Ryder was entranced by what he saw.

The match was rather one-sided, the British team winning by 13½ matches to 1½, but the idea of national team golf at matchplay over the finest courses on each side of the Atlantic seemed to Sam Ryder to contain the seeds of greatness. He

decided to donate a trophy – a magnificent trophy of solid gold – to be competed for by the professionals of the two nations every other year. And then the Ryder Cup was launched.

The following year, 1927, the first British team sailed for America aboard the luxury liner *Aquitania* to compete at Worcester, Massachusetts. Sadly Abe Mitchell, appointed captain, was taken ill with appendicitis and could not sail with the team. At Wentworth he had beaten U.S. Open Champion Jim Barnes 8-and-7 and partnered by George Duncan, Scotland's best player, had defeated Barnes and the great Walter Hagen 8-and-7. Now at Worcester the British were to meet the first of many, many reverses.

The United States won 9½ to 2½. In these early days all matches were over 36

Opposite page *The U.S. team, Worcester, Mass., 1927. Left to right: Mehlhorn, Espinosa, Sarazen, Golden, Hagen (capt), Diegel, Farrell, Turnesa and Watrous.*

Left *Ted Ray, Great Britain's non-playing captain, congratulates the American team on their victory in 1927.*

Below *Moortown 1929: George Duncan (right) in a filmed interview with Sam Ryder and Walter Hagen.*

Bottom *The British team thrashed at Scioto, Ohio, in 1931.*

holes, with four foursomes (four players, two balls) on the first day and eight singles the next. This format was not changed until 1961, when the length of the matches was reduced to 18 holes. Fourball matches were introduced in 1973.

At Moortown, Leeds, in 1929 the British took their expected revenge 7–5. Few in England imagined that in the next 20 years the United States would win eight times or that in the three decades that followed Great Britain and Ireland would win only once. The slow but dramatic improvement that was to come to American golf was not foreseen and for a long time never understood.

At Moortown George Duncan, the mercurial Scot, beat the equally mercurial Walter Hagen 10-and-8 – the largest margin ever achieved by anyone in Ryder Cup matches. Archie Compston defeated Gene Sarazen 6-and-4. And the young Henry Cotton beat Al Watrous 4-and-3. The concensus seemed to be that you won at home, but lost abroad. It was understandable.

In 1931 at Scioto, Ohio, the Americans won easily once again, 9–3. Walter Hagen beat Charlie Whitcombe 4-and-3 while Densmore Shute thrashed Bert Hodson 8-and-6. But the temperature during this match reached 100°F, so the British felt they had a reasonable excuse – 'In this weather golf is not a game: it's a form of torture,' their manager remarked.

What was not then appreciated was that golf in the United States was changing radically. The steel shaft had become

Above *U.S. Open champion Ralph Guldahl driving in his 8-and-7 defeat of Alf Padgham in the 1937 match at Southport & Ainsdale.*

Below, left *Byron Nelson, left, and Henry Picard, Ryder Cup rookies, at the 1937 match at Southport.*

Below, right *Newcomer Sam Snead (left) and Ryder Cup ever-present Horton Smith at Southport.*

and heathland courses, British golfers tended to play the 'bump-and-run' game. But Americans were learning to play target golf. It all made a difference.

The extent of that difference was not immediately obvious. In 1933 at Southport and Ainsdale Great Britain won again, although only narrowly (6½ to 5½): Abe Mitchell beat Olin Dutra 9-and-8; Percy Alliss beat Paul Runyan 2-and-1; Arthur Havers beat Leo Diegel – he of the arms-akimbo putting style – 4-and-3. In the foursomes Alliss and Whitcome halved with Hagen and Sarazen. And the match reached a thrilling climax when Denny Shute missed his putt on the 18th but Syd Easterbrook sank his to win the match and the Cup. But an awful long time was to pass before Britain tasted victory again.

At Southport the great J. H. Taylor was non-playing Captain and he had had his men out running on the sands every morning from 6.30 to 7am. But no amount of physical exercise would have availed in 1935 at Ridgewood, New Jersey, where the Americans gave the British team a severe drubbing. Walter Hagen was the United States captain for the fifth time and he and Gene Sarazen beat Alf Perry and John Busson 7-and-6 in the morning foursomes; Paul Runyan and Horton Smith were even more merciless to Bill Cox and Eric Jarman, beating them 9-and-8. Only Percy Alliss managed to win his

standard. The 1.68 in. ball had been made mandatory. Courses were designed differently, with less rough in front of the tees and more in front of the greens. The weather, somewhere in the United States, was always warm. And not only were Americans beginning to play a different game but they now had more good players to choose from and these good players played many more competitions than British pros. Even American college golfers played more tournaments than most British pros.

With the smaller ball, often in cold weather – the optimum temperature for a golf ball is said to be 72°F – and on links

match in the singles. Possibly the British team missed the inspiration of Henry Cotton. At this time he was pro at the royal Belgian Waterloo Club and under the strict terms of the trust deed setting up the Cup was ineligible for selection. (Later he was to miss another match because of a disagreement with the PGA.)

Cotton was present in 1937 at Southport and Ainsdale, however, and won his single 5-and-3. But Dai Rees was the only other British singles winner, beating the great Byron Nelson 3-and-1. Instead of achieving the expected victory Great Britain went down by 8 to 4.

Post-war U.S. domination

War clouds were gathering in 1939 and although the Americans picked a team for the Cup no match was played. By the end of 1941 the United States was in the war too and all such engagements were put aside until the wars in Europe and in the Far East were over.

When the Ryder Cup was played for once again, in 1947 at Portland, Oregon, conditions on either side of the Atlantic were utterly different. The gap between living standards and between competitive opportunities in Britain and America widened the existing disparities between the two competing teams. The matches would not have been revived, at least for a decade, but for the generosity of a Portland businessman, Robert Hudson, who financed the event.

Ben Hogan and Henry Cotton captained the respective teams. But Cotton and

Arthur Lees went down 10-and-9 in the first foursome to Porky Oliver and Lew Worsham, setting the scene for almost total disaster. Dai Rees and Charlie Whitcombe managed a half in the foursomes with veteran Gene Sarazen and Densmore Shute and Sam King halved with Shute in the singles, otherwise Great Britain lost every match. Sam Snead beating Henry Cotton 5-and-4.

Things looked up at Ganton in 1949, Great Britain won three of the four foursomes and there was optimism in the air. Then in the first singles match Dutch Harrison, playing Max Faulkner, opened with four consecutive birdies and went on to win by 8-and-7. Only Dai Rees and James Adams won their matches and the side went down 7 to 5.

By now, that wasn't a bad beating, even for a home fixture. But in 1951 at Pinehurst, North Carolina, Britain and Ireland

lost heavily once again. The American team was one of the strongest ever, including as it did Ben Hogan, Sam Snead, Jimmy Demaret, Lloyd Mangrum, Jack Burke and Porky Oliver. Arthur Lees was the only British singles winner.

Henry Cotton came in as non-playing Captain in 1953 when the match went to Wentworth and once again there was a very close finish. Everyone in the British team left the course shaking their heads and saying, 'We should have won'. The foursomes had been lost 3–1, but Cotton pepped up his team and the singles began to go Britain's way. Fred Daly of Ireland beat Ted Kroll 9-and-7; Harry Weetman beat Sam Snead on the final green after

Above *The powerful U.S. team at Wentworth, 1953. Left to right, standing: Turnesa, Burkemo, Haas, Douglas, Oliver and Kroll. Seated: Middlecoff, Mangrum (capt) Snead and Burke.*

Right *Bernard Hunt and the agony of the putt that didn't drop. His was the final singles, with Dale Douglas. Had the putt gone in Great Britain would have halved the 1953 match.*

finding himself 4-down with 6 to play; Eric Brown beat Lloyd Mangrum by two holes. It was all going Britain and Ireland's way. Then lack of top-level match practice or just the occasion beat the two youngest members of the side. Peter Alliss who was just off the 18th green in two, would have won with a birdie, could have halved with a par – but took four to get down. Bernard Hunt, also with a chance to clinch the match at that hole, only managed a half. But it was a close-run thing.

Then in the next match, at the Thunderbird Golf and Country club in California, it was the same old story again. Great Britain lost 8 to 4. Only John Jacobs shone: he won both his matches in his only Ryder Cup appearance.

But in 1957 at Lindrick, Yorkshire, came victory – after 34 years. Britain and

Ireland lost the foursomes 3–1. However, captained with flair by Dai Rees and cheered on by a huge crowd, the home team took the singles 6½ to 1½ to win. Eric Brown beat Tommy Bolt 4-and-3; Peter Mills beat Jack Burke 5-and-3; Ken Bousfield beat Lionel Hebert 4-and-3; Dai Rees beat Ed Furgol 7-and-6; Bernard Hunt beat Doug Ford 6-and-5; and Christy O'Connor beat Dow Finsterwald 7-and-6. It was a crushing victory. The only trouble was the partisanship of the large crowd. The famously irascible Tommy Bolt re-marked, 'This isn't golf; it's war'.

Britain and Ireland were never to win the Ryder Cup again. When the Americans were beaten 28 years later it was by a European not a British team, Jack Nicklaus having proposed to Lord Derby, President of the PGA, that the area of selection be widened to save the Cup from fading gradually into oblivion. But even that change did not come for 20 years.

In 1959 at the Eldorado Club in California, GB and I once again lost heavily, 8½ to 3½. Only Eric Brown maintained his record of never suffering defeat in a singles match; he beat Cary Middlecoff 4-and-3. Everyone felt it was time something was done to even things up. And so a complete change of format was decided on. Matches would be over 18 holes instead of 36. And there would be two sets of foursomes on the first day and two sets of singles on the second, bringing more players into the game.

The format was introduced at Royal Lytham and St Anne's in 1961. The Americans won the foursome 6-2 – and foursome golf was a game they never experienced at home – but the 16 singles matches were shared. In this match Arnold Palmer made his first appearance. In the foursome he and Billy Casper beat Dai Rees and Ken Bousfield in the morning and John Panton and Bernard Hunt in the afternoon. Next day in the singles Peter Alliss halved with Palmer in the morning but Tom Haliburton was beaten by him in the afternoon. Dai Rees beat both Jay Hebert and Doug Ford, while Neil Coles halved with Gene Littler in the morning and beat Dow Finsterwald in the afternoon. It certainly wasn't a massacre.

But at Atlanta, Georgia, in 1963 it *was* a massacre. Play was extended to cover three days and fourball golf was intro-

duced. The main aim was to recapture the interest of the American golfing public. This aim was not achieved. And the Americans won by 23 points to 9. The British won only one of the eight fourball matches and only one of the foursomes. In the first group of singles Great Britain and Ireland won four matches and halved one and things seemed to be looking up. But in the afternoon the Americans won every match but one and they halved that one.

Opposite, bottom *Johnny Fallon of Great Britain drives the first ball of the match at Thunderbird, in the Californian desert, in 1955. It was a close-run thing although the final team score was 8 to 4 in America's favour. Welshman Dai Rees was British captain; John Jacobs, now a famous coach, won both his matches.*

Left *Victory at last! Max Faulkner congratulates Dai Rees (right) at Lindrick in 1957: Great Britain had won the cup for the first time for 34 years, 7½ to 4½.*

Below *Great Britain's successful 1957 Ryder Cup team. Left to right, standing: Harry Bradshaw, Peter Mills, Peter Alliss, Bernard Hunt, Harry Weetman. Seated: Max Faulkner, Eric Brown, Dai Rees (capt), Ken Bousfield and Christy O'Connor.*

Right *Two sportsmen shake hands: Jack Nicklaus congratulates Tony Jacklin after losing to him by 4-and-3 in the first singles match at Birkdale in 1969. In the afternoon Nicklaus was to concede a 2½ ft putt to Jacklin which tied the whole match.*

Below *Arnold Palmer encourages Jack Nicklaus at Muirfield in the 1973 match, when they beat Maurice Bembridge and Eddie Polland 6-and-5 in the foursomes.*

The half was achieved by Peter Alliss, playing Tony Lema. Alliss had the distinction of beating Arnold Palmer by one hole in the morning. But overall it was a far from distinguished performance by the team as a whole.

At Royal Birkdale in 1965 the British side put up a much better performance but they still lost 19½ to 12½. Peter Alliss, playing majestic golf, won both his singles, the first against Billy Casper in the morning and the second against Ken Venturi in the afternoon. In the first foursomes Dave Thomas and George Will beat Arnold Palmer and Dave Marr 6-and-5; and Alliss and Christy O'Connor beat Ken Venturi and Don January 5-and-4. In the afternoon the same two beat Casper and Gene Littler. Next day in the fourballs they lost one and won one, their opponents on each occasion being Palmer and Marr. Neil Coles beat Billy Casper in the afternoon singles, and Lionel Platts beat Tommy Jacobs; but otherwise there was little else to cheer about. It wasn't terribly bad: it simply wasn't good enough.

The British side went to Houston, Texas, in 1967 in high hopes of achieving something in America at last. Once again, however, those hopes were to be dashed and mercilessly so. The end result was the United states 23½ and GB and I 8½. But there was light at the end of the fairway – Tony Jacklin and Neil Coles beat Doug Sanders and Gay Brewer in the morning foursomes, then Jacklin and Dave Thomas beat Gene Littler and Al Geiberger in the afternoon. Next day they lost to the same pair in the morning fourballs but halved in the afternoon ones.

In the singles Arnold Palmer beat Jacklin in the morning and Brian Huggett in the afternoon. For Great Britain and Ireland Neil Coles beat Doug Sanders twice and Huggett beat Julius Boros once so it was by no means a whitewash. But it was very disappointing. And the perplexing question was, why? Why couldn't British golfers distinguish themselves in America?

Part of the answer was given during the next Cup match, although in England not in America. Tony Jacklin had won the Open two months earlier, now he and Peter Townsend beat Dave Hill and Tommy Aaron in the morning foursomes and Billy Casper and Frank Bear in the afternoon. In the fourballs Jacklin and Neil Coles beat Jack Nicklaus and Dan Sikes in the morning and halved with Lee Trevino and Miller Barber in the afternoon. Then in the singles Tony Jacklin beat Nicklaus 4-and-3 in the morning and halved with him in the final match of the afternoon.

The fact was that Tony Jacklin had not only been toughened by his experience in the USA – he had won the Jacksonville Open – but he had learned how to play the Americans at their own game. He had learned to use his legs. And he had learned target golf. With just one more Jacklin in the team Great Britain and Ireland would have won. As it was, the match became famous for Jack Nicklaus's gesture in conceding Jacklin's final putt (a 2½- to 3-footer) to halve not only their match but the Ryder Cup match as a whole – a gesture wholly alien to Nicklaus's style on the U.S. tour, but wonderfully in keeping with Sam Ryder's ambitions for his competition.

Their faith in themselves restored, the British did much better in 1971 at St Louis, Missouri, in spite of the searing heat. They managed only 1½ points in the fourballs but won 3½ in the foursomes and looked like making a real fight of it. Tony Jacklin and Brian Huggett beat Jack Nicklaus and Dave Stockton in the foursomes. They halved with Lee Trevino and Mason Rudolph in the afternoon. On the final morning Jacklin lost to Lee Trevino on the 18th, but Bernard Gallacher halved with Stockton, while Brian Barnes beat Rudolph and Peter Oosterhuis beat Gene Littler 4-and-3. It looked good. But in the afternoon singles only Oosterhuis and Neil Coles managed to win and the side went down 18½ to 13½.

Neil Coles, who has an aversion to flying, took ship across the Atlantic and drove half way across the United States to get to St Louis. There was also an unusual incident involving Arnold Palmer, Gardner Dickinson, Peter Oosterhuis and Bernard Gallacher. On one hole, Gallacher's caddie, a local American, asked Palmer's caddie in a whisper what club his man had hit. Dickinson heard this and complained to the referee who awarded the Americans the hole. The British pair would otherwise almost certainly have won that hole, though nobody could claim it made much difference to the match, Palmer and his partner winning 5-and-4. But the incident rather soured the atmosphere.

At Muirfield in 1973 there was a very similar result. The British team was doing well when, very unfortunately, Bernard Gallacher was taken ill and the pairings chosen by captain Bernard Hunt were thrown into disarray. Brian Barnes and Gallacher had beaten Lee Trevino and

Billy Casper in the foursomes and then Jack Nicklaus and Tom Weiskopf in the fourballs; Jacklin and Oosterhuis had beaten Tom Weiskopf and Casper in the foursomes and Gay Brewer and Casper in the fourballs. Gallacher soldiered on but lost both his singles. Jacklin won one and lost one, as did Barnes. It was an honourable defeat.

Two years later at Laurel Valley, Pennsylvania (not far from Arnold Palmer's home in Latrobe), the Americans once again gave the British side a drubbing. They won by 21 points to 11. A feature of the match was that big Brian Barnes beat Jack Nicklaus twice in one day, 4-and-2 in the morning and 2-and-1 in the afternoon. Jacklin, who in the fourballs teamed with Peter Oosterhuis had beaten Billy Casper and Ray Floyd, and in the afternoon had halved with Casper and Johnny Miller, lost both his singles. Only Peter Oosterhuis joined Barnes as a double winner.

The feeling grew that Britain would never win, certainly not on American soil. It seemed clear that the Americans as a whole were not only technically superior to the British but that, at the crunch, their temperaments, honed in the tough, hugely competitive school of the U.S. tour, were much more resilient than those of the British. There was some talk of scrapping the biennial matches. It was the low point in the history of the Ryder Cup.

Nineteen seventy-seven was a year of

Great things were expected of the Scots partnership of pipe-smoking Brian Barnes and Bernard Gallacher at Laurel Valley, Pennsylvania in 1975. But they, like every other British pairing, lost their foursomes in the morning to set up an American victory again, this time by 21 to 11. Barnes, however, had the glory of beating Jack Nicklaus twice in one day!

singles altogether. As one of the team remarked, 'There may be 10 better players in Britain than Tony Jacklin, but I doubt it'. However, more importantly for the future, this match at Royal Lytham saw the arrival on the scene of a new talent: Nick Faldo (in partnership with Peter Oosterhuis) beat Ray Floyd and Lou Graham in the foursomes and then Nicklaus and Ray Floyd in the fourballs; and then in the singles he beat Tom Watson (who had recently, and majestically, won the Open at Turnberry) by one hole.

Europe v. United States

The 1977 contest proved to be the end of an era. At Jack Nicklaus's suggestion, the terms of the trust setting up the competition were changed to admit continental Europeans to the formerly British and Irish team. It had become obvious that Britain and Ireland alone were unlikely ever again to muster the strength in depth that the United States could command. So in 1979 for the first time, at the Greenbrier Club (Sam Snead's country) in West Virginia, two Spanish players won their spurs – Antonio Garrido and Severiano Ballesteros.

Although the Americans won again, this – everyone agreed – was much more like it. Once again, however, the format was changed. The first two days were divided between foursomes and fourballs, then on the third day there were 12 singles. The first day seemed pretty disastrous for Europe, but on the second Tony Jacklin and Sandy Lyle beat Lee Elder and John Mahaffey (Elder being the first black golfer to take part in the Ryder Cup); Nick Faldo and Peter Oosterhuis beat Andy Bean and Tom Kite 6-and-5; and Bernard Gallacher and Brian Barnes beat Fuzzy Zoeller and Mark Hayes 2-and-1. In the afternoon fourballs Gallacher and Brian Barnes beat Zoeller and Lee Trevino, while Faldo and Oosterhuis repeated their success over Elder and Hayes.

Although the Europeans lost the singles heavily on points – 8½ to 3½ – most of the matches went to the final green and Faldo, Ken Brown and Gallacher all won their games. When Peter Oosterhuis lost to Hubert Green it was his first defeat in eight games.

In 1981 the West German Bernhard Langer appeared in the European side for

Above *Jacklin and Lyle congratulate each other after their match with Trevino and Morgan at the Greenbrier Club, White Sulphur Springs, in 1979. But the Americans won once more, even though Europeans were brought into the visiting side for the first time. For the United States Larry Nelson won five matches out of five.*

Right *Peter Oosterhuis, seen here with Nick Faldo at Walton Heath in 1981, had one of the best British Ryder Cup records of all: he played 28 matches, won 14 and lost 11. At Walton Heath America's Larry Nelson kept his perfect record; this time he won four out of four.*

anti-climax. It was decided to play only 18 holes a day, an experiment which proved unpopular with the players. Brian Huggett, the captain, had a public argument with Tony Jacklin after the latter, in company with Eamonn Darcy, had lost to Dave Hill and Dave Stockton 5-and-3 – and then left Jacklin out of the final day's

the first time and after the first day Europe was actually leading. This match was held at Walton Heath, Surrey, the first time it had come to the south of England for nearly 30 years.

The second and third days were disappointing for the crowds as well as for the players. In the foursomes and fourballs only Bernhard Langer and Manuel Pinero managed a win. Finally in the singles Sam Torrance, Sandy Lyle, Mark James, Des Smyth, José-Maria Canizares, Eamonn Darcy and Peter Oosterhuis all lost their matches. Only two of the younger players won – Nick Faldo (fashioning a superb Cup record) and Howard Clark.

Part of the trouble, perhaps pretty certainly, was that both Seve Ballesteros and Tony Jacklin were left out of the team. Ballesteros had been involved in an argument with the British PGA over appearance money; Jacklin was told he was too old (he was 37).

For the Americans Larry Nelson maintained his extraordinary record, four wins out of four matches making his Ryder Cup total nine wins out of nine. Lee Trevino also scored four wins. Tom Kite was 10-under par when he beat Sandy Lyle (who had scored eight birdies!) 3-and-2 in one of the greatest matches in Cup history.

Turn of the Tide

Going to Palm Beach Gardens, Florida, for the 1983 Ryder Cup Tony Jacklin was made Captain for the first time; his oppo-

site number was Jack Nicklaus. Jacklin, U.S. Open winner in 1970, had more experience of American golf than any other British player. He had learned from that experience much about golf psychology. He agreed to lead the team only if they all travelled first-class and were treated like VIPs. He also felt he had developed a special relationship with Jack Nicklaus following the match at Birkdale in 1969 when Nicklaus had conceded him the final putt and the two teams tied. This, he felt, was the spirit in which these matches should be played. Jacklin arranged for each team member of his team to receive engraved Waterford crystal tankards to mark the occasion. When he told Nicklaus of his intentions the American captain said he would provide his team members with special golf-club heads made of Tiffany glass.

One consequence of all this was that a new and better spirit permeated the Ryder Cup matches. Jacklin's pairings seemed inspired. Ballesteros initially felt uncomfortable playing with young Paul Way; he said he felt like a father-figure. 'Exactly', said Jacklin, 'that's why I paired you with him'. Bernhard Langer felt he was off-form and should be left out. Jacklin put him with Nick Faldo to steady him and they won three out of four matches. Jack Nicklaus rang the changes with his pairings with equal success. Everything eventually depended on the singles.

Ballesteros halved with Fuzzy Zoeller; Faldo beat Jay Haas; Langer beat Gil Morgan. Then Gordon Brand lost to Bob Gilder, Sandy Lyle to Ben Crenshaw, Brian Waites to Calvin Peete. But young Paul Way beat Curtis Strange, and Sam Torrance halved with Tom Kite. Then Craig Stadler beat Ian Woosnam, and José-Maria Canizares had to surrender half a point to a fighting Lanny Wadkins, who on the final hole hit a 70-yard wedge to 12 inches from the pin. Ken Brown took Ray Floyd 4-and-3. In mounting excitement Tom Watson was victorious over Bernard Gallacher, who missed a shortish putt on the 17th. The result: USA 14½, Europe 13½ – and a new confidence suddenly began to surge through European golf as a whole.

The Europeans started badly in the 1985 event at The Belfry. They lost the morning foursomes 3–1. Nick Faldo,

Above *Paul Way was one of the successful youngsters in the European side at Palm Beach Gardens, Florida. Europe came within one point of victory. The tide was turning.*

Left *Bernhard Langer of West Germany driving at the Belfry in the famous match in 1985 when Europe won for the first time since 1957. Europe won 7 of the final 12 singles and halved one.*

paired again with Bernhard Langer, went straight to Jacklin after their defeat by Calvin Peete and Tom Kite and told him that he (Faldo) was not playing well and suggesting Sandy Lyle should take his place. By the end of the second day things has been evened up: all was going to depend on the results in the 12 singles.

The first match could prove crucial. Manuel Pinero, who seemed to sense his hour had come, begged Jacklin to let him open, confident that he would be drawn against Lanny Wadkins – himself a superbly pugnacious matchplay golfer. So it proved – and an inspired Pinero closed out Wadkins 3-and-1 in a marvellous contest. Ian Woosnam then lost to Craig Stadler, but Paul Way beat Ray Floyd, and Ballesteros halved with Tom Kite after being three down. Excitement mounted. Then Sandy Lyle beat Peter Jacobsen, Langer beat Hal Sutton and Sam Torrance beat Andy North with a long, curling birdie putt on the final green. The Cup was won!

The result of that match was not reflected just in the scoreline – Europe 16½, USA 11½ – but in the confidence and enthusiasm with which the next team travelled to Jack Nicklaus's course at

Top *Manuel Pinero set the scene for Europe in the singles at the Belfry in 1985 by beating Lanny Wadkins, seen here congratulating the Spaniard, who won 3-and-1.*

Above *The 10th hole at the Belfry. As it measures only 275 yards, most of the pros can drive the green if they wish to, but few attempt it with any certainty in their hearts.*

Right *Sam Torrance approaches the 18th at the Belfry in 1985, about to make the putt that won the Ryder Cup. But it was his drive on this hole that really set up the victory – very long, very safe and with the right touch of draw to set him up for a birdie.*

Muirfield Village, Ohio, in 1987. The confidence may have received a shock when Europe went behind in all the morning foursomes, but the enthusiasm shone through as this set of matches was halved, the partnerships of Nick Faldo and Ian Woosnam – the latter hitting tee-shots of such exorbitant length that, even on the long par-4s, he often needed only a wedge for his second shots – and Seve Ballesteros and José-Maria Olazábal both winning their matches. Then in the afternoon Europe won *all* the fourballs to lead 6-2.

On the Saturday morning the United Stated won the foursomes 2½ to 1½ and in the afternoon shared the fourballs. There was some extraordinary golf played. America's top pair Tom Kite and Curtis Strange, parred the first five holes – and found themselves five down to Faldo and Woosnam, who reached the turn in 29 and won 5-and-4. In the last fourball Sandy Lyle and Bernhard Langer were involved in a pulsating match with Lanny Wadkins and Larry Nelson. The climax began when Lyle hit a 3-iron some 230 yards to within 20 feet of the 15th hole – then sank the putt for his second eagle of the week. And this on one of the most difficult courses in America! That put the

European pair three up with three to play. Now it was Wadkins' turn. He brilliantly birdied the 16th and 17th, winning both holes. All four hit superlative approach shots to the final green. But Langer, going last, struck a magisterial 8-iron to within 10 inches to clinch it.

On Sunday Europe needed four points to retain the trophy. And they had to fight for them. Howard Clark won. Sam Torrance halved, but heroes Faldo and Woosnam both surprisingly went down by one hole to Mark Calcavecchia and Andy Bean. Ben Crenshaw broke his putter in a fit of pique with it and Eamonn Darcy (who had thrown away a three-hole lead) eventually sank a nasty, curling 5-footer on the 18th to turn the tide. Bernhard Langer then got a half and Europe could not now lose. Appropriately, it was Ballesteros who made sure of victory by beating Curtis Strange more easily than 2-and-1 might suggest. And so Europe had won in the United States at last.

Back at the Belfry in 1989 the match proved to be one of the most enthralling in the Cup's history. On the first morning the Americans started fast, winning two of the foursomes and halving the other two; but Europe fought back after lunch

The long and the short of victory – Nick Faldo and Ian Woosnam at Muirfield Village, Ohio, in 1987, when Europe beat the United States on its home ground for the first time.

Right *Scotland's Sandy Lyle and West Germany's Bernhard Langer plot their way to a last-green victory over Lanny Wadkins and Larry Nelson in the exhilarating final fourball of the 1987 match.*

to take all the fourballs. Next day honours were even, Paul Azinger and Chip Beck defeating Ian Woosnam and Nick Faldo in one of the greatest fourballs in Cup history. As at Muirfield Village the partnership of Severiano Ballesteros and José-Maria Olazábal proved inspired.

On the Sunday morning before the 12 singles, then, Europe led 9–7 – not enough in the opinion of many home supporters. And halfway through the day's play their worst fears seemed about to be realised:

the Americans led in seven matches and were level in all but one of the others. Azinger beat Ballesteros on the 18th; Faldo, Langer and Woosnam would all eventually lose; and Kite wiped out Howard Clark by 8 and 7. Two factors transformed the situation: Olazábal led Europe's foot-soldiers – Mark James, Christy O'Connor, Jr, Ronan Rafferty and José-Maria Canizares – in a final charge; and the Americans developed an obsessive attraction for the water at the 18th.

Near right *Seve Ballesteros and young José-Maria Olazábal made an emotional and fiercely competitive pairing in foursomes and fourballs at Muirfield Village.*

Far right *Ireland's Eamonn Darcy sinks the all-important putt that made European victory a certainty – all of five feet but on a wickedly sloping green on the course Jack Nicklaus designed.*

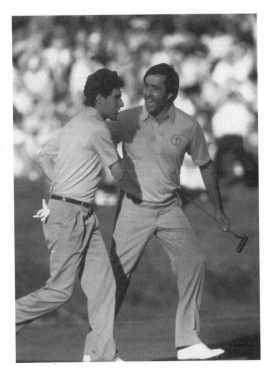

Far left *The finest golf in the 1989 Cup was played by rookies Paul Azinger and Chip Beck in the Saturday fourballs: they were heading for a nett 60 when they beat Nick Faldo and Ian Woosnam at the 17th.*

Near left *Top scorer on either side was José-Maria Olazábal who dropped only half a point in his five matches. Here he's on his way to beating Payne Stewart.*

Below *An Irish apotheosis: Christy O'Connor, Jr offers up silent thanks after beating Fred Couples on the 18th green. He had set up his birdie with a heroic 2-iron to three feet.*

Eventually Europe scraped together the five points needed to tie the match and so retain the Cup. Olazábal was top scorer on both sides, unbeaten on four and a half points; Beck, unflashy but manifestly a player of the highest class, topped the American list with one point less.

MOST APPEARANCES IN THE RYDER CUP
10: Christy O'Connor

YOUNGEST TEAM MEMBER
Nick Faldo: 20 years, 1 month, 28 days

OLDEST TEAM MEMBER
Ted Ray: 50 and 2 months (1927).

MOST WINS FOR BRITAIN AND EUROPE
14: Peter Oosterhuis; Tony Jacklin, Bernard Gallacher and Nick Faldo each had 13 wins up to 1989.

MOST WINS FOR UNITED STATES
22: Arnold Palmer
20: Billy Casper

The Walker Cup

A dress-rehearsal for the Walker Cup took place in 1921 with an informal match at Hoylake.

Below *The United States side. Standing: Francis Ouimet, Frederick Wright, Jesse Guilford, Chick Evans. Seated: J. Wood Platt, William Fownes, Bobby Jones, Paul Hunter.*

Bottom *Great Britain. Standing: Tommy Armour (then a Scottish amateur), Gordon Simpson, Roger Wethered, R.H. de Montmorency. Seated: Ernest Holderness, J.L.C. Jenkins, Cyril Tolley and C.C. Aylmer.*

The oldest of the national team events between British and United States golfers, this is the amateurs' equivalent of the Ryder Cup. It has long been dominated by Americans who, in many cases, have gone on to stardom on the pro tours. . . .

The Walker Cup – the amateurs' Ryder Cup – started almost by accident in a rather haphazard manner. Its roots lie in two matches arranged between the Royal Canadian Golf Association and the USGA in the years immediately after the end of World War I. At the same time the American Bob Gardner reached the final of the British Amateur at Muirfield before losing to Cyril Tolley at the 37th. Then Tolley, Roger Wethered, Lord Charles Hope and Tommy Armour (still a Scot then and an amateur) sailed off to compete in the U.S. Amateur. The idea of possible international team matches was very much in the air. Meanwhile the Executive Committee of the USGA set sail for Scotland to discuss the unification of the Rules of Golf with the Royal and Ancient Golf Club at St Andrews.

The President of the USGA was George Herbert Walker and the net effect of all these developments on him was a proposal for an international amateur team championship. Since the ball had started rolling following the U.S.-Canadian matches he wished it to be open to all countries. And for this purpose he donated an International Challenge Trophy. The newspapers immediately christened it 'the Walker Cup', rather to his annoyance. In 1921 he invited all golfing countries to compete but none accepted. Later that year William Fownes (son of the designer/owner of the great Oakmont championship course) took an unofficial team to Britain which played a British team before the Amateur Championship, and the Americans won 9–3.

This roused the R & A and it announced that it would indeed send a team to compete for the Walker Cup in 1922. Since no other country sent a team the match became a direct confrontation between the British and the Americans. The American team was captained by Fownes and included Bobby Jones, Francis Ouimet, 'Chick' Evans and Jess Sweetser. The British team included Cyril Tolley and Roger Wethered, but the British champion Ernest Holderness was unable to make the trip. Bernard Darwin went with the team as golf correspondent of *The Times* and when the captain Robert Harris fell ill Darwin took his place. He beat the American captain 3-and-1, but the British side went down 4–8. And this was to become a familiar story.

The American sides have always been stronger than the British. Partly this may be because American amateurs, particularly those at universities, play much more competitive golf than the British, many of whom have literally been weekend golfers. For many years there was also a wide gap between the standards of living in the two countries, making golf in the big-time relatively more expensive for the British in an age when amateurs paid their own way. Nine golfers who later

went on to win the United States or the British Open have played for America in the Walker Cup – Francis Ouimet, Bobby Jones, Johnny Goodman (last amateur to win the U.S. Open), Lawson Little, Gene Littler, Ken Venturi, Jack Nicklaus, Bill Rodgers and Jerry Pate. Only one Briton has achieved a similar feat – Sandy Lyle.

The 1923 match at St Andrews was, however, a very close-run thing. The British won three of the four foursomes and on the second day led in most of the

Above *The year is 1924. The U.S. captain, Robert Gardner receives the Walker Cup from Wyant Vanderpeel, president of the USGA. In the centre is the British captain, the big-hitting Cyril Tolley.*

Left *Bobby Jones (right) and Rex Hartley stride up the fairway at Sandwich in the 1930 match. Jones maintained his 100 per cent singles record and in his match with Roger Wethered he won 9-and-8. That year he also won the U.S. and British Amateurs and Opens.*

singles. Indeed at one point the U.S. team was, collectively, 24 holes down. But Francis Ouimet, two down to Roger Wethered with three to play made threes on the 16th and 18th to halve the match. In doing so he holed an 18-foot putt around a partial stymie. In the final singles Dr O. F. Willing of the United States defeated William Murray on the 17th to give the Americans victory. The Chairman of the USGA's international matches committee in his report to headquarters wrote: 'Your committee is of the opinion that international competition in golf has done as much for the development of the game as any other factor.' The matches have always been played in that spirit.

Up until, and including, 1924 the matches had been played annually. But this was placing too much of a financial strain on many of the players, and in future it was decided to play in alternate years, as with the Ryder Cup. In 1926 the match went to St Andrews again and once more there was a narrow victory for the Americans. But Bobby Jones, who never lost a singles match, this time defeated Cyril Tolley 12-and-11 in what should have been a 36-holes match. Jess Sweetser won the Amateur at Muirfield that year and Jones won his first British Open.

Bobby Jones now took over the captaincy and the United States promply won the next two matches by 11 to 1 and 10 to 2. The 1930 match was held at Royal St George's, Sandwich, and Jones himself beat Roger Wethered 9-and-8. The most astonishing win was that of the American Don Moe who was playing Bill Stout. Stout lived up to his name in the first half of the match, going round Sandwich in 68. He then started the second half with three 3s to go 7-up. Moe immediately won seven

holes in a row and got a birdie three on the 36th hole to win the match. He had been round in 67.

After the 1932 match at the Country Club, in the Boston suburb of Brookline, John P. English wrote: 'The biggest dent the British made was by Leonard G. Crawley. He not only won the only point for [his] side ... but his errant shot to the 18th hit the Cup on the fly. The Americans won the dented cup, 8 to 1.'

In 1934 at St Andrews the British side was skippered by the Hon. Michael Scott who at 56 was the oldest player. He had won the British Amateur the year before. Then at Pine Valley, New Jersey, in 1936 the British failed to win a single match.

But golf is a strange game. You never can tell. And in 1938, after the disaster at Pine Valley, Britain won the Walker Cup for the first time. Captain John Beck had the British players out practising at St Andrews and held a series of trials. The tactic paid off. Britain won the foursomes 2½ to 1½. Next day the Americans needed to win five singles: they could only win three of them. St Andrews went wild.

World war now cut short the series. It was not until 1947 that another match was played and then, although it was Britain's turn to go to America, the Americans agreed to return to Britain and St Andrews. They won handily, although they were behind in three of the four foursomes at the half way stage on the first day. Ronnie White was the best of the British players. Then at Winged Foot, New York, in 1949 White won both his singles and his foursomes (partnering Joe Carr), the only points the British side gained. In 1951 at Royal Birkdale, Ronnie White beat Charlie Coe in the singles, Joe Carr beat Frank Stranahan and Alec Kyle beat Willie Turnesa – but still the British lost.

In 1965 there was a tie, the first and only one of the series. The match was at Five Farms, Baltimore. The British held the lead in five matches on the second afternoon but the Americans clawed their way back into the match and Clive Clark was left needing to hole a 30 foot putt to avert another defeat. He made it!

It was not until 1971 that the British won again. Once more the match was at St Andrews. By this time the format had been changed and matches were now over 18 holes with a set of foursomes and a set of singles played on each of the two

dale in 1987 the home side had high hopes. But the United States won the first day's foursomes 4–0 and the singles 5–3 and on the second day won 3–1 and 4½–3½ in the relevant matches. The young Americans, too, were on their way to the professional tour.

In 1989, the GB & I team journeyed to the sweltering heat of Atlanta to do battle at exclusive Peachtree club. They felt a good deal more confident this time, and with Peter McEvoy, Garth McGimpsey, Eoghan O'Connell and the mighty Russell Claydon they lacked little in mental or physical sinew. On the other hand the Americans included the ageless Jay Sigel, the 19-year-old southpaw prodigy Phil Mickelson, and Robert Gamez, the most brilliant player on either team.

At the end of the first day GB & I led by 7½ to 4½, having taken the singles by 5 to 3. When they won the foursomes by 3½ to ½ the following morning it seemed all over bar the shouting. But the Americans came out fighting for the final session of singles – to such effect that in the final match Jim Milligan (who had been blown away 7 and 6 by Gamez the previous day) needed to halve with Sigel but found himself two down with three to play. In an

Above *At Muirfield in 1959 a beefy 19-year-old called Jack Nicklaus joined the American team for the first time. It was perhaps the most powerful amateur team of all time and won easily, 9-3.*

Right *Dr David Marsh on the tee at St Andrews in 1971. It was his 220-yard 3-iron second shot to the 17th that enabled him to go dormie-1 against Bill Hyndman and assured Great Britain and Ireland of victory.*

days. At lunch-time on the second day the British were two points adrift but won six of the afternoon singles to win the Cup. Four matches were won on the 18th and in the other two the 17th was the vital hole, as it so often is at St Andrews. One crucial stroke was Dr David Marsh's superlative 3-iron to the 17th green which made him dormie-1 against Bill Hyndman.

In 1973 at the Country Club, Brookline, the British again did well in the singles but were crushingly defeated in the foursomes and lost 14–10. The familiar story was repeated in the years that followed, although in 1983 at Hoylake the British (and Irish) team were tied 8-all before the final afternoon's singles. And this time they lost those singles 5½–2½.

The matches were getting closer and in 1985, again at Pine Valley, almost 50 years after that first disaster, the two teams ended the first day level. The hosts then won the morning foursomes handsomely, and although Britain and Ireland won the singles 4½ to 3½ it just wasn't good enough to win the Cup.

So when the match came to Sunning-

authentic nail-biter Milligan got a winning birdie with a super chip at the 16th, chipped in for another win at the 17th, and secured a safe half at the 18th before being engulfed by his team-mates.

Top *Last-gasp heroics: Jim Milligan chips in at the 17th at Peachtree to square his match with Jay Sigel. His half at the final hole of the final singles ensured victory in the 1989 match.*

MOST MATCHES PLAYED FOR GREAT BRITAIN AND IRELAND
25: Michael Bonallack

MOST MATCHES PLAYED FOR THE USA
27: Jay Sigel

MOST CONSECUTIVE APPEARANCES (USA)
8: Francis Ouimet

MOST CONSECUTIVE APPEARANCES (GB & I)
9: Joe Carr

BEST PLAYING RECORD
Bobby Jones won all five singles he played in and four out of five foursomes.

Left *British hopes for 1989 had received a tremendous boost with the emergence of Englishman Russell Claydon. He nearly toppled the great Greg Norman in the 1989 Australian Masters, coming home second, ahead of many familiar figures on the pro tour.*

The Curtis Cup

Below *The two golfing sisters who began it all – Margaret and Harriet Curtis. They originally offered to put up a trophy for American and British women golfers in the year 1905.*

Bottom *Jean Donald of Scotland led the British ladies to their first-ever Cup victory at Muirfield in 1952. Only a week before she had won the Scottish Ladies' title next door at Gullane for the third time.*

Another U.S.-British biennial confrontation, this time for lady amateurs. As with the Ryder Cup, long years of American triumphs have been reversed by a generation of British golfers equal to their rivals in skill and competitive steel. . . .

The origins of the Curtis Cup – the 'Woman's Walker Cup' – actually predate not only the Walker but the Ryder and the World cups as well. It was in 1905 that two golfing sisters from the United States, Harriet and Margaret Curtis, came over with several other American woman golfers to compete in the British Women's Amateur at Cromer, Norfolk. The British champion Lottie Dodd arranged an unofficial team game before the championship. Playing in this so delighted the Curtis sisters that they offered to put up a trophy for regular competitions, originally for women golfers 'of many lands.'

Periodic discussions took place over the next couple of decades, but it was not until 1 May 1930, when another unofficial match took place, this time at Sunningdale, that the concept took wings at last. Rather unexpectedly several thousand spectators flocked to the course to see the great match. So the Ladies Golf Union opened an International Match Fund, while in America the USGA agreed to finance an official American team for biennial matches. A silver bowl – the Curtis Cup – was commissioned to a design that had been originally made by the Bostonian silversmith and independence hero Paul Revere. It was inscribed: 'To stimulate friendly rivalry among the women golfers of many lands'.

In 1932 the first match took place at Wentworth, between the United States and Great Britain and Ireland. Joyce

Wethered (Lady Heathcoat-Amory), who was coming to the end of her golfing career, beat her great friend and rival Glenna Collett Vare 6-and-4 in the singles. But Glenna and her partner Mrs Hill had their revenge in the foursomes, beating Wethered and Wanda Morgan by one hole. For the British and Ireland side Enid Wilson and Diana Fishwick also won in the singles but lost in the foursomes, and America was victorious by 5½ to 3½.

After that the event adopted the same basic formula as the Walker Cup. There was a tie in 1936 on the King's Course at Gleneagles, Scotland, but it was not until 1952 at Muirfield that the British ladies team recorded their first win. The irony of the occasion was not lost on the ladies: the Honourable Company of Edinburgh Golfers at Muirfield allows no lady members and provides no facilities for them. The LGU felt it had made a valid point – though the original choice of venue seems curious. The heroines on this occasion were Frances Stephens, Jeanne Bisgood and Elizabeth Price.

At Merion, Pennsylvania, in 1954 the British lost only narrowly 4–5. Then at Prince's, Sandwich, in 1956 the scores were exactly reversed, Frances Stephens, now Mrs Smith, beating the American Polly Riley on the 36th hole to win a thrilling match.

Mrs Smith – 'Bunty' to her host of friends – faced Polly Riley again at the

Brae Burn Country Club, outside Boston, in 1958 in the very last match. She arrived at the 18th dormie and won the hole to finish 2-up. This victory halved the whole match for the British and Irish. It was the first time any British golf team – amateur or professional, male or female – had avoided defeat in the United States.

But in 1960 at Lindrick the Americans regained the cup – and they held on to it firmly for another quarter of a century. At Broadmoor in Colorado in 1962 the British ladies went down 8–1. A change to 18-hole matches in 1964 made no difference: at Royal Porthcawl in Wales the home team was defeated 10½–7½; back in America two years later the hosts won 13–5 at Virginia Hot Springs. And so it went on. In 1968 at the beautiful Royal County Down course in Northern Ireland even the weather favoured the visitors – that is, it was warm and sunny, just as it had been in Virginia – and the United States won yet again.

At Western Gailes, Ayrshire, in 1972 two famous young golfers halved a tremendously exciting match – Michelle Walker and Laura Baugh, both of whom later turned professional. They met again in a foursome which Mickey Walker and her partner won. But once more the team went down, this time 8–10.

Nancy Lopez played for the first time in 1976 when the match was at Royal Lytham & St Anne's. For some strange reason she was picked for only two matches, both of which she won; and the Americans prevailed by 11½–6½.

Above *Victory, sweet victory! Jesse Valentine and Elizabeth Price clasp hands and Mrs Smith (Bunty Stephens) and Philomena Garvey hug each other after Mrs Smith's putt had assured the Great Britain and Ireland side of victory at Princes, Sandwich, in 1956.*

Left *Elizabeth Price hits a big drive. She beat Grace de Moss in the historic victory for Great Britain and Ireland at Muirfield.*

Above *Julie Wade and Linda Bayman at Royal St George's, Sandwich, in 1988, when Great Britain and Ireland for once started favourites for the cup.*

Right *At Muirfield again, this time in 1984. Vicky Thomas watches Claire Hourihane splash out of the sand. It was nail-biting time. Britain and Ireland nearly squared the match. They said one putt was the difference. But who knows? In golf, every shot counts one.*

In 1982 in Denver, Colorado, the 50th anniversary was celebrated. Forty-seven former players attended, including Glenna Collett Vare and Enid Wilson. But the match was somewhat one-sided, the Americans winning again, 14½–3½.

One putt decided the match in 1984, when the ladies returned to Muirfield –

but the putt went in favour of the United States. Laura Davies made her first and only appearance in this match, winning one single but losing in one foursome. The final score was 9½–8½. Things at last seemed to be looking up.

Then came the famous year – 1986. The British side ventured to Prairie Dunes, Kansas, and won the Cup, the first official team of British golfers ever to win in the United States, male or female. The British and Irish ladies made a clean sweep of the first morning's foursomes. Then they won the afternoon singles 3½–2½. In the second set of foursomes next day the Americans could only scrape one half, and then they lost the singles 2–4. The young Patricia (Trish) Johnson won all four of her matches. The captaincy of Mrs Diane Bailey was a vital factor in the victory. 'I never want to be able to tell whether you are up or down in a match,' she told her players. 'Walk tall. Stride out, and keep worrying the opposition.'

At Royal St George's, Sandwich, in 1988 the British actually started as favourites, although the Americans had considerably strengthened their team. But not only is St George's the type of course Americans rarely play: the weather was unusually chill by American standards; and by now

the home team really believed in itself. Once again Mrs Bailey assumed the captaincy, instilling a determined team spirit into her players and seeing that they were treated as stars. She was also strong-minded herself. She did not feel able to give the Irish star Claire Hourihane (heroine of many previous Cup matches) a single game, so she did not do so. This was an immensely disappointing decision for the Irish girl, but one she accepted with grace. (Claire Hourihane reached the semi-finals of the British Amateur the very next week, defeating one of the best American Curtis Cup players on the way, which was some consolation.) The youngest member of the British side, 18-year-old Susan Shapcott, the English and French Junior champion, won three points out of a possible four. In a fine team performance, Julie Wade's superlative swing, Linda Bayman's gritty singles win against Pearl Sinn, Sue Shapcott and Karen Davies' fine foursomes partnership, and June Thornhill's 8 out of 12 points in her three Cup appearances all helped towards the 11-7 victory. Belle Robertson, at 50 the senior player of the side that had won in Kansas, commented afterwards on the change that has come over women's golf in Europe in the past few years.

Most women are now taking up careers outside the home, and the most talented girl golfers have thoughts of making golf their careers, just like the young men. This could drastically change the whole amateur scene.

It is almost incredible to recall that in 1893, when it was first proposed to form a Ladies' Golf Union, a 'distinguished player' who was asked for his advice replied to the lady who became the LGU's first Treasurer, 'Don't do it.' He said women were bound to quarrel and that 'constitutionally and physically women are unfitted for golf.' That kind of imbecility has been decisively exposed by the Curtis Cup. Golf is a game for everyone.

Above *Sue Shapcott, the baby of the British side, plays from the rough at Royal St George's, 1988. She had a fine match, winning three points out of four.*

MOST APPEARANCES
16: Mary McKenna (GB & I)

YOUNGEST PLAYER
Jane Connachan (GB & I): 16 years

OLDEST PLAYER
Belle Robertson (GB & I): 50 years

MOST MATCHES PLAYED
30: Mary McKenna (GB & I)
20: Anne Quast Sander (USA)

Left *Great Britain and Ireland's victorious 1988 team at Sandwich, captained by Mrs Diane Bailey.*

The World Cup

Two-man national teams battling for honours over 72 holes of strokeplay, the World Cup has been held at venues as far apart as Wentworth and Hawaii. Today it struggles to find a place on tour schedules congested by new, big-money events. . . .

Above *Julius Boros, the 'easy swinger', who won two U.S. Opens and was an early stalwart in the U.S. World Cup team.*

Right *The British public had few chances to see the great Ben Hogan in action. But in 1956 he and Sam Snead showed all the power and the majesty of American golf when they won the World Cup, Hogan also taking the individual honours.*

The World Cup – originally the Canada Cup – was founded by an American industrialist John Jay Hopkins in 1952 and first competed for the following year in Montreal, Canada. Its founder's aim was 'to further good fellowship and better understanding among the nations of the world through the medium of international golf competition.'

Increasingly successful through a quarter of a century, it began to run out of steam in the early 1980s as more and more sponsors paid out more and more money to lure the world's top golfers to special events between the seasons of the major professional tours. Run by a non-profit-making body, the International Golf Association, the World Cup was never seen as a commercial event. Yet it had to face that competition or perish. The IGA decided to reshape the event, put it in the hands of an experienced sports promoter, call in new sponsors and, after one year's 'sabbatical' in 1986, present it once again to the world as a major tournament. In future there would be a million-dollar purse which would include a bonus for the golf authorities in the winning country for the betterment of golf there.

The format remains the same. All recognised golfing countries can compete. There are 22 'seeds' deriving from the previous year's results. The other countries play-off for the other 10 places in a 32-nation field. Each country nominates its own two golfers and the winning team is that with the lowest combined stroke-

Left *The attraction of the World Cup has always been that it truly is an international event. Here Eric Brown of Scotland tees off at the Kasumigaseili Country Club in Japan in 1958.*

play score over four rounds. There is also a prize for the lowest individual score.

In the inaugural event, however, only seven teams entered and play was over 36 holes. Argentina came first with a team total of 297, the winning pair being Roberto de Vicenzo and Antonio Cerda; Cerda won the individual title with a score of 140. Participants included Julius Boros, winner of the United States Open that year, and Bobby Locke, who on this occasion played for England.

In 1953, 25 countries entered teams and the 72-hole format was inaugurated. The event was again played in Montreal. Winners that time were the Australian pair, Peter Thomson and Kel Nagle, with a total

of 556. Argentina, again represented by de Vicenzo and Cerda, came second four strokes behind.

Again, in 1955, 25 countries entered for the tournament. That year it was held in Washington, DC, and the American team of Ed Furgol and Mel Harbert won with 560. There was a four-way tie for the individual title, and Furgol won on a play-off.

By this time the concept was catching on and in 1956 at Wentworth, England, huge crowds turned out to watch the main attractions, Ben Hogan and Sam Snead. They duly obliged by winning handsomely for the United States. Four shots behind was the South African pair,

Below *Christy O'Connor, Sr, 'wristy Christy', the great Irishman known universally in the golfing world as Himself, swings confidently toward an Irish victory in 1958 in Mexico City.*

Right *Sam Snead in 1960, when he partnered Arnold Palmer. In the following year he won the individual title at the age of 50, partnering Jimmy Demaret.*

Below *Ben Crenshaw, 'gentle Ben', the golf historian among professionals, winning the individual prize in Australia in 1988. The Japanese were second, the Australians third.*

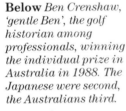

Bobby Locke and Gary Player. Hogan won the individual title with 277.

There were 30 entries in 1957 when the event was held in Japan, and the Japanese team of 'Pete' Nakamura and Koichi Ono won by nine shots from the United States, Makamura taking the individual; the Americans were represented by Sam Snead and Jimmy Demaret.

Ireland won in Mexico City in 1958 (Harry Bradshaw and Christy O'Connor), Australia in 1959 (Peter Thomson and Kel Nagle), and the United States (Arnold Palmer and Sam Snead) in 1960, when the tournament was held at Portmarnock, Dublin. After that the Americans dominated the tournament for a decade, the only interruptions to their rule being made by South Africa (Player and Harold Henning) in Madrid in 1965 and by Canada (Al Balding and George Knudson) in 1968.

Individual winners included not only the Big Three of the time (Jack Nicklaus, Arnold Palmer, Gary Player) and veteran Sam Snead but also Flory van Donck (Belgium), a familiar face in Britain, and George Knudson and Al Balding of Canada. At Melbourne, Australia, in 1972 the Taiwanese team won the Cup, Hsieh Min Nam taking the individual prize.

The World Cup had by this time become an international event of some importance, attracting the world's best players. But gradually and ironically, as world interest in golf increased, the attractions of the World Cup diminished for several of the leading players. New tournaments appeared, offering huge amounts of prize money; players' schedules grew more and more congested, and some top players suffered from exhaustion. In the United States it seemed easier to some to stay at home and take the

chance of winning half a million bucks in a nine-hole 'skins' game. Other 'world cups' appeared on the scene – the Kirin and the Dunhill for instance – with different formats and with instant international television appeal.

When it was learned that there would be no World Cup of the traditional kind in 1986 many people concluded that John Jay Hopkins' original idea was dead. But this was not the case. The IGA under the chairmanship of Howard L. Clark had been regathering its strength. A new executive director, Burch Riber, a man with an impressive track record in sports promotion, had been appointed. The Parallel Media Group of London put in about a million pounds to underwrite the restoration of the tournament, and a team of sponsors was recruited.

The contest was revived in style in 1987 at Kapalua, Maui, Hawaii. They put the flags out in a literal sense as 64 golfers paraded the 32 national colours at the opening ceremony, rather in the spirit of the Olympics. Besides the big golfing nations, Fiji, Korea, Hong Kong, Singapore and Colombia were there. In the pro-am before the tournament the team playing with the two Colombian pros won the amateur section of the event, while Scotland's Sandy Lyle and Sam Torrance won the professional section.

In the World Cup proper Wales won a splendid victory, with Ian Woosnam, Europe's Golfer of the Year, putting the finishing touches to his *annus mirabilis*, taking the individual prize by the length of a street. In the team event Scotland, led by Sandy Lyle, was runner-up, with the United States third and Ireland fourth.

In 1988 Ian Woosnam disappointed his Welsh colleagues and dismayed many of the golfing public when he decided not to compete but rather to defend his title in the Sun City 'Million Dollar Challenge', a singularly uningratiating event in southern Africa whose only notable feature is the size of the purse. More to the point, Masters Champion Sandy Lyle was not there; England's Nick Faldo was not there; U.S. Open Champion Curtis Strange was not there; Open Champion Severiano Ballesteros was not there; even Greg Norman, No. 1 in the world rankings at the time, was not there. The world's top five golfers were either at home resting or competing elsewhere. It was a bitter blow.

Some very fine golfers were, nonetheless, at the Royal Melbourne club. Former Masters champion Ben Crenshaw won the individual title with scores of 68, 67, 66 and 74, and with his partner Mark McCumber he won the team prize. Japan's famous golfing brothers, Tateo and Masashi Ozaki, were only one shot behind. And they were just one shot ahead of Australia's Peter Senior and Roger Mackay (who broke the course record with a 63 on the second day). Scotland were fourth, represented by Gordon Brand, Jr and Colin Montgomerie (Britain's 'Rookie of the Year'). England, represented by Mark James and Barry Lane, tied for 15th place with Thailand. The Netherlands finished last, behind Indonesia.

The competition was televised in all five continents; but some major golfing countries (including Britain) did not take the programme. However, the organisers remained determined to get the World Cup back to what they consider its rightful place, among the majors. Las Brisas, Spain, was chosen as the venue for 1989, with possibly the United States or Japan to follow. Prize money would be increased. Then, with the growth of satellite television and the proliferation of channels devoted to sport, it was hoped that the whole golfing world would be looking in.

Above *In 1987 in Hawaii Ian Woosnam led Wales to a famous victory in a contest in which 32 golfing nations took part.*

Left *Ben Crenshaw and Mark McCumber celebrate after winning the trophy in 1988.*

The Dunhill Cup

An end-of-season event played every year on the Old Course at St Andrews, the Dunhill is a knock-out tournament of medalplay singles matches between three-man national teams. It has proved popular with both players and spectators. . . .

Latest of the international tournaments, the Dunhill Nations Cup brings three top players from each of 16 countries (after qualifying rounds) to the Old Course at St Andrews for contests at 'medal matchplay.' Each individual match between two players is decided not on the number of holes won as in normal matchplay but on their medal scores over 18 holes. In the event of a tie, further holes are played until there is a result. There being three a side, the team that wins at least two matches wins that round.

So far this unusual competition has been held in the autumn, with the threat of rough weather looming ever in the background. But so far the promoters have been lucky. And already it seems that the players, even from the tropical countries, like the format and respect the Old Course. From the viewpoint of spectators and TV viewers it is a great attraction to know that all matches go at least to the 18th hole with the distinct possibil-

Below *David Graham, Graham Marsh and Greg Norman show how pleased they are to win the first Dunhill Nations Cup in 1985.*

Right *Greg Norman putts on the 17th on his way to a 65 – and to Australia's victory – at St Andrews in the 1985 Dunhill Cup.*

ity that in a close match there could be a dramatic upset at the marvellously perilous 17th (Road Hole).

Before the inaugural contest in the third week of October 1985 there were gales so severe that the tented village threatened to blow away. But on the first day the sun came out and a more kindly wind dried the course. Scoring was not easy but when Australia beat the United States in the final Greg Norman fired a superb 65. Australia also won the second Dunhill, beating Japan in the final. The wind rose and the scores soared like kites.

Greg Norman's 73 was the best score of the day. Rodger Davis was round in 76 and David Graham in 81.

Asked if he wasn't ashamed at winning with 81, Graham replied he wouldn't mind winning with 101 if his opponent took 102. (Naomichi Ozaki had indeed taken 82). England this time went out to Argentina, despite scores of 70, 70, 69. You never can tell just what's going to happen on the Old Course.

In 1987 in the qualifying rounds Denmark surprisingly beat Wales 2–1. They were then beaten by France. The French were then beaten by Ireland. Australia met Sweden in the first round and won by the skin of their teeth. In the second round much the same thing happened to them against Canada, only perhaps more so. Greg Norman had to go to the 23rd hole before he beat Richard Zokol and Peter Senior had to go to the 19th. Rodger Davis had a record 63 which lasted all of one day. For in the play-off for third place Curtis Strange of the United States scored a magnificent 62.

In the semi-finals Scotland beat the United States 3–0, while Australia lost to England in a most unlikely fashion. With the first match on the 16th tee they stood in total 13 under par and well ahead in all games. England's Howard Clark drove out of bounds; his opponent Peter Senior drove into the Principal's Nose bunker. When he managed to extricate himself he too hit out of bounds and took a 9 on the hole, Clark finishing in 7. Then Rodger Davis came to grief at the 17th and lost to Nick Faldo by one shot.

Happily the final was worthy of the Old Course. Scotland, led by Sandy Lyle scored 68, 69, 69. But England led by Nick Faldo, won with 66, 64, 73.

In 1988 the weather once again cleared only just in time: the Wednesday Pro-Am was literally washed-out, the first players, drenched, being called in after five holes. But the luck of the tournament held and play started on time, as if nothing had happened. The only trouble was that when the winds died on semi-final day the Scottish *haar* (the cold sea-fog) drifted in and closed down the proceedings at a vital moment. In this semi-final England met Ireland and in the crucial match Nick Faldo, playing Des Smyth, felt unable to play his final approach because he could not see the bottom of the flag. Des Smyth had already played his second to the 18th green, and there was a hostile reaction from part of the crowd. Since Faldo was 1-down at the time and his team desperately needed a win, and since Smyth's approach had found the green and thus put pressure on him, Faldo's decision to wait was quite justified. Next morning he played a fine shot to eight feet, but missed the vital putt. Maybe justice was done.

Ireland went on to a strange but famous victory over Australia. The crux came when Rodger Davis, striving for distance from the 17th tee, sliced his drive into the hotel grounds beyond the one-time railway sheds. Des Smyth beat him 71–73. Ronan Rafferty beat David Graham 69–74. So Greg Norman's superb 63 to beat Eamonn Darcy availed him nothing. But all the world enjoyed the Irish victory.

In truth – as one spectator remarked – the Old Course at St Andrews had won yet again.

Top *England's hero Gordon J. Brand drives off in the 1987 Dunhill Nations Cup which England won, defeating Scotland in the final.*

Above *Des Smyth jigs with delight on the 18th green at St Andrews after beating Australia's Rodger Davis in 1988. Ronan Rafferty beat David Graham, so that Greg Norman's amazing round of 63 to beat Eamonn Darcy went for nought.*

THE EVOLUTION OF TECHNIQUE

There are as many theories about the way to hit a golf ball as there are golfers. But in the past century some basic principles have emerged as golf-swing mechanics have become better understood.

The basic requirements for a good golf shot remain as they have always been:

- *Strike the ball with the 'sweet spot' on the clubface.*
- *Do so at the appropriate speed and force along the correct line.*
- *Angle the clubface at impact so that the ball flies in the intended manner along the intended path to the intended target.*

If you can do this consistently, time after time, it is of absolutely no consequence *how* you do it or whether it is pretty to watch. Technique, therefore, is to a great extent individual.

On the other hand, almost every golfer, whether a Tour star or a 20-handicap hacker, develops firmly held theories about how to

Left *Severiano Ballesteros hits 'into the bow', a supple young man's action. It is not advised for the over-50s.*

Right *This is the old-fashioned, firm-left-leg finish as demonstrated by 'the Silver Scot' Tommy Armour. It is an enduringly reliable action Armour used in winning the British and U.S. Opens.*

hit a golf ball; and such theories have changed during the past century as the laws of physics and mechanics, as applied to the golf swing, have become better understood. A modern player can develop or adapt his or her swing within the limits set by those laws, and many of today's top golfers do so.

Jack Nicklaus has markedly flattened his swing and reduced his flying right elbow since his early days on tour; a few years ago Severiano Ballesteros changed his take-away; Gary Player, passing 50, altered his wrist action; Sandy Lyle disciplined his left arm; Nick Faldo remodelled his entire swing.

With early equipment, a very full, flat, slashing two-handed action seemed necessary on all full shots. Clubs were usually gripped in the palms with both thumbs around the shaft. Playing the game was easy and amusing enough – but to play it well demanded genius. As now, the ball was small, and the 'sweet spot' on the clubface was little bigger than the smallest coin of the realm. Club-shafts of ash or hazel often flexed and twisted unaccountably. And yet, absolute precision of strike was imperative.

The first professional (in the modern sense) was Allan Robertson, who reached his peak in the mid-19th century. Old Tom Morris started his working life in golf as Robertson's assistant. His son Young Tom Morris, might have had a profound influence on technique but for his tragic death at the age of 24. Young Tom, they said, had found the secret.

But it was to be Harry Vardon, the under-gardener from the island of Jersey, who revolutionised the golf game in the last years of the 19th century. The sheer grace of his upright swing captivated players and spectators alike. He epitomised the virtues of rhythm and tempo, effortlessly driving the ball great distances for those days with clubs that were usually shorter and lighter than those of his contemporaries. He was also deadly accurate with his fairway woods. Said a contemporary, Andrew Kirkaldy, the professional at the R & A: 'His play was enough to break the heart of an iron horse.'

Vardon popularised, although he did not originate, the overlapping grip which bears his name. Many other great golfers have used different grips – Gene Sarazen interlocked the index finger of his left hand and the little finger of his right, and also had his left thumb hanging free outside the shaft. Jack Nicklaus (who has small hands) also interlocks. But the Vardon grip remains standard to this day and is preferred by most teachers.

Vardon 'cupped' his left wrist, holding it bent in a concave fashion throughout his swing. He dragged the clubhead away hands-

Left *At and just after impact: a study in two different styles. Henry Cotton (left) felt his right hand brush past his left at this point. Bernard Hunt (right) had a short, controlled swing and felt little in the way of hand action; but he derived more power from his legs.*

have not grasped is his interpretation of *how* to swing the clubhead.' The simple thesis seemed to him to beg too many questions.

Modern swing theories

Even when he first visited the United States, Cotton noted that swing theory was beginning to discourage an independent role for the hands. The steel shaft had just arrived. Many Americans had taken to swinging rather in the manner which much later became

first, initiating a sort of whiplash action. He also bent his left arm more than modern teachers would like. The cupped-wrist action, although not always the very bent left arm, was used by many fine golfers after him – Jimmy Thomson, Tommy Armour, Bobby Jones, Walter Hagen and even the very individualistic South African Bobby Locke. For a long time that, too, was the accepted norm.

Such a swing stresses positive use of the hands. It requires the clubface (and thus also the hands, wrist and forearms) to roll 'open' on the backswing; the clubhead at the top of the backswing points almost vertically to the ground. A reverse roll, closing the clubface, was necessary on the downswing.

Bobby Jones, a true golfing genius, although using the cupped wrist action, made two changes: he made sure that his hands were slightly ahead of the ball at impact, which had not been the case with Vardon; and he pulled the club-head down and through in a way that allowed him to 'freewheel' through the ball.

The young Henry Cotton exchanged several letters with Bobby Jones in discussing this point. Cotton was the archetypal 'hands player': he always insisted there must be a *hit* within the swing, and that it was the hands that applied the hitting force. No golf ball ever travelled far, he said, unless it was hit hard.

Cotton also exchanged words with another Jones, Ernest Jones the teacher, who emigrated from England to the United States in the 1920s and became famous for his simple slogan: 'Swing the clubhead.' Cotton commented: 'What I

> ### From a letter to *The Times* (London):
>
> It is what a good follow-through implies about the contact with the ball that is important.
>
> A follow-through, as the term suggests, means that the club/bat follows the ball on its path. Thus, contact with the ball and the force of the club are applied for longer.
>
> Mathematically, the relevant equation is: $F \times t = m(v-u)$, where F = force applied to the ball; t = length of time for which it is applied; m = mass of the ball; v = velocity with which the ball leaves the club/bat; u = velocity of the ball before contact. (In golf $u = 0$.)
>
> Thus, for a given force (say, the greatest force which a particular sportsman can exert) the critical factor in determining the speed at which the ball moves down the fairway or across the outfield is the time for which the ball and club/bat are in contact. Hence the importance of the club/bat following the ball along its course.
> Yours faithfully,
> CHARLES HOUSE

THE VERY FIRST GOLF TIPS

The oldest known instruction manual dates back to 1687. It was found in the *Journal* of Thomas Kincaid, an Edinburgh man-about-town.

His main recommendations were these:
- Take your stance as if you were fencing, left foot turned out.
- Position the ball opposite the left chest.
- Pivot from the legs.
- Keep your eye on the ball.
- Hit through the ball, making the swing one continuous movement.
- Turn as far to the left at the finish as you did to the right on the backswing.

Plus ça change, as golfers say.

known as 'square-to-square', which requires keeping the left wrist in line with the forearm at the address and throughout the swing. Cotton called it 'playing push shots all the time' and kept to his own artistic, open-to-closed, wristy swing.

A little later in the United States two Texans made particularly important contributions to the further development of technique: Byron Nelson and Ben Hogan. Nelson totally redesigned his own swing over a six-year period from 1938 to 1944, even though he had already won the Masters with his old swing in 1937. He now stood closer to the ball, kept his left arm ramrod straight, and adopted a 'one-piece' take-away. On the downswing he turned his left wrist square to his arc 30 inches before impact; then dragged the clubhead through using what seemed then to be a somewhat exaggerated leg action. The total effect, he believed, was to guarantee him a straight hit every time. There were few to argue with him when in 1945 he won 18 tournaments, 11 of them in a row.

Active leg action became standard for almost all American golfers thereafter and later for much of the rest of the world. Both South Africa's Gary Player and Britain's Tony Jacklin, when they first ventured to the United States, found they had to alter their styles in this way. Without more active use of the legs they could not reach the longer American par-5s in two shots. And Jack Nicklaus has always attributed his great length off the tee to his strong legs and powerful back muscles. Scientists analysing the golf swing support this view. So instead of hitting against a firm left side golfers

Right *Byron Nelson was rated the first of the great 'modern swingers'. He kept his left arm ramrod straight, stood very close to the ball and used his legs to drag the clubhead through for a considerable distance along the target line.*

Below *Gary Player at the top of his backswing. His clubshaft is exactly parallel to his line-of-aim, he is 'on-plane', and his legs are preparing to swing his club through impact with increasing force.*

began to 'hit into the bow' (the shape the body assumes on completion of the full swing).

Technically, the most influential golfer has been that other genius, Ben Hogan. Hogan himself reverted to the old-fashioned cupped left wrist method in his most successful years – it guaranteed him against a fierce hook which had plagued him in his early days – but he did not recommend the action to others. He made no mention of it in his most famous book, *The Modern Fundamentals of Golf*. Instead, his most vital contributions to the understanding of technique was his emphasis on the swing-plane and on full right-arm extension.

Hogan visualised the plane as an imaginary pane of glass sloping down from the golfer's shoulders to the ball. The golfer was to keep his hands and club immediately below the glass, at every point of the swing, in the exact plane determined by the slope of the glass. Modern understanding has the hands and the clubshaft actually lying on the surface of the glass, with teachers stressing the 'Law of the Parallels'.

During the swing, whenever the club-shaft is parallel to the ground – half-way up the backswing, at the top of the full backswing, half-way down again, on the follow through after impact, and so on – it must also be parallel to the intended direction of shot. Similarly, at the point on the backswing and downswing when the club-shaft points directly upwards, its angle to the ground must be exactly the same as the angle of the shaft at address.

The Law of the Parallels holds good whether the plane is upright or flat. Indeed almost all golfers change the angle of their plane for the downswing; and, of course, it changes as the golfer changes clubs in progressing from tee to green. But the law still applies: in a good swing the clubshaft always moves on the surface of a plane.

Right-arm extension adds thrust to clubhead speed at impact. Hogan once asked the writer and commentator Henry Longhurst why British golfers of his day did not extend the right arm but bent it quickly on the backswing. Americans, he pointed out, kept the left arm straight on the backswing and the right arm straight on the throughswing. Why didn't the British do the same? Longhurst, of course, had no answer. The fact is that, in technique, the British had not yet caught up. They have now. A first-class example of full extension can be seen, for example, in the economical swing of Ian Woosnam.

So most modern swings now include these elements:
- Commitment to the plane.
- Dragging the clubhead down and through, using the power of the legs.
- Striking with a firm, flat left wrist.
- Extending the bent right arm at and after impact.
- Using a moderate backswing but a very full finish.

Today among the top players the lower body, rather than the hands and arms, drives the swing. Hands tend to be used in reflex, without conscious thought, to generate extra speed at impact. For the average player, indeed, one of the most sensible pieces of advice is: 'Forget

Below *Australia's Jan Stephenson shows how the correct action can produce accuracy and distance from quite a petite frame. Note her right-arm extension and the controlled turn of the forearms on the follow through. A fine example of power and grace combined.*

IT TAKES ALL SORTS

In 1988 a 50-years-old former Albanian hairdresser, using a 47-inch driver and (in his own words) 'a terrible swing', qualified for the Seniors Tour in the United States.

His name is **Agim Bardha** and he is 5ft 5in in height. At the qualifying school at Prestancia, Florida, he tied 9th among the 16 fresh players who made it to the tour.

'My swing may be funny', he says, 'but I can get the ball in the hole.' However, he carries a pair of barber's scissors in his travel bag. After all, you never know.

the hands!' The difference in the angles formed between club-shaft and left fore-arm at address and at the top of the swing ensures that a whiplike acceleration of the club-head automatically occurs as it approaches the point of impact with the ball. A conscious effort to control this natural acceleration by means of deliberate hand-action usually has two effects, both destructive: first, it tends to make the acceleration occur too early or too late; second, it almost invariably deflects the club's path from the correct swing plane.

However, it remains as true today as it always was that if one fulfils the basic requirements – strikes at the appropriate speed along the chosen line with a correctly angled clubface – just how one swings is immaterial.

Golf still is a game for individuals.

GLOSSARY

ACE A ball holed with a single shot.

ADDRESS The position taken when preparing to swing. It is not completed officially until the golfer has grounded the club, except in a hazard where it may not be grounded.

AIR SHOT Hitting at but failing to make contact with the ball.

ALBATROSS A score of three-under-par on a hole; in the United States, a double-eagle.

APPROACH A shot within range of the green from fairway or rough.

APRON The area edging the green, mown shorter than the fairway but not as short as the green; also known as 'fringe'.

AWAY A player is 'away' when it is his or her turn to swing.

BAFFY A hickory-shafted fairway wood, equivalent to a modern 4-wood.

BETTER BALL A fourball match in which the lower score of either partner in each pair determines whether a hole is won, lost or halved.

BIRDIE A score of one-under-par on a hole.

BISQUE A handicap stroke which may be claimed at the discretion of the recipient.

BLIND HOLE A hole in which the flagstick is out of sight from the tee and/or fairway.

BOGEY Once the British term for a reasonable score by an imaginary good player; but now, Americanised, universally applied to a score of one-over-par on a hole. A 'double bogey' is two-over-par, and so on.

BORROW The extent to which a putted ball will deviate from a straight line on a sloping green; in United States usually called 'break'.

BRASSIE A wooden-headed club with a brass soleplate used in earlier times; equivalent to a modern 2-wood.

BUNKER A hollow in the ground largely filled with sand which is officially a hazard; often called a 'sand-trap' in the United States.

CARRY The distance a ball flies before it hits the ground.

CASUAL WATER A temporary pond, pool or superfluity of water from which a ball may be lifted and dropped clear without penalty.

CHIP A low, running shot to the green.

CLEEK A shallow-faced hickory-shafted club equivalent to a modern 2-iron.

CLOSED Of the stance, aimed right of the line-of-aim (with right-handers); of the clubface, aimed left.

CLUBFACE The striking surface of the clubhead.

CROSS BUNKER A bunker lying more or less at right-angles across the fairway.

CUT A faded or sliced shot. To 'make the cut' in tournaments, however, is to qualify for the final two rounds.

DIVOT A piece of turf cut from the ground by a club when it strikes the ball.

DOG-LEG A hole that changes direction abruptly at a point between tee and green.

DORMY When in matchplay a player leads by the same number of holes as there are left to play. Not applied if extra holes will be played to determine a winner.

DRAW A shot which (for right-handers) curves left in a controlled manner.

DRIVE The shot from the teeing ground.

EAGLE A score of two-under-par on a hole.

ECLECTIC A record of the best score a player has achieved, over a period, at each of the 18 holes.

ETIQUETTE Golf's code of good behaviour. Provides the first section of the Rules of Golf.

FACE That part of the club-head surface used to strike the ball.

FADE A shot that (for right-handers) curves gently right.

FAIRWAY The mown surfaces on a golf course between tees and greens.

FAT A shot is hit 'fat' when the clubhead strikes the ground before the ball.

FOLLOW-THROUGH The forward movement of the club after the ball has been struck.

FORE The golfer's cry when a ball flies dangerously toward someone else.

FOURBALL A two-a-side team game in which each player plays his own ball. Called a 'foursome' in the United States.

FOURSOME A two-a-side team game in which partners play shots alternately with the same ball. In the United States, 'Scotch foursomes'.

FREE DROP When under the rules a ball may be lifted and dropped clear of trouble without penalty.

GIMME A putt left close enough to the hole for the next to be conceded. Legal only in matchplay.

GREEN Traditionally the whole golf course. Now understood as the specially mown area where players putt.

GREENSOME Like a foursome except that all players drive. Having chosen the better drive, partners then play shots alternately.

GRIP Covering round the shaft where the player holds it. Also the manner in which the player holds it.

GROUND UNDER REPAIR An area of the golf course that is being repaired or otherwise restored. It will be clearly marked as such, sometimes by the initials GUR.

HALF A drawn hole or match.

HANDICAP The number of strokes a player deducts from his gross score over 18 holes to establish a 'net score'. The aim is to enable all players of whatever level of skill to compete on fair terms.

HAZARD Any bunker, pond or watercourse.

HEEL That part of the club-head nearest the shaft.

HOLE (*Verb*) To hit the ball into the hole. (*Noun*) The hole must be 4¼ inches (107.9 mm) in diameter and four inches (101.6 mm) deep. (The whole area between tees and green is also called a hole) a full-size course has 18 holes.

HONOUR The right to play first from the tee. On the opening hole, properly decided by draw or by lot; thereafter according to which player won the previous hole.

HOOK To cause the ball to curve strongly left (for right-handers).

HOSEL The lower extension of an iron club shaft to which the head is fitted.

IMPACT The instant when the clubface contacts the ball and compresses it.

IN PLAY A ball is 'in play' the moment it has been struck and until holed out or picked up.

IRON A metal-faced club, usually steel, with a blade rather than a rounded clubhead.

JIGGER A once-popular shallow-faced iron club useful for chipping, pitching and playing out of rough.

LINKS Seaside courses originally laid out on the rolling dunes and adjacent commonland.

LOFT The angle of slope in a club face. A 1-iron will commonly have a loft of 18°, a sand-wedge 56° or more.

MASHIE Old term for a 5- or 6-iron; the more lofted mashie-niblick was equivalent to a modern 7-iron.

MATCHPLAY Games decided on the number of holes won.

MEDAL PLAY A competition decided on the number of strokes taken.

MOVE A ball has officially 'moved' if it leaves its position and comes to rest in another place, however short a distance away. If a player has already addressed the ball, such movement counts as one stroke.

MULLIGAN American term for a bad opening shot which can be discarded, the player driving again without penalty. *Not allowed by the rules.*

NASSAU A match in which three points are scored, one for each nine holes and one for the match.

NIBLICK A small-faced hickory-shafted iron, equivalent to a modern 9-iron, used for pitching and bunker shots.

PAR The score a scratch golfer should make on each hole, allowing two putts per green. Determined by distance, not difficulty.

PITCH A lofted shot to the green.

PROVISIONAL A shot taken with a second ball when the player is unsure whether his first is lost or out-of-bounds.

PUTT The stroke made to hole the ball on or near the green.

ROUGH Thicker grass, scrub, etc, along the sides of the fairways.

RUB OF THE GREEN Lucky or unlucky happenings to the ball which are not catered for in the rules and which must be accepted.

SCRATCH A zero handicap. The very best players have 'plus handicaps'. When playing the less expert they must add shots to their score.

SHANK A shot hit off the hosel (*qv*).

SLICE A shot curving (for right-handers) strongly right.

SOLE That part of the clubhead that rests on the ground at address.

SPOON Old name for a fairway wood equivalent to a modern 3-wood.

SQUARE Of the stance, parallel to the target line; of the clubface, at right-angles to it.

SSS Standard Scratch Score: the gauge for handicaps. What a scratch player should score in a round. Unlike the equivalent par figure, it is based not only on the length of the holes but also on their relative difficulty.

STABLEFORD A game in which players get one point for a bogey, two for a par, three for a birdie, and so on.

STROKEPLAY A game decided on the players' nett number of strokes per round. Also called 'medal play'.

SUDDEN DEATH A play-off in which one or more extra holes, rather than a complete round or rounds, are used to determine a winner after two or more players have tied when the scheduled rounds have been completed.

TAKEAWAY The first movements of the backswing.

TEE Where the drive is taken on each hole. Also the peg on which the ball may be placed when driving from the teeing ground.

TEXAS SCRAMBLE A team game in which the best tee shot is chosen and all members play second shots from there. Then the best second shot is chosen and all play on from there and so on until the hole is completed. But there is a limit to the number of times each individual's 'best ball' may be selected in each phase of the game.

TEXAS WEDGE The putter when used from off the green.

TOE That part of the club-head farthest from the shaft.

WEDGE The short-range pitching club. A sand-wedge is used in bunkers.

WOOD Traditionally, a wooden-headed club used for the longer shots from tee or fairway. Now often of metal or composite, and sometimes lofted like short irons.

YIPS Nervous twitches on the putting green, making it very difficult to strike the ball correctly.

INDEX